Main

This is a **FLAME TREE** book
First published 2012

Publisher and Creative Director: Nick Wells
Names Research and Selection: Dawn Laker
Project Editor: Catherine Taylor
Layout Design: Jane Ashley
Art Director: Mike Spender
Digital Design and Production: Chris Herbert
Picture Research: Polly Prior and Giana Porpiglia

Special thanks to Joseph Kelly, Laura Bulbeck, Giana Porpiglia and Chelsea Edwards.

This edition published 2016 by
FLAME TREE PUBLISHING
6 Melbray Mews, Fulham
London SW6 3NS, United Kingdom

www.flametreepublishing.com

16 18 20 19 17
5 7 9 10 8 6 4

ISBN 978-1-84786-986-9

A CIP record for this book is available from the British Library upon request.

Printed in China

All pictures are courtesy Shutterstock and © the following photographers: Cienpies Design: 1; FOTOCROMO: 3; Losevsky Pavel: 4; ansar80: 8; Christophe Testi: 9; Golden Pixels LLC: 10; restyler: 11 & 103; Julie Campbell: 12; AM-STUDiO: 22; Johanna Goodyear: 26; rickt: 28; Jakob: 33; Melissa King: 37, 147; Renata Osinska: 47; Kavring: 50; Tobkatrina: 56; Salim October: 63; Cheryl E. Davis: 64; Supri Suharjoto: 77; greenland: 82, 109; Kim Ruoff: 89, 127; Plechi: 95; Olinchuk: 104; Kristina Postnikova: 115; Sashkin: 116; joshhhab: 118; karen roach: 119, 112; Jiri Hera: 123; Haywiremedia: 128; Philip Date: 137; Nadezda Verbenko: 139; Tjerrie Smit: 141; Jamey Ekins: 142; Linor: 144; Warren Goldswain: 155; Vasina Natalia: 160; Aspen Photo: 164; mypokcik: 168; Gelpi: 177; Christopher Parypa: 183; Caroline RW: 188; Kitch Bain: 192; Raia: 195; Anatoliy Samara: 203, 254; Ivonne Wierink: 204; Sean MacD: 208; Kimberley McClard: 211; HannaMonika: 215; Africa Studio: 220; Dmitri Melnik: 225; Andreja Donko: 229; DenisNata: 235; michaeljung: 241; Strakovskaya: 246; Yaruta Igor: 248; Ilya Andriyanov: 251; MNStudio: 130-131; Oleg Kozlov: 14-15; DelaLane Photography: 5bc; Elena Schweitzer: 5bl & 69 & 256, 79, 199; Adrov Andriy: 5br & 73, 156; Easyshoot: 5tl & 60; Kuznetsov Dmitriy: 5tr & 172; Senol Yaman: 6bc; Ipatov: 6r.

Babies' Names

Foreword by **Justine Roberts**

Introduction by **Maryanna Korwitts**

**FLAME TREE
PUBLISHING**

Contents

Foreword

Picking out a name is probably one of the first choices you and your partner will make together as parents, and quite likely the first parenting decision you'll argue about.

Many mothers on Mumsnet feel a kind of visceral indignation when they discover that their partners are expecting to have a significant say in the naming of the forthcoming child. But partners should of course have their say – it is their child too. Fear not, though. Hitherto happy couples need not be fissured by forthcoming offspring. Yet. There are some ways to approach the deadlock even in the face of someone who has devoted absolutely no imaginative energy to the topic, who stands around saying "Er, I quite like Emily [substitute name of old girlfriend here]" and expects to be given air time.

First, one of you should draft a reasonably long and liberal list of all the names you like and then the other chooses from said list. If you're feeling ruthless you could try drafting the list yourself and try inserting the name you really want amongst a string of unlikely contenders, thus:

Duke	**Chappy**	
Melvyn	**Beelezebub**	
Spongebob	**Kermit**	
Thomas		

Alternatively sit down together with this book and shout out any name that you like. The other person must count to twenty before providing a considered response to the name. Or you can both draw up lists from the book, exchange the lists, cross out all unacceptable names on each other's lists and create a master list which you both then consider together.

If that fails you could just talk and talk. You may feel you will never get anywhere at all with someone whose first suggestions are Winifred and Norman, but days and weeks of debate will eventually move him or her on. Hopefully.

Bear in mind that even if the name you end up with is a compromise name in the sense that it isn't the one you have lovingly cherished since childhood, it will be the name of your child and chances are it will therefore be lovely.

And do remember you have middle names as your secret weapon. Middle names are often the graveyard where ugly family names go to die or at least to be preserved until a future generation finds them alluring again. And if you have some entertaining frivolous names you want to use somewhere, bung them in as well. But maybe not too many.

If after all that you really can't both agree on one definite winner, then your best bet is to draw up a shortlist of acceptable names and then one of you (and we're not saying who as that would be sexist) should point out in no uncertain terms that the person who has carried the baby for 40 weeks and then gone through a three-day labour gets the casting vote. RIGHT? The only proviso being that you can't use the names of past lovers or current crushes.

Good luck.

P.S. If you're seriously contemplating calling your child Moonbat, remember it's probably the preggie hormones speaking and your partner is right to say no.

Justine Roberts
Founder of Mumsnet.com

Introduction

Will it be William George III, after daddy and grandpa, or Grace, after a real Princess? Is it best to go with a popular moniker like Olivia or Harry, or might it be fun to boldly choose a unique spelling like Berezekiah or Zyndalee? One of the biggest responsibilities every parent faces is that of naming a baby. Since a name is meant to last a lifetime, finding just the right sound, look and significance is no easy matter. Today, more than ever, parents need a little help with the naming process, and *Babies' Names* provides that help in a big way.

What's in a Name?

Over the past couple of decades, naming trends have evolved dramatically. It used to be that parents would safely settle on classic first names that have been around for centuries. Many still do. But with a desire to give their children ever more unique and meaningful identities, a significant number of parents are opting for monikers that don't fit old moulds. Some children are now named after cities like Paris or London, others after natural elements like River, Ocean and Apple. It has even become common for names to outright represent the characteristics mums and dads want as a baby's destiny. Thus, first names such as True, Serenity and Charisma have popped up on the scene. Even when naming a baby after a cherished relative, favoured saint, war hero or movie star, there

is a growing sense that the influence of a name runs deep. In other words, there is a growing belief that there's more to a name than meets the eye and ear. The truth is ... there's much more.

A Name's Energy

Beyond its spelling, there resides an actual energy in a name, which fuels the person who bears it. We have evidence that energy exists, through a bevy of psychological studies suggesting everything from names that begin with a C or D produce poorer students, to the suggestion that certain names predict certain occupations. If you are like many parents, determined to give your baby a name that is more than just a convenient label, you'll want to know what a name does, along with how it looks.

So how do you discover and define that elusive energy before finalizing your baby's birth certificate? How do you make sure the name you pick will be a good fit? Begin by researching a name's roots and origins, along with the lives of the people who wore it. In so doing, you will have a good awareness of how that name will play out in your child's life. In addition, you will also be able to provide your offspring with a greater appreciation of their name identity.

Know the Background to a Name

Consider what a difference it can make for a little girl to be told she's called Charlotte, not only because the name means 'womanly', but also because it has encouraged others like Charlotte Brontë and Queen Charlotte to be strong and persevering. Even Charlotte, the intelligent little spider in the children's classic *Charlotte's Web*, was a great motivation to others. Out-fitted with the details of her name story, a modern day Charlotte can grow in the knowledge that she has been gifted with a name that not only has a lovely feminine sound, but also carries inspirational power.

Likewise for the young lad who bears his great granddad's name, Arthur. If told nothing other than that he's carrying on family tradition, this little guy might feel he's stuck with a rather tired, boring moniker. On the other hand, he might truly revel in the knowledge that many before him wore this name and were able to impressively express the 'bear-like' bravery and strength suggested by its Welsh etymology.

As you scan through *Babies' Names* in search of the perfect fit for your baby, keep in mind that you are looking for more than a name. You are seeking a rich identity for your child, an identity that will add an important chapter to your family's history. You are searching for the name that begins your child's story.

Matching First Name to Surname

Since a first name continuously partners with the family surname, consider how the two names will blend when spoken or written together. A long surname will be more compatible with a short first name, and vice versa. If your son's last name will be Smith, steer clear of a common first name like Bob or Joe, perhaps picking something like Thaddeus or Sebastian. On the other hand, a surname like Theobald is begging for a one-syllable first name such as Rhys or Jake. A first name that ends with a vowel, will literally 'melt', sound-wise, into a last name that also begins with a vowel. So if your surname is Ashdown, think twice about going with Ava as a first name.

Don't Forget Middle Names in the Mix

As an added caution, disregarding how the middle name mixes into the full name could have your child disowning that middle name later in life. Bartholemew Phineas Lancaster is bound to tell no one what that middle initial 'P' stands for, even if he decides to go by Bart as an adult.

Abbreviations and Nicknames

Whether a name is long or short, it's a good bet that nicknames will play a role in a child's identity. Some names are especially nickname-prone. Thinking of going with the first name

Bradford but dislike the nicknames Brad and Ford? Then you'd best consider what name your son will use on an everyday basis. Or, if you love the name Alex but are tempted to put Alexander on the birth certificate, why not just make the preferred name the formal given name?

Do what you can to be sure your final pick doesn't lend itself to teasing, since it will be your responsibility as your little one grows up to deal with any and all forms of cruel 'name tampering'. If the potential for such tampering is especially strong, look for an alternative name that is similar but more tease-free. Belle could become Belly on the playground, but Ella is likely to avoid such a fate. Do your best to try getting into the mind of a child, and you may see some of those favourite choices on your initial baby name list in a different light.

Initials

It is more important than you might think to consider your baby's initials as you're going through the naming process. Be sure those initials don't spell a word that could bring grief later in life. Hailey Anne Gordon has a great sound, but the initials HAG won't be appreciated by your daughter when she sets out to purchase her first set of monogrammed towels. Likewise, avoid initials that spell out a negative acronym, such as KKK.

A 1999 study carried out by psychologists suggests that negative initials such as PIG or DIE can decrease life expectancy, most likely because self-image is negatively affected. Neutral initials have no such effect. Finally, remember that your daughter is likely to change her surname someday, so do some heads-up planning and avoid first and middle initials that could be problematic when combined with a popular last name initial.

Twins

It is difficult enough naming just one baby, but special considerations come into play when expecting twins. The babies will enjoy a special bond through life as a result of sharing the same birthday, so it can be valuable to let their names express and enhance that bond. You might opt for two names that appear different yet have the same meaning, like Eve and Zoe (both mean 'life'). Or you might go with anagrams, as in Aidan and Nadia. Another way to create a twin link could involve choosing two names that have equal association around revered historical figures.

Since having a unique identity is just as important to twins as it is to other children, steer clear of choosing two names that sound almost the same such as Marian and Marcia. Even beginning each child's name with the same letter could bring regret as you go to label lunches and school bags with identical initials. And keep the length of the two names similar so that one child won't be forced into having a nickname before being out of diapers! Even if you have identical twins, avoid using the beginning letters of their names to show birth order, since later in life Andrew may think he has the edge on his brother Byron because A comes before B in the alphabet!

A Lifelong Gift

There is a multitude of ways your baby's given name will affect future experiences, relationships, job choices and personality development. While some effects, such as the sight and sound are obvious, others may not be evident until the name is in use. However, exerting due diligence while searching for the perfect moniker is bound to pay off. After all, babies' names are one of the greatest gifts we can give to the next generation!

Aaron
Variants: Arn, Aaran
Origin: Biblical
Meaning 'bright' or 'high mountain', this name was popular with Puritans in the seventeenth century. Still popular with both Christians and Jews, it enjoyed a peak in popularity in the 1970s and 1980s.

Abasi
Origin: Swahili
Meaning 'stern'.

Abbott
Variants: Abbitt, Abott, Abotte
Origin: Hebrew
Meaning 'father', from which the English word comes for the religious rank and title of abbott.

Abdi
Origin: African
Meaning 'servant'.

Abdul
Variants: Ab, Abdel, Abul
Origin: Arabic
Meaning 'servant'.

Abe
See Abraham

Abiah
Origin: Hebrew
Means 'God is my father'.

Abraham
Diminutives: Abe, Ham, Bram
Variants: Abram, Avrom (Yiddish)
Origin: Hebrew
From the Hebrew Avraham, itself from Hebrew *av hamon*, meaning 'father of many nations'. Adopted by the Puritans in the seventeenth century, it is now uncommon outside Jewish communities.

Absolom
Variants: Absolon (French)
Origin: Hebrew
Meaning 'father of peace', name of King David's favourite son in the Bible. Until the nineteenth century, it was still in irregular use, but is now highly unusual.

Ace
Variants: Acey
Origin: Latin
Latin for 'unity', rather than 'top' or 'number one'.

Achim
Origin: Hebrew and Polish
In Hebrew, this means 'God will establish'; in Polish, 'the Lord exalts'.

Ackerley
Origin: English
Meaning 'oak meadow', this is also used as a surname.

Adair
Origin: Irish
Meaning 'oak wood', this is usually interpreted as 'dweller by the oak wood', in reference to the druids of Celtic folklore. Also a Scottish variant of Edgar.

Adam
Diminutives: Ad, Adie
Origin: Hebrew
From the Hebrew *adama*, meaning 'earth', this is sometimes traced back to the Hebrew for 'red', from the colour of the earth from which Adam was traditionally made.

Addison
Origin: Hebrew and English
Meaning 'son of Adam'.

Aden
See Aidan

Adley
Origin: Hebrew
Meaning 'fair-minded'.

Adnan
Origin: Arabic
From the Arabic *adana*, meaning 'to settle down', this name predated Islam, though it appears as the name of a descendant of Ibrahim and is common throughout the Arab world.

Adrian
Diminutives: Ade, Addie, Adie
Origin: Latin
From the Roman name Hadrian, from the Latin for 'man from Adria'. Especially popular in the 1960s, it is now less common. A famous bearer of the name is the fictional character in Sue Townsend's *The Secret Diary of Adrian Mole, Aged 13¾*.

Aelwyn
Origin: Welsh
Meaning 'fair-browed'. The feminine equivalent is **Aelwen**.

Ahmed
Variants: Ahmad, Ahmet
Origin: Arabic
From the Arabic *hamida*, meaning 'to praise' and interpreted as meaning 'more praiseworthy'.

Aidan
Diminutives: Adie
Variants: Adan, Aden, Edan
Origin: Irish
An Anglicized version of the Irish Aodan, a diminutive of **Aodh**, the name of a Celtic sun god and one that means 'fire'. The Anglicized version succeeded the Irish version and became popular among English speakers towards the end of the century.
See also **Haydn**

Ainsley m/f
Variants: Ainslee, Ainslie
Origin: Old English
From the place name, itself from the Old English *an* ('one') and *leah* ('wood' or 'clearing'), interpreted as meaning 'lonely clearing' or 'my meadow'. In the 1990s, the name enjoyed a boost through TV chef Ainsley Harriott.

Ajay
Origin: Sanskrit
Meaning 'unconquerable', this is an Indian name.

Akash
Origin: Sanskrit
Meaning 'sky', this is an Indian name.

Akbar
Origin: Arabic
Meaning 'the greatest'.

Akeem
Origin: Arabic
Meaning 'wise' or 'insightful'.

Akira
Origin: Japanese
Meaning 'intelligent'.

Akiva
Origin: Hebrew
Meaning 'to shelter' or 'to protect'.

Aksell
Origin: Scandinavian
Meaning 'father of peace'.

Akshar
Origin: Sanskrit
This Indian name comes from the Sanskrit, meaning 'imperishable'.

Alan
Variants: Alun, Allan, Allen
Origin: Celtic
Meaning 'concord' or 'harmony', this comes from the Celtic *alun* and can also be translated as 'shining', this name was revived in the nineteenth century. Most widespread in the 1950s, it has since gone into decline.

Alastair
Diminutives: Aly
Variants: Alasdair, Alister
Origin: Greek
This name comes via the Greek and is the Scottish Gaelic variant of **Alexander**. The name spread from Scotland in the nineteenth century and remained popular, though it has gone into decline since the 1950s.

Alban
Diminutives: Albie, Alby
Variants: Albany, Albin
Origin: Latin or Celtic
Deriving originally from the Latin

albus ('light'); alternatively, from the Celtic *alp*, meaning 'crag' or 'rock'. Usually translated as meaning 'white hill'. It enjoyed a minor revival in the nineteenth century.

Albert

Diminutives: Al, Bert, Bertie
Variants: Alberto (Spanish), Albrecht (German), Elbert
Origin: Old German
From *adal* ('noble') and *berht* ('famous' or 'bright'), records of this name go back to the Norman invasion. The name did not become popular in its modern form until the nineteenth century.

Alden

Variants: Aldwin, Aldwyn, Eldin
Origin: Anglo-Saxon
Meaning 'wise old friend', someone friends can rely on.

Alder

Origin: Anglo-Saxon
Meaning 'at the alder tree'.

Aldous

Variants: Aldus, Aldo
Origin: Old German
Meaning 'old' (from *ald*), this was popular during the thirteenth century, but has never been common, even after a minor resurgence in the nineteenth

century. Probably the most famous bearer of the name was writer Aldous Huxley.

Aldwyn

Variants: Aldwin
Origin: Anglo-Saxon
Meaning 'old friend', this Anglo-Saxon name has recently been revived.

Alec

Diminutives: Lec
Variants: Alic, Alick, Aleck
Origin: Greek
This is a diminutive of Alexander that developed at the end of the nineteenth century and was especially popular in Scotland, but has since been eclipsed by Alex. Notable bearers of the name have included actor Sir Alec Guinness.

Aled

Origin: Welsh
Meaning 'offspring', this name was effectively exported from Wales in the 1980s through the Welsh soprano opera singer, Aled Jones.

Aleron

Variants: Aileron, Alerun, Ailerun
Origin: Latin
Meaning 'a child with wings'.

Alexander

Diminutives: Alex, Alec, Sanders, Sandy, Sasha, Zandra, Lex, Xander
Variants: Alessandra (Italian), Alejandra (Spanish), Alastair, Iskander
Origin: Greek
From the Greek *alexein*, meaning 'to defend', and *aner* 'man'), translated as 'defender of men'. The name has been widespread since the Middle Ages. Famous bearers of the name have included inventor Alexander Graham Bell and bacteriologist Alexander Fleming.

Alexei

Origin: Greek
A Russian variant of Alexander.

Alfonso

Variants: Alphonse, Alphonso, Alonso, Alfons
Origin: Teutonic
Meaning 'noble and ready'.

Alford

Origin: Old English
From the Old English, meaning 'from the old ford'.

Alfred

Diminutives: Alf, Alfie, Fred
Origin: Old English
Derived from the Old English

Aelfraed, itself from *aelf* ('elf') and *raed* ('counsel') and usually translated as meaning 'inspired advice'. Alternatively, it could be derived from Ealdfrith, meaning 'old peace'. It was revived in the nineteenth century but has since fallen into decline.

Algernon
Diminutives: Algie, Algy
Origin: Norman
From the Norman French *als gernons*, meaning 'with whiskers', and was originally employed as a nickname. Popular in the nineteenth century, famous bearers of the name have included poet Algernon Swinburne and writer Algernon Blackwood.

Ali
Origin: Arabic
Derived from the Arabic *ali*, meaning 'sublime' or 'elevated', it is widespread among Muslims as the name of Muhammad's cousin and the first convert to Islam.

Alonso
See Alphonse

Alphonse
Diminutives: Fonsie, Fonzie
Variants: Alfonse, Alphonsus, Alfonso, Alonso
Origin: Old German

From the Old German *adal* ('noble') and *funs*, meaning 'prompt' or 'ready'; or from *ala* ('all') and *hadu* ('struggle') or *hild* ('battle').

Alselm
Variants: Anse, Ansehlm, Ansellm
Origin: Old German
Meaning 'divine protector', this name comes from the Old German.

Alvie
See Alvin

Alvin
Diminutives: Al, Alvie
Variants: Alwyn, Aylwyn
Origin: Old English
From the Old English name Aelfwine, from *aelf* ('elf') and *wine* ('friend'), it made only rare appearances before the twentieth century. Notable bearers of the name include singer Alvin Stardust.

Alwyn
See Alvin

Ambrose
Origin: Greek
From the Roman name Ambrosius, from the Greek *ambrosios*, meaning 'divine' or 'immortal'. This name dates back to the eleventh century and enjoyed a revival in the nineteenth, but is now rare.

Famous bearers of the name have included satirist Ambrose Pierce.

Amijad
Origin: Arabic
Meaning 'glorious'.

Amil
Origin: Arabic and Sanskrit
Meaning 'industrious' and 'invaluable'.

Amitabh
Variants: Amitav
Origin: Sanskrit
This is one of the names for the Buddha, from the Sanskrit meaning 'limitless splendour'.

Amos
Origin: Hebrew
Usually interpreted as meaning 'carried by God', Amos is possibly from the Hebrew meaning 'borne' or 'carried'; alternatively, it could be from the Hebrew meaning 'courageous' or 'strong'. It remained in use until the nineteenth century, but it has since fallen into decline.

Anakin
Origin: American
Meaning 'warrior', this name was made famous by the character Anakin Skywalker in the *Star Wars* films.

Anand
Origin: Hindi
Meaning 'peaceful'.

Anders
See **Andrew**

Andrew
Diminutives: Andy, Andie, Drew
Variants: Anders
(Scandinavian), Andreas (German)
Origin: Greek
From the Greek *andreia*, meaning 'manliness', this was in regular use among English speakers by medieval times. In use ever since, it enjoyed a recent peak in the 1960s and 1970s.

Angel
Diminutives: Ange
Variants: Angelo (Italian)
Origin: Greek
Originally from the Greek *angellos*, meaning 'messenger', thus meaning 'God's messenger' or simply 'angel'. This name has made only rare appearances since the seventeenth century. A recent bearer of the name is the character Angel from the the series *Buffy the Vampire Slayer*.

Angelo
See **Angel**

Angus
Diminutives: Gus

Variants: Aonghas, Aonghus, Innes
Origin: Scottish
From the Gaelic *aon* ('one') and *ghus* ('choice'), this name remains distinctly Scottish, though English speakers adopted the name towards the end of the nineteenth century. Famous bearers of the name include TV presenter Angus Deayton.

Anil
Origin: Sanskrit
This Indian name comes from the Sanskrit word for 'wind' and is the name of a Hindu god.

Anthony
Diminutives: Tony
Variants: Antony
Origin: Obscure, possibly Etruscan
This is descended from the Roman name Antonius, and in its modern spelling was in use by the seventeenth century, but has been in decline since the 1950s. Notable bearers of the name have included Prime Minister Anthony Eden.

Aodh
See **Eugene**, **Hugh**, **Innes**, **Egan**

Aramis
Origin: French
Meaning 'fire'.

Archibald
Diminutives: Archie, Baldie
Origin: Old German
The Norman French Archambaud came from the Old German *ercan* ('genuine') and *bald* ('bold'), meaning 'truly brave'. In Scotland, it was seen as an anglicized version of Gillespie. Famous bearers of the name have included poet Archibald MacLeish.

Ardal
Origin: Irish
Meaning 'high valour', famous bearers of this Irish name include actor and comedian Ardal O'Hanlon.

Arden
Origin: Latin
Meaning 'loyal', 'sincere' or 'fiery'.

Aric
Diminutives: Rick, Rickie, Ricky
Origin: Anglo-Saxon and Scandinavian
Meaning 'sacred ruler' in Anglo-Saxon, or 'king of all' in Scandinavian (a form of Eric).

Ariel m/f
Variants: Arel
Origin: Hebrew
Meaning 'lion of God'.

Arion
Diminutives: Ari, Arie
Variants: Ariohn, Arrian
Origin: Greek
Meaning 'enchanted'.

Aris
Origin: Greek
Meaning 'best figure'.

Arkin
Diminutives: Ark
Variants: Arken
Origin: Scandinavian
Meaning 'son of the eternal king'.

Arlen
Origin: Irish
This name is derived from the Irish Gaelic word meaning 'to pledge' or 'to promise'.

Arley
See **Harley**

Armand
See **Herman**

Arnold
Diminutives: Arn, Arnie
Origin: Old German
Derived from the Old German *arn* ('eagle') and *wald* ('ruler'). In the nineteenth century it was revived, but has become less popular since the early twentieth. Famous bearers of the name include actor and politician Arnold Schwarzenegger.

Art
Origin: Celtic
Originally evolved as a diminutive of **Arthur**, at the end of the nineteenth century it became popular, especially in the USA. Particularly associated with the jazz fraternity, famous bearers of the name include saxophonist Art Tatum and singer Art Garfunkel.

Artemus
Variants: Artemas
Origin: Greek
This name is thought to have developed from the feminine name Artemis, the name of the mythological Greek goddess of the moon and the hunt. Mentioned in the New Testament, it was taken up by Puritans in the seventeenth century, but it has since been rare.

Arthur
Diminutives: Art
Variants: Artair (Scottish Gaelic)
Origin: Probably Celtic
Possibly from the Celtic *artos* ('ear') or the Irish *art*, meaning 'stone'; alternatively, it could be derived from the Roman clan name Artorius. Famous bearers of the name have included the third son of Queen Victoria, Prince Arthur.

Arun
Origin: Hindi
Meaning 'sun'.

Ashby
Variants: Ashbey, Ashton
Origin: Anglo-Saxon
Meaning 'ash-tree farm'.
See also **Ashton**

Asher
Origin: Hebrew
Meaning 'laughing one'.

Ashley m/f
Diminutives: Ash
Origin: Old English
From the Old English *aesc* ('ash') and *leah* ('wood', 'clearing'), this surname was taken up as a surname in the nineteenth century and enjoyed a huge boost in the mid-twentieth century thanks to *Gone with the Wind* character Ashley Wilkes.

Ashton
Origin: Anglo-Saxon
Meaning 'one who lives at the ash-tree farm'.
See also **Ashby**

Ashwani
Origin: Hindi
Meaning 'the first of twenty-seven galaxies orbiting the moon'.

Atarah
Origin: Hebrew
Meaning 'crown', perhaps to
bestow a regal air on the bearer.

Atwell
Origin: English
Meaning simply 'from the well'.

Aubrey m/f
Diminutives: Aub
Variants: Oberon
Origin: Old German
From the Old German *alb* ('elf')
and *richi* ('power' or 'riches'),
meaning 'elf ruler', this name
was revived in the nineteenth
century. Notable bearers of the
name have included artist
Aubrey Beardsley.

Auden
Origin: Old English
Meaning 'old friend'.

Audley
Origin: Old English
Meaning 'prospering'.

August
Variants: Augustus, Austin,
Auguste
Origin: Latin
Meaning 'exalted one', though it
could also be named simply for
the month of August.

Aurelius
Origin: Latin
Meaning 'golden friend'.

Avery
Origin: Anglo-Saxon
Meaning 'elf ruler'.
See also Alfred, Aubrey

Aviv
Origin: Hebrew
Meaning 'spring'.

Axel
Variants: Acke
Origin: Teutonic
Meaning 'father of peace'.

Ayers
Origin: Old English
Originally form the Old English
word for 'heir', this name is now
also associated with Ayers Rock
(Uluru) in Australia.

Aylmer
Variants: Ailmer
Origin: Old English
Meaning 'famous noble'
(*aethel*, meaning
'noble' and *maere*,
meaning 'famous'),
this name was in use
before the Norman
invasion but fell from
use after the medieval
period. In the
nineteenth century it enjoyed a
minor revival.
See also Elmer

Aymon
Origin: Old French
Meaning 'home'.

Aziz
Origin: Arabic
Meaning 'beloved' or 'invincible'.

Azriel
Origin: Hebrew
Meaning 'Angel of the Lord'.

Bachir
Origin: Arabic
Meaning 'welcome'.

Baha
Origin: Arabic
From the Arabic meaning 'glory' or splendour', this name is common throughout the Arab world.

Bahar
Origin: Arabic
Meaning 'sailor'.

Bailey
Variants: Baillie, Bayley, Baily
Origin: French
Meaning 'guardian' or 'trusted steward' of other people's property.

Bakari
Origin: Swahili
Meaning 'promise' or 'hope'.

Bala m/f
Origin: Sanskrit
This Indian name comes from the Sanskrit *bala*, which means 'young', and appears in ancient texts, sometimes referring to the young Krishna.

Baldwin
Variants: Maldwyn (Welsh), Baudouin (French)
Origin: Old German
From the Old German *bald* ('bold') and *wine* ('friend'), thus interpreted as meaning 'bold friend', this name was introduced from Flanders in the twelfth century but fell into decline in the Middle Ages. It was revived in the nineteenth century.

Balvinder
Origin: Hindi
Meaning 'compassionate', 'merciful'.

Bannon
Origin: Irish and Welsh
From the Irish, meaning 'a descendant of O'Babain, this is also the name of a Welsh river.

Baptiste
Variants: Baptist (English and German), Battista (Italian)
Origin: Greek
This French name ultimately derives from the Greek *batistes* ('baptist'). It has a long history in connection with Christians because of its biblical associations.

Barack
Origin: African
From the African word meaning 'blessed', this name has been made famous in recent years by US president Barack Obama.

Baram
Origin: Hebrew
Meaning 'son of the nation'.

Barden
Variants: Bardon
Origin: Old English
Meaning 'from the valley of barley'.

Barend
Origin: Dutch
Meaning 'firm bear', the ultimate meaning of this name is obscure.

Bari
Origin: Arabic
Meaning 'the maker'.

Barnabas
Diminutives: Barney
Variants: Barnaby
Origin: Aramaic
Derived ultimately from the Aramaic name Barnebhuah, meaning 'son of consolation', this was the name of one of St Paul's companions and was in use among English speakers during the Middle Ages. It was eventually eclipsed by Barnaby.

Barnes
Origin: English
Meaning 'son of Barnett' ('from the land cleared by burning').

Baron
Variants: Barron
Origin: Anglo-Saxon
Meaning 'noble warrior', the lowest rank of the peerage.

Barry
Diminutives: Baz, Bazza
Variants: Barrie
Origin: Gaelic
Derived from either the Gaelic *bearach* ('spear') or from the Irish Barra, a diminutive of Fionnbarr (*see* Finbar). This name was at a peak in the 1950s. Famous bearers of the name include comedian Barry Humphries and singer Barry Manilow.

Bartholomew
Diminutives: Bart
Origin: Aramaic
This biblical name is derived from the Aramaic for 'son of Talmai' (Talmai means 'abounding in furrows'). This name has been in occasional use among English speakers since medieval times.

Bashir
Origin: Sanskrit
Meaning 'a bringer of good news'.

Basil
Diminutives: Bas, Baz
Variants: Vasili (Russian)
Origin: Greek
Evolved originally from the Greek *basileus* ('king') and thus translated as meaning 'royal'. The name was revived in the nineteenth century. Popular in the 1920s, it has been in decline since. A famous bearer of the name is Basil Fawlty in the TV series *Fawlty Towers*.

Baxter
Diminutives: Bax, Baxie
Variants: Baxther
Origin: English
Meaning simply 'baker'.

Baz
See Barry, Basil

Beagan
Origin: Irish
Meaning 'little'.

Beaman
Origin: Anglo-Saxon
Meaning 'the bee-keeper'.

Beattie
Origin: Gaelic
Meaning 'public provider', someone who would supply food and drink for a town's inhabitants.

Beau
Origin: French
Taken straight from the French word for 'handsome', this name only started to appear regularly after the publication of *Beau Geste* by P. C. Wren in 1924. Famous bearers of the name include actor Beau Bridges.

Beck
Variants: Bec
Origin: Anglo-Saxon
Meaning simply 'brook'.

Bela
Origin: Hungarian
Meaning 'within'. Arguably, the most famous bearer of the name was actor Bela Lugosi.

Belden
Variants: Beldon
Origin: Anglo-Saxon
Meaning 'one who lives in the beautiful glen'.

Bellamy
Origin: Old French
Meaning literally 'handsome friend', this was a surname before being adopted for occasional use as a first name.

Benedict
Variants: Benedick, Bennett, Benoit
Origin: Latin
From the Latin *benedictus*, meaning 'blessed'. This name

enjoyed a revival in the 1980s and 1990s, but lost favour in the USA due to Benedict Arnold, a US Revolutionary soldier who colluded with the British.

Benjamin
Diminutives: Ben, Benny, Benji
Origin: Hebrew
With various interpretations as to its meaning, this is often seen as meaning 'favourite'. It was taken up by Puritans in the seventeenth century and is well established as a Jewish name. Notable bearers of the name have included prime minister Benjamin Disraeli.

Benoit
See Benedict

Benroy
Origin: Hebrew
Meaning 'son of a lion'.

Benson
Origin: Hebrew
Meaning 'son of Benjamin'.
See Benjamin

Bentley
Variants: Bently
Origin: Old English
A place name in various areas of England, this name is derived from the Old English *beonet* ('bent grass') and *leah* ('wood',

'clearing'), so meaning 'place of coarse grass', this was taken up as a surname and then an occasional first name.

Benton
Origin: Anglo-Saxon
Meaning 'from the town on the moors'.

Berg
Variants: Bergren, Burgess
Origin: Teutonic
Meaning 'mountain'.

Bert
Variants: Burt, Bertie
Origin: Various roots
This developed as a diminutive of such names as Albert, Bertram and Herbert. Between the nineteenth century and the middle of the twentieth, it was popular, but it has since declined. Famous bearers of the name include actor Burt Reynolds.

Berthold
Variants: Barthold, Bertolt
Origin: Old German
From the Old German *berht* ('bright' or 'famous') and either *wald* ('ruler') or *hold* ('lovely' or 'fair'). Famous bearers of the name have included playwright Berthold Brecht.

Bertram
Diminutives: Bert, Bertie, Burt
Origin: Old German
From *beraht* ('famous' or 'bright') and *hramn* ('raven'), which has been interpreted as 'wise person'. Common among English speakers during the Middle Ages, it was revived in the nineteenth century, but was eclipsed by its diminutives from the early 1900s.

Berwick
Origin: Old English
Meaning 'barley grange'.

Bharat
Origin: Sanskrit
This is an Indian name which is derived from the Sanskrit *bharata*, meaning 'being maintained'. In Indian mythology, it is an alternative name for Agni, god of fire, and of the son of King Dushyanta.

Bhaskar
Origin: Sanskrit
From the Sanskrit *bhas* ('light') and *kara* ('making'), meaning 'shining', the name appears in Indian mythology as one of Shiva's names and was the name of a medieval astronomer and mathematician.

Bildad
Origin: Hebrew
Meaning 'beloved'.

Blaine
Origin: Obscure
This Scottish surname has been in occasional use as a first name since the early twentieth century, likely a modern variant of Blane, a much older name borne by a sixth-century bishop.

Blake m/f
Origin: Old English
From *blaec* ('black') or *blac* ('white'), this has been used as a first name since at least the nineteenth century. Famous bearers of the name include film director Blake Edwards.

Blas
Variants: Blaze
Origin: German
Meaning 'firebrand'.

Blue
Origin: English
Simply named after the colour.

Bond
Origin: English
Meaning 'tied to the earth'.

Booth
Origin: Old Norse
From the Old Norse meaning 'shed' or 'hut', this was a surname before being adopted as a first name.

Boris
Diminutives: Boba, Borya
Origin: Old Slavonic or Tartar
From Old Slavonic *bor* ('struggle' or 'fight'), but more likely from the Tartar name Bogoris, meaning 'small'. The nineteenth century saw it taken up by English speakers and it has remained in irregular use to the present day. Famous bearers of the name include poet Boris Pasternak and tennis player Boris Becker.

Bosley
Origin: Old English
Meaning 'tree grove'.

Boyce
Origin: French
This English surname comes from the French for 'wood' (*bois*) and has been used as a first name since the early twentieth century.

Boyd
Origin: Scottish
From the Gaelic *buidhe*, meaning 'yellow', this Scottish surname has been in use as a surname on an irregular basis since the early twentieth century. *Gone with the Wind* by Margaret Mitchell includes a character named Boyd Tarleton.

Bradley
Diminutives: Brad
Origin: Old English
From the Old English *brad* ('broad') and *leah* ('wood' or 'clearing'), it has been used as an occasional first name since the nineteenth century, mainly in the USA. A famous bearer of the diminutive Brad is actor Brad Pitt.
See also Leigh

Brady
Origin: Irish
This name is likely to have derived from the Irish *bragha*, meaning 'chest' or 'throat', thus translated as 'large-chested'.

Bram
See Abraham or Bramwell

Bramwell
Diminutives: Bram
Origin: English
Place name meaning 'place of brambles' that was taken up as a surname and first name. Famous bearers of the name have included Bramwell Brontë, brother of the celebrated sisters.

Bran
Origin: Celtic
Meaning 'raven', which is the symbol of eternal youth.

Branson
Origin: English
Meaning 'son of Brand'.

Breck
Origin: Irish
Meaning 'freckled'.

Brandon
Variants: Brendon
Origin: Old English
From *brom* ('broom' or 'gorse')

and *dun* ('hill'), this was taken up as an occasional first name, perhaps under the influence of the Irish name Brendon. Most popular in the USA, a recent bearer of the name was actor Brandon Lee, son of Bruce Lee.

Brennan
Origin: Gaelic
Meaning 'teardrop'.

Brett
Variants: Bret
Origin: English from French
This name was given to Breton settlers in medieval times and its use as a first name has been increasing, especially in the USA, since the mid-twentieth century.

Brewster
Diminutives: Brew
Variants: Brewer
Origin: English
Meaning 'brewer'.

Brian
Diminutives: Bri
Variants: Brien, Bryan, Brion, Bryant
Origin: Irish Gaelic
Originally from the Gaelic *brigh*, meaning 'power' or 'strength'; famous bearers of the name include singer Bryan Ferry and actor Brian Blessed.

Brigham
Origin: English
English place name from the Old English *brycg* ('bridge') and *ham* ('homestead'). It is usually associated in the USA with the Mormon leader Brigham Young.

Brinley
Origin: English
Meaning 'tawny-coloured'.

Broderick
Origin: Old German
An English name meaning 'son of Roderick'. The influence of Roderick probably contributed to its use as a first name.

Brodie
Variants: Brody
Origin: Scottish
This name is derived from the Gaelic for 'ditch'. It was in use as a surname before being adopted as a first name.

Brook
Origin: English
Meaning 'dweller by a brook', this was taken up as a surname near the end of the nineteenth century. Initially adopted by African-Americans, it has since become more widespread.

Brooklyn m/f
Origin: English
Named for the district in New York City, this name came to prominence in 1999 when David and Victoria Beckham selected it for their son.

Bruce
Origin: Norman
Originally a Scottish surname, taken from the Norman French baronial name de Brus. Recently a generic word for men in Australia, famous bearers of the name include rock star Bruce Springsteen.

Bruno
Origin: Old German
Derived from the Old German

brun, originally reserved for people with brown hair, the name was in use in medieval times and was revived near the end of the nineteenth century.

Bryden
Origin: Irish
Meaning 'strong one'.

Bryn m/f
Variants: Brin
Origin: Welsh
This name is derived from the Welsh *bryn*, meaning 'hill', also used as a diminutive of Brynmor. It is likely to have been a twentieth-century introduction, and famous bearers of the name include opera singer Bryn Terfel.

Buck
Origin: English
Taken from the ordinary vocabulary word for a male deer or goat, suggesting a lively and spirited person. Early in the twentieth century it was quite popular in the USA, promoted by the fictional character Buck Rogers.

Burke
Origin: French
Meaning 'fortified settlement'.

Burl
Origin: French
Meaning 'knotty wood'.

Burleigh
Origin: English
Meaning 'from the clearing of knotted tree trunks'.

Buster
Origin: American
Meaning 'puncher', this is usually a nickname.

Byron
Variants: Byren, Biron, Biryn
Origin: Old English
Originally from *aet thaem byrum*, meaning 'at the byres', this has made occasional appearances as a first name quite recently. Usually associated with the poet Lord Byron.

Cailean
Origin: Scottish
From the Gaelic meaning 'victorious warrior'.
See also Colin

Calder
Origin: Gaelic and English
From the Gaelic meaning 'one who lives by the oak' and the English meaning 'from the cold stream'.

Caldwell
Origin: English
Meaning literally 'from the cold well'.

Caleb
Origin: Hebrew
Derived from the Hebrew Kaleb, which has been interpreted in a variety of ways, including 'bold', 'dog' or 'intrepid', taken to suggest a doglike devotion to God. Because of its biblical associations, it was taken up by the Puritans after the Reformation and was popular in the USA.

Calhoun
Origin: Gaelic
From the Scottish Gaelic meaning 'from the forest strip'.

Calum
Diminutives: Cal, Caley, Cally
Variants: Callum

Origin: Roman
This Scottish name derives from the Roman Columba, meaning 'dove'. Its associations with St Columba mean it is closely linked with Scotland, though it has been increasing in popularity since the mid-twentieth century, with a peak in the 1990s.
See also Malcolm

Calvin
Diminutives: Cal
Variants: Kelvin
Origin: Latin
From the Latin *calvus* ('bald') via the French *chauve*, this was taken up as a name by English speakers in the sixteenth century in tribute to theologian Jean Calvin.

Camden
Origin: Gaelic
Meaning 'from the winding valley'.

Cameron m/f
Origin: Gaelic
From the Gaelic *cam shron*, meaning 'crooked nose', it has been in use among English speakers since the early twentieth century. Retaining its links with Scotland, it has become increasingly popular among English speakers since the 1990s.

Campbell
Origin: Gaelic
From the Gaelic *cam beul*, meaning 'crooked mouth', this name has been in use for centuries, primarily in Scotland.

Carey m/f
Origin: Various roots
Developed as a variant of Cary in the nineteenth century; the Irish use may be derived from *O Ciardha* (meaning 'descendant of the dark one'). It can be traced back to the Welsh place name Carew. Until the 1950s, it was used as a boys' name but is now given almost exclusively to girls.

Carl
Variants: Karl (German)
Origin: Old English
Derived from the Old English *ceorl*, meaning 'free man', or as a diminutive of Carlton. In the middle of the nineteenth century, it was taken up by English speakers, enjoying a surge in popularity in the 1970s and 1980s. Notable bearers of the name have included astronomer Carl Sagan.
See also Charles

Carlton
Diminutives: Carl
Origin: Old English

From the Old English *ceorl* ('free man') and *tun*, meaning 'settlement', used as a surname and then as a first name at the end of the nineteenth century.

Carson
Origin: English
This name may have been based on a place name which remains unidentified and records of its use as a name go back to the thirteenth century. It is mainly associated with people with Scottish or Irish connections.

Carter
Origin: English and Scottish
As an English name, the meaning of this is self-explanatory in that it once denoted a person who transported goods by cart. In Scotland, it is sometimes treated as an anglicization of the Gaelic Mac Artair.

Carver
Origin: Cornish
This name comes from the Cornish meaning 'great rock'.

Cassidy
Origin: Irish
This name derives from the Irish *O Caiside* and is quite a recent introduction as a first name. It is mainly confined to the USA.

Cecil
Origin: Latin
From the Roman Caecilius, from the Latin *caecus*, meaning 'blind', or the Welsh *seissylt*, from the Latin *sextus*, meaning 'sixth'. It was not in use as a first name until the nineteenth century. Popular in the early twentieth century, it has since become rare.

Cedric
Origin: English or Welsh
Either from the Old English name Cerdic, the meaning of which is uncertain, or the Welsh *ced* ('bounty') and *drych* ('pattern'), meaning 'pattern of generosity'. It is thought that Sir Walter Scott misspelled the name in *Ivanhoe*.

Chadwick
Diminutives: Chad
Origin: Anglo-Saxon
Meaning 'town of the warrior'.

Chandler
Origin: English
The traditional name for a candle maker, this name enjoyed a boost in the 1990s thanks to the character Chandler in the TV series *Friends*.

Charles
Diminutives: Chas, Charlie, Chay, Chick
Variants: Tearlach

Origin: Old German and Irish
From the Old German *karl*, meaning 'free man', though also used as an anglicization of the Irish name Cearbhall. The mid-nineteenth century saw a peak and its use has continued. Famous bearers of the name include Charles, the Prince of Wales.
See also Carl

Chase
Origin: English
Derived from a nickname used in medieval times for a hunter, this name comes from the ordinary vocabulary word and is used mainly in the USA.

Cheney
Variants: Chaney, Cheyney
Origin: French
Meaning 'a woodman', 'one who lives in the oak wood'.

Chesney
Diminutives: Ches, Chet
Origin: English
This surname has been in use as a first name since the early twentieth century. Notable bearers of the name have included comedian Chesney Allen.

Chester
Diminutives: Chet

Origin: Latin
This name comes from the English place name, which derives from the Latin *castra*, meaning 'fort' or 'camp'. It has made occasional appearances as a first name since the end of the nineteenth century and famous bearers of the name have included US president Chester A. Arthur.

Chet
See **Chesney**, **Chester**

Christian
Diminutives: Chris, Kit
Origin: Latin
Taken from the Roman name Christianus, this was adopted by English speakers in the seventeenth century and was promoted by the character Christian in John Bunyan's *The Pilgrim's Progress*. Famous bearers of the name include actors Christian Slater and Christian Bale.

Christopher
Diminutives: Chris, Christy, Kit, Chip, Kris
Variants: Kester
Origin: Greek
Derived from the Greek *kristos* ('Christ') and *pherein* ('to bear'), this can be interpreted as meaning 'bearing Christ', a reference to St Christopher. The name enjoyed a revival in the twentieth century. Famous bearers of the name have included architect Christopher Wren and actor Christopher Plummer.

Chrysander
Origin: Greek
Meaning 'golden man'.

Cian
Variants: Kean, Keane
Origin: Irish
This Irish name comes from the Gaelic meaning 'ancient one', this name was borne by the son-in-law of Brian Boru.

Ciaran
Variants: Kieran
Origin: Irish
Meaning 'dark-haired one'.

Clarence
Diminutives: Clarrie, Clancy
Origin: Latin
This name means 'of Clare' and was adopted as a ducal title in the fourteenth century. It was used as an occasional first name in the nineteenth century, partly as a tribute to Queen Victoria's grandson, Albert Victor, Duke of Clarence.

Clark
Variants: Clarke
Origin: English
Taken from the ordinary vocabulary word, this has been used as a first name since the end of the nineteenth century, mainly in the USA. Famous bearers of the name have included actor Clark Gable.

Clayton
Diminutives: Clay
Origin: Old English
From the place name taken from the Old English *claeg* ('clay') and *tun*, meaning 'settlement', this was used first as a surname and then as a first name.

Clement
Diminutives: Clem
Origin: Latin
From the Latin *clemens*, meaning 'merciful', this name was common in medieval times and has survived to the present day, though it is now rare. Famous bearers of the name have included Prime Minister Clement Attlee.

Clifford
Diminutives: Cliff
Origin: English
This place name was taken up as a personal name in the

nineteenth century and comes from the Old English *clif* ('cliff' or 'riverbank') and *ford*, meaning simply 'ford'. Popular in the first half of the twentieth century, especially in the USA, it has since become less common.

Clint
Origin: English
Derived from the surname Clinton, which may come from the same source as Clifton, this meaning 'town on a cliff', this was initially adopted by English speakers in the USA in tribute to the Clinton family, but is now more associated with the actor and director Clint Eastwood.

Clive
Origin: English
This place name was adopted as a first name around the mid-nineteenth century. The place name was based on *clif* ('cliff' or 'riverbank'). It is likely the first bearer of the name was the character Clive Newcombe in Thackeray's novel *The Newcombes* in 1853–55. A modern bearer of the name is TV presenter Clive Anderson.

Clyde
Origin: Scottish
Taken from the name of the river in Scotland, this was adopted as a first name in the nineteenth century. The name itself has been translated as 'the washer' and has ancient origins. It was initially popular among African-Americans and the twentieth century saw it become more widespread.

Cody m/f
Variants: Codey, Kodey
Origin: Probably Irish
This is thought to have come from the Irish name meaning 'a descendant of a helpful person' and is more common in the USA than in the UK.

Coleman
Variants: Colman
Origin: Latin
Based on the Latin for 'dove', this name developed from the Roman Columba.

Colin
Variants: Coll, Collin, Colyn, Collwyn, Cailean
Origin: Greek
Originally found as Col, a diminutive of Nicholas, this is now regarded as a name in its own right. In Scotland, it can be seen as an anglicization of Cailean, meaning 'whelp' or 'puppy'. This name was revived in the twentieth century.

Coll
Origin: Celtic
Originally from the Scottish Gaelic Colla, from the Celtic word for 'high', this is often found as a diminutive of Colin.

Colley
Origin: Irish
This Irish name translates as 'swarthy'.

Comfort m/f
Origin: English
Fairly popular after the Reformation, it seems likely it is now defunct as a first name.

Connor
Diminutives: Con, Conn
Variants: Conor
Origin: Irish
This name was originally given to hunters, as it comes from the Irish Gaelic Conchobar or Conchobhar, which is thought to mean 'hound lover' or 'wolf lover'. It was the name of a legendary Irish king.

Consuelo
Diminutives: Chelo, Suelo
Variants: Consuela (f)
Origin: Spanish
Meaning simply 'consolation', a friend in need; also attributed to the Spanish name for the Virgin Mary ('Our Lady of Consolation').

Corey
Origin: English
Since the 1960s, this has been used occasionally as a first name, chiefly among African-Americans.

Cornelius
Diminutives: Corney, Cornie, Corny
Origin: Probably Latin
This biblical name probably has as its root the Latin word *cornu*, meaning 'horn'. It came from the Netherlands in the fifteenth century and was popular in the nineteenth.

Courtney m/f
Variants: Courtenay
Origin: English, from Norman
From the Norman place name, meaning 'domain of Curtius', this has been a name for boys since the mid-sixteenth century. Famous bearers of the name have included jazz musician Courtney Pine.

Craig
Origin: Scottish
Derived from the Gaelic *creag*, meaning 'crag', this has been used as a first name since the mid-nineteenth century. It was once uniquely Scottish but has now become more widespread. Famous bearers of the name include actor Craig McLachlan.

Crispin
Variants: Crispian
Origin: Roman
This name is derived from the Roman Crispinus, from the nickname Crispus, meaning 'curly-haired'. Adopted by English speakers in the seventeenth century, it remained popular into the twentieth, but has since suffered a decline.

Curt
See CurtisCurtis
Diminutives: Curt
Origin: French

Derived from the Old French *curteis*, meaning 'courteous', this has been in occasional use since the eleventh century. It also derives from the Middle English *curt*, meaning 'short', and *hose* ('hose' 'leggings'). A famous bearer of the name is musician Curtis Mayfield.

Cyril
Origin: Greek
This name is derived from the Greek *kurios* ('lord') via Kyrillos and was borne by several early saints, including St Cyril, inventor of the Cyrillic alphabet. It has been in decline since the 1920s and is now rare. Famous bearers of the name include politician Sir Cyril Smith.

Cyrus
Diminutives: Cy
Origin: Biblical
This biblical name probably derived from the Greek *kurios* ('lord') via Kyros; alternatively, it may have evolved from the Persian meaning 'sun' or 'throne'. English speakers have used the name since the seventeenth century and it enjoyed a modest peak in the USA in the nineteenth.

Daegal
Origin: Scandinavian
Meaning 'a boy born at dawn'.

Daegan
Origin: Irish
Meaning 'dark-haired one'.

Dafydd
See David

Dahab
Origin: Arabic
Meaning 'gold'.

Dai
Origin: Celtic
This Welsh name is derived from the Celtic *dei*, meaning 'to shine', but it is often considered to be a diminutive form of David. Since the nineteenth century, it has come to be known as a definitively Welsh name, and is virtually unknown outside Welsh-speaking areas.

Daithe
Variants: Dahy
Origin: Irish
Meaning 'capable', this is often anglicized to Dahy, its phonetic pronunciation.

Dakota m/f
Origin: Native American
Meaning 'friend' or 'partner', this is the name of a Native American tribe.

Dale m/f
Origin: English
From the ordinary vocabulary word 'dale', meaning 'valley', this was adopted by English speakers, primarily in America, in the nineteenth century. Initially a boys' name, it was later adopted as a name for girls.

Dalton
Diminutives: Dal, Dalt, Tony
Origin: Anglo-Saxon
Meaning 'from the farm in the valley'.

Dalziel
Origin: Scottish
Pronounced 'Dee-el', this means 'from the small field'.

Damek
Origin: Slavonic
Meaning 'man of the earth'.

Damian
Variants: Damien (French), Damon
Origin: Greek
From the Greek *daman* ('to subdue', 'to rule') via Damianos, use of this name was irregular until the twentieth century.

It enjoyed a peak in the 1970s, partly due to the popularity of the character Damien from the film *The Omen*.

Damon
Origin: Greek
Originally a diminutive of Damian, Greek mythology tells the story of Damon and Pythias. Famous bearers of the name include racing driver Damon Hill.

Dan
Origin: Various, depending on root name.
Derived from the Hebrew Dan, meaning 'judge', but more often regarded as a diminutive of Daniel, the name appears in the Bible as the name of one of Jacob's sons. Famous bearers of the name include actor Dan Ackroyd.

Dana m/f
Origin: Hebrew
Regarded as a diminutive of Daniel in the nineteenth century, but can also be traced back to the identical surname. Now mainly reserved for girls, as a diminutive of Donna and Danielle.
See also Dane

Danby
Origin: Norse
Meaning 'from the Danish settlement'.

Dane
Origin: English
Thought to have developed as a variant of Dean, this name has increased in frequency since the early twentieth century, but it is rare outside the USA.
See also Dana

Daniel
Diminutives: Dan, Dana, Danny
Origin: Hebrew
Meaning 'God has judged' or 'God is my judge', this name is popular in Ireland, where it is seen as an anglicized version of Domhnall; in Wales, it may be seen as an English version of Deiniol, meaning 'charming' or 'attractive'. Notable bearers of the name have included writer Daniel Defoe and singer Daniel O'Donnell.

Dante
Origin: Latin
From the Latin *durare*, meaning 'to endure', the most famous bearers of this name have been poet Dante Alighieri and artist Dante Gabriel Rossetti.

Dara m/f
Variants: Darach
Origin: Irish and Hebrew
Derived from the Gaelic Mac Dara, this is sometimes anglicized as Dudley. Among Jewish communities, it is a girls' name and is traced back to the Hebrew for 'pearl of wisdom'.

Darby
Origin: Old Norse or Irish
This name, based on the English place name Derby, from the Old Norse *diur* ('deer') and *byr* ('settlement'), and is sometimes seen as an anglicization of Dermot.

Darcy
Variants: D'Arcy
Origin: Norman
From the Norman surname d'Arcy ('from Arcy'), this has been in occasional use since the nineteenth century. The name was given a boost by the character Fitzwilliam Darcy in Jane Austen's *Pride and Prejudice*, published in 1813.

Dario
Origin: Persian
From the Persian *daraya* ('to hold' 'to possess') and *vahu* ('well', 'good'), so meaning 'wealthy' or 'protector', via the Roman name Darius.

Darius
See Dario

Darragh
Origin: Irish
Meaning 'dark oak'.

Darren
Diminutives: Daz
Variants: Darran, Darrin, Darin
Origin: Probably Norman
Thought to have developed as a variant of Darryl, this name first appeared in the 1920s in the USA. The 1960s and 1970s saw a peak in its popularity, but it has since been in decline.

Darrick
Origin: Old German
Meaning 'power of the tribe'.

Darryl m/f
Variants: Daryl, Darel, Darell, Darrell
Origin: Norman or Old English
From the Norman d'Airelle, a baronial surname, this has been in use as a name for both girls and boys since the early twentieth century. Other sources suggest the name comes from the Old English *deorling*, meaning 'darling'. A male bearer of the name is singer Daryl Hall.

Darshan
Origin: Hindi
Meaning 'vision'.

Darwin
Variants: Derwin
Origin: Old English
Meaning 'dear friend', this is most commonly associated with the naturalist Charles Darwin.

Dashiell
Origin: French
Meaning 'page boy'.

David
Diminutives: Dave, Davey, Davie
Variants: Dafydd, Dewi, Daibhidh (Gaelic), Taffy, Tay
Origin: Hebrew
Believed to mean 'beloved' or 'darling', this biblical name has remained one of the most popular of boys' names since medieval times. The patron saint of Wales, notable bearers of the name include rock star David Bowie.
See also David

Davin
Origin: Scandinavian
Meaning 'brightness of the Finns'.

Davis
Origin: Anglo-Saxon from Hebrew
Meaning 'David's son'.
See also David

Dayton
Origin: Old English from Hebrew
Meaning 'David's place'.

Dean
Variants: Deane, Dene
Origin: Old English
This name has been in use as a surname since the nineteenth century. It can be traced to *denu*, meaning 'valley' or it could also relate to the rank of dean. Probably used as a first name initially in the USA. Famous bearers of the name have included singer and actor Dean Martin.

Declan
Origin: Irish
This is an English version of the Irish Deaglan, but the meaning is uncertain. It became popular as a first name in the 1940s and, from the 1980s, it became more widespread.

Deems
Origin: Anglo-Saxon
Meaning 'the judge's son'.

Deepak
Variants: Deepan
Origin: Indian
Meaning 'illumination'. Famous bearers of the name include the writer Deepak Chopra.

Delaney
Origin: Gaelic
Meaning 'descendant of the challenger'.

Delroy
Origin: French
Derived as a variant of Leroy, which itself can be traced to the French 'le roy', meaning 'king'. It has been fairly popular since the mid-twentieth century.

Demas
Origin: Greek
Meaning 'popular person'.

Dempsey
Origin: Gaelic
This English name has its roots in the Gaelic word for 'proud descendant' and was a surname before being adopted as a first name.

Denholm
Variants: Denham
Origin: Old English
Derived from the Old English *denu*, meaning 'valley', and *holm* ('island'). Famous bearers of the name have included actor Denholm Elliott.

Denley
Origin: English
Meaning 'from the valley clearing'.

D

Babies' Names ✤ Boys

Dennis

Diminutives: Den, Denny
Variants: Denis, Denys
Origin: Greek
From the Greek Dionysios, the god of wine, this name has been less popular since the seventeenth century. Revived in the early twentieth century, it has fallen from favour since the 1970s.

Denzel

Variants: Denzil, Denzyl
Origin: Cornish
Thought to mean 'fort' or 'fertile upland', from the Cornish place name Denzell, records of this name go back to the sixteenth century. Famous bearers of the name include actor Denzel Washington.

Deon

Origin: Greek
Meaning 'of Zeus'.

Derek

Diminutives: Del, Derry, Derk, Dirk
Variants: Derrick, Deryk, Deryck, Derrick
Origin: Old German
Ultimately derived from the Old German name Theodoric, meaning 'ruler of the people', it is believed this name came to England with Flemish immigrants in the fifteenth century. It gained purchase in the nineteenth century but has never been popular in the USA.

Dermot

Variants: Diarmid, Diarmuid, Diarmad (Scottish)
Origin: Gaelic
This name probably derives from the Gaelic *di*, meaning 'without', and *airmait* ('envy'). With the spelling of Dermot, it appeared in Ireland in the nineteenth century and retains its Irish connections even when used outside Ireland itself.
See also Jeremiah

Derry

See Darius, Derek

Desmond

Diminutives: Des, Dez, Desi
Origin: Gaelic
Derived from the Gaelic surname Deas-Mhumhan, meaning 'from south Munster' it came to England near the end of the nineteenth century, but since the mid-twentieth century, it has become less used. A notable bearer of the name is anthropologist Desmond Morris.

Dev

Variants: Deb, Deo
Origin: Sanskrit
This name is derived from the Sanskrit *deva*, which means 'god'.

Devereux

Origin: Norman French
This surname, from the Norman French *de Evereux* ('from Evreux'), has made occasional appearances as a first name, mainly in the USA.

Devlin

Origin: Gaelic
This Irish name means 'fiercely brave'.

Devon m/f

Origin: English
Named for the county of Devon, this name is popular among African-Americans, making more of an appearance during the latter half of the twentieth century.

Devyn

Origin: Irish
Meaning 'poet'.

Dewi

Variants: Dewey
Origin: Welsh, from Hebrew
This name has ancient roots and made a comeback in the twentieth century. It is a Welsh equivalent of David.

Dialo
Variants: Diallo
Origin: African
Meaning 'bold'.

Dickon
See Richard

Didier
Diminutives: Didi
Origin: Latin
This French name is derived from the Latin *desiderium* ('longing') via the Roman Desiderius.

Diego
Origin: Probably Greek
Thought to be derived from the Greek *didakhe* ('teaching'), this Spanish name is often treated as a variant of Santiago. Famous bearers of the name include footballer Diego Maradona.

Dieter
Origin: Old German
From the Old German *theuth*, meaning 'race' or 'people', and *hari* ('army' or 'warrior').

Digby
Origin: Old Norse
From the Lincolnshire place name, itself from the Old Norse *diki* ('ditch') and *byr* ('settlement'), translated as 'farm by a ditch', this has been used as a first name since the nineteenth century.

Dion
Origin: Greek
Either from the Greek name Dionysios, or from another Greek source, Dion was adopted as a first name in the sixteenth century and remains in use, but is uncommon, most popular with African-American communities in the USA.

Dirk
See Derek

Dixon
Origin: English, from Old German
Meaning 'son of Dick'.
See also Richard

Dodd
Origin: Teutonic
Meaning 'of the people'.

Dolan
Origin: Gaelic
Meaning 'black-haired'.

Dominic
Diminutives: Dom, Nic
Variants: Dominique (m/f)
Origin: Latin
Ultimately derived from the Latin *dominus* ('lord') via the Roman name Dominicus. In medieval times, it was popular among English speakers, often reserved for children born on a Sunday. In Ireland, it is often treated as an anglicization of Domhnall.

Donaghan
Origin: Celtic
Meaning 'dark-skinned'.

Donahue
Diminutives: Don, Donn, Donnie, Donny
Origin: Gaelic
Meaning 'warrior dressed in brown'.

Donald
Diminutives: Don, Donny
Origin: Celtic
This name derives from the Gaelic name Domhnall, from *dubno* ('world') and *val* ('rule', 'mighty'). The final 'd' could be the influence of Ronald or from attempts by non-Gaelic speakers to pronounce it. It has close associations with Scotland but made in the 1920s it became popular elsewhere and has remained in use. Famous bearers of the name include actors Donald Pleasance and Donald Sutherland.

Donnacha

Variants: Donagh
Origin: Celtic
Meaning 'brown-haired fighter' in the Irish Gaelic, it is also an Irish variant of the Scottish name Duncan.

Donovan

Diminutives: Don, Donny
Origin: Irish
This name is derived from the Gaelic *donn* ('brown') and *dubh* ('black', 'dark'), referring to a person's eye colour, hair or complexion. It was adopted by English speakers in the early twentieth century, including those with no Irish connections.

Dorian m/f

Variants: Dorien, Dorrien
Origin: Greek
This name comes from the Greek Dorieus ('person from Doris'), via the Roman Dorianus. It seems to have made its first appearance in the Oscar Wilde novel *The Picture of Dorian Gray*.

Dorsey

Origin: French
From the French d'Orsay.

Dory

Origin: French
Derived from the French meaning 'golden'.

Dougal

Diminutives: Doug, Dougie
Variants: Dugald, Doyle
Origin: Gaelic
This is an anglicized version of Dubhgall or Dughall, from the Gaelic *dubh* ('black') and *gall* ('stranger'), and originally referred to the dark-haired Danish settlers in Ireland. Later adopted in Scotland, it became more widespread in the early twentieth century.

Douglas

Diminutives: Doug, Dougie
Origin: Scottish
Derived from the Gaelic *dubh* ('black') and *glas* ('stream'), this was adopted as a first name in the nineteenth century. Originally a gender-neutral name, it has been reserved exclusively for boys since the seventeenth century. In the twentieth century, it became less common.

Doyle

See Dougal

Drake

Origin: English
From the surname meaning 'dragon', this name is uncommon.

Drew m/f

Origin: Uncertain
Either a diminutive of Andrew or from the Old German name Drogo, this name established itself in Scotland initially, and was adopted elsewhere in the 1940s. It is usually a name for boys.

Driscoll

Variants: Driscol
Origin: Irish
Derived from the Gaelic for 'interpreter'.

Drystan

see Tristram

Duane

Variants: Dwayne, Dwane
Origin: Gaelic
This is derived from the Gaelic *dubh* ('black'), via Dubhan and became popular among English speakers in the 1940s. Reaching a peak in the 1970s, it is often associated with the 1950s, as famous bearers of the name include guitarist Duane Eddy.

Dudley
Diminutives: Dud
Origin: Old English or Irish
From the Old English 'clearing or wood of Dudda', this was originally a surname and was adopted as a first name in the nineteenth century. It is also found as an anglicized version of Dubhdara or Dara. Famous bearers of the name have included actor Dudley Moore.

Dugan
Variants: Doogan, Dougan
Origin: Gaelic
Meaning 'dark-skinned'.

Duke
Origin: English or Celtic
This is found as a diminutive of Marmaduke or derived from the rank or title of 'duke'. It was adopted in the early twentieth century, mainly in the USA. Notable bearers of the name have included jazz musician Duke Ellington.

Duncan
Diminutives: Dunk, Dunkie, Dunky
Origin: Celtic
An English version of the Scottish Gaelic Donnchadh, from *donn* ('dark') and *cath* ('battle'), thus meaning 'dark warrior', this name was adopted widely outside Scotland in the twentieth century and enjoyed a peak in the 1960s. It is now less common, and famous bearers of the name include swimmer Duncan Goodhew.

Dunham
Origin: Celtic
Meaning 'dark man'.

Dunstan
Origin: Old English
From the Old English *dun* ('dark') and *stan*, meaning 'stone', this was originally a surname and used as a first name from medieval times, mainly among Roman Catholics because it was the name of a tenth-century saint.

Durant
Variants: Dante, Durand
Origin: Latin
Meaning 'enduring', suggesting long-lasting friendships.

Dustin
Origin: Uncertain
This has been in use as a first name since the early twentieth century, perhaps deriving from Old Norse or Old German. The most famous bearer of the name is undoubtedly actor Dustin Hoffman.
See also Dusty

Dusty m/f
Origin: English
Either a feminine version of Dustin or simply from the ordinary vocabulary word 'dusty'.

Dwight
Origin: Uncertain
This name was probably derived from the French name Diot and has made occasional appearance as a first name since the late nineteenth century, mainly in the USA. It has also been suggested that it comes from Dionysius (*see* Dennis).

Dyani
Origin: Native American
Meaning 'eagle'.

Dylan
Origin: Probably Celtic
This name can probably be traced to the Celtic word for 'sea' via the Welsh *dylif* ('flood'), perhaps meaning 'son of the wave' or 'influence', as has been put forward by some. Probably the most famous bearer of the name was poet Dylan Thomas.

Eachan

Variants: Eachann
Origin: Scottish
This name is derived from the Gaelic *each* ('horse') and *donn* ('brown'), and sometimes considered to be the Gaelic equivalent of Hector.

Eagan

Origin: Irish
Meaning 'mighty'.

Eamonn

See Edmund

Earl

Origin: Old English
This name is from the aristocratic title 'earl', from the Old English *eorl* ('chieftain' or 'nobleman'). It became popular in the seventeenth century, especially among African-Americans. A well-known bearer of the name is actor James Earl Jones.

Easton

Variants: Easten
Origin: English
Meaning 'town in the east'.

Eben

Origin: Hebrew
Meaning 'rock', suggesting a reliable personality.

Eckhard

Variants: Eckhardt, Eckehard
Origin: Old German
Derived from the Old German *ek* ('edge') and *hardu* ('hardy', 'brave').

Eden

Origin: Old English and Hebrew
This name comes from the Old English name Edon or Edun, from *ead* ('riches') and *hun* ('bear cub'). The Hebrew *eden*, meaning 'paradise' or 'delight', was adopted by Puritans in the seventeenth century, though it has never been common.

Edgar

Diminutives: Ed, Eddie
Origin: Old English
Derived ultimately from the Old English *ead* ('riches') and *gar*, meaning 'spear', this name translates as 'owner of many spears'. Revived in the nineteenth century, it has been in decline since the early twentieth. Famous bearers of the name include the character Edgar from Shakespeare's *King Lear*.
See also Adair, Garek

Edmund

Diminutives: Ed, Eddie, Ned, Ted, Teddy
Origin: Old English

From the Old English *ead* ('riches') and *mund* ('protector'), this name translates as meaning 'protector of wealth'. In its modern spelling, it was in use in medieval times, but it is much less common since the early twentieth century.

Edric

Origin: Old English
Derived from the Old English *ead* and *ric* ('riches' and 'power' respectively), this name means 'rich and powerful'. In Anglo-Saxon times, it was common, but now it is much less so.

Edward

Diminutives: Ned, Eddie, Ed, Ted, Teddy, Iorwerth (Welsh)
Origin: Old English
From the Old English *ead* ('riches') and *weard* ('guard'), the name was revived in the nineteenth century and reached a peak in the 1920s. Famous bearers of the name include the youngest son of Queen Elizabeth II, Prince Edward.

Edwin

Diminutives: Ed, Eddie, Ned
Variants: Edwyn, Edwy
Origin: Old English
Based on the Old English name Eadwine, from *ead* and *wine*

('riches' and 'friend' respectively), it was revived in the nineteenth century, but is now quite rare. A well-known bearer of the name is musician Edwyn Collins.

Egan
Origin: Irish
This name is derived from Aogan, from **Aodh**, meaning 'fire'.

Egon
Origin: Old German
This name is derived from the Old German *ek*, meaning 'edge', usually interpreted to mean 'swordpoint'. Notable bearers of the name include food writer Egon Ronay.

Elbert
See **Albert**

Elfred
Origin: Welsh
Meaning 'autumn'.

Elgin
Origin: Scottish
Meaning 'earldom of the Bruces of Scotland', this could also be taken directly from the town of the same name.

Eli
Variants: Ely
Origin: Hebrew
Meaning 'exalted' or 'high', this

name appears in the Bible and was adopted by English speakers in the seventeenth century. In the nineteenth century, it enjoyed a peak, but the twentieth century saw it lose ground.

Elias
Variants: Ellis
Origin: Greek, from Hebrew
This is a Greek version of the Hebrew **Elijah** and was adopted by English Puritans in the seventeenth century. It became less popular after the nineteenth century.
See also **Elliott**

Elijah
Variants: **Illias**
Origin: Biblical
From the Hebrew name Eliyahu, meaning 'God is Yah'. It was adopted by the Puritans in the seventeenth century but it was irregular until the nineteenth. It has now become rare except in Black Muslim communities in the USA.

Elliott
Variants: Eliot, Eliott
Origin: Ultimately from Hebrew
This surname came from the French Norman **Elias**. It reached a peak in the 1990s, possibly as a result of the character of the same name in the film *E.T. The Extra-*

Terrestrial in 1982. Famous bearers of the name include actor Elliott Gould.
See also **Elias**

Elmer
Diminutives: Elm, Elmy
Origin: Old English
This name was derived from the Old English *aethel* ('noble') and *maer*, meaning 'famous', and was adopted as a first name, mainly in the USA, in the nineteenth century. A famous bearer of the name is the cartoon character Elmer Fudd.
See also **Aylmer**

Elmore
Origin: English
Meaning 'riverbank with elms', perhaps the most famous bearer of this name is writer Elmore Leonard.

Elton
Origin: Old English, from German
Derived from the Old English for 'Ella's settlement', this has made a few appearances as a first name in recent years. The most famous bearer of the name is singer Elton John.

Elvin
Variants: Elven
Origin: Old English
Meaning 'of the elves'.

Elvis

Origin: German or Irish
This name is derived from Elwes, itself from *Eloise*, but may have its roots in Ireland, from the Gaelic Ailbhe. The most famous bearer of the name in recent years was singer Elvis Presley.

Emanuel

Diminutives: Manny, *Manolo*, Mano
Variants: Emmanuel
Origin: Hebrew
Derived from the Hebrew Immanuel, meaning 'God with us', this was adopted by English speakers in the seventeenth century.

Emerson

Origin: English, from Old German
Meaning 'Emery's son', a famous bearer of the name is racing driver Emerson Fittipaldi.

Emile

Variants: Emil, Emilio (Spanish)
Origin: Latin
From the Latin for 'eager' or 'striving' via the Roman name Aemilius. In the nineteenth century, it came into irregular use and has remained sporadic.
See also *Emlyn*

Emlyn

Origin: Latin or Celtic
This name is derived either from the Roman name Aemilius or from some unknown Celtic source. This is a Welsh name and is rarely found outside Wales. Well-known bearers of the name have included footballer Emlyn Hughes.
See also *Emile*

Emmet

Origin: Old German
This was originally a surname derived from *Emma*, appearing in medieval times. Well-known bearers of the name include the character in the *Back to the Future* series of films, Dr Emmet Brown.

Ennis

Origin: Gaelic
Meaning 'the only choice'.
See also *Angus*, *Dennis*

Enzo

Origin: Old German and Latin
This Italian name is derived from the Old German *ent* ('giant'), but is also found as a diminutive of Lorenzo (*see* *Laurence*.)

Eoghan *See* *Owen*
Erhard

Origin: Old German
Derived from the Old German *era*, meaning 'respect' or 'honour', and *hardu* ('brave' or 'hardy').

Eric

Variants: Erik
Origin: Old Norse
Derived from the Old Norse name Eyrekr, from *ei* ('ever', 'always') or *einn* ('one') and *rikr*, meaning 'ruler'. Well-known bearers of the name include comedian Eric Sykes and musician Eric Clapton.

Ernest

Diminutives: Ern, Ernie
Origin: Old German
This name is derived ultimately from the Old German *eornost*, meaning 'seriousness' or 'earnestness'. Records of its use go back to the accession of George I of Hanover and was popular until the early twentieth century. Famous bearers of the name have included comedian Ernie Wise.

Errol

Origin: Scottish
This name may have evolved from *Earl*, and proved popular with African-Americans in the twentieth century. Famous bearers of the name include musician Errol Brown and actor Errol Flynn.
See also *Earl*, *Harold*

Erskine

Origin: Scottish
Derived from the Scottish place name, this has been used as a first name since the nineteenth century. Famous bearers of the name have included novelist Erskine Caldwell.

Esteban

See Stephen

Ethan

Variants: Etan (Jewish)
Origin: Hebrew
This biblical name is derived from the Hebrew Eythan, meaning 'firm', 'constant', 'strong' or 'long-lived'. Its popularity increased slightly in the nineteenth century. Famous bearers of the name include actor Ethan Hawke.

Etienne

see Stephen

Eugene

Diminutives: Gene
Variants: Yevgeni (Russian)
Origin: Greek
This name, which was borne by several early Christian saints, is derived from the Greek *eugenes* ('well-born', 'noble'), though in Ireland, it is considered to be an anglicization of such names as Aodh and Eoghan.
See also Owen

Eustace

Diminutives: Stacy
Origin: Greek
Derived from the Greek name Eustakhios, meaning 'good harvest'. Brought to England by the Normans in the eleventh century, it was less frequent in the Middle Ages but was revived in the nineteenth century.

Evan

Variants: Ewan, Ifan, Keon
Origin: Hebrew
This Welsh name is derived from Iefan or Ieuan, from John, and seems to have been in use by 1500. Popular in Wales in the nineteenth century, the twentieth century saw it become more widespread, though it is still distinctly Welsh.

Evander

Origin: Greek and Gaelic
Derived from the Greek *eu* ('good') and *aner* ('man'), this name was especially popular in Scotland, where it was also seen as an anglicization of Iomhair. Famous bearers of the name include boxer Evander Holyfield.

Everett

Variants: Everitt
Origin: Probably Old German
This surname, thought to have evolved from Everard, was adopted as a first name near the end of the nineteenth century.

Ewan

See Evan

Ewart

Origin: Old English
Either derived from Edward or from the Northumbrian place name, this was adopted as a first name in the nineteenth century. Its popularity increased slightly in tribute to Prime Minister William Ewart Gladstone.

Ezra

Origin: Hebrew
Meaning 'help', this biblical name was taken up by Puritans in the seventeenth century, on both sides of the Atlantic. Famous bearers of the name have included poet Ezra Pound.

Fabian
Variants: Fabio, Fabien
Origin: Latin
Derived from the Latin *faba*, meaning 'bean', thus translating as 'bean grower', evidence for use of this name before the sixteenth century is sparse.

Fabrice
Origin: Latin
Ultimately derived from the Latin *faber*, meaning 'craftsman', via the Roman name Fabricius.

Fadil
Variants: Fadl
Origin: Arabic
Meaning 'virtuous' or 'generous'.

Fadoul
Origin: Arabic Meaning 'honest'.

Fagan
Variants: Fagen, Fagin, Fegan
Origin: Irish
From the Irish meaning 'small and fiery'. Probably the most famous bearer of the name is the character Fagin from Charles Dickens' *Oliver Twist*.

Fahim
Origin: Arabic
This Indian name comes from the Arabic *fahim*, meaning 'scholar' or 'learned man'.

Fairfax
Diminutives: Fax
Origin: English
Meaning 'blond-haired'.

Faivish
Variants: Faivel
Origin: Greek
This Jewish name was probably derived from the Greek Phoibos or Phoebus. Possibly the first Jews to be given the name were slaves captured by the Greeks.

Falkner
Variants: Faulkner, Faulkener, Fowler
Origin: Anglo-Saxon
Meaning 'falcon trainer'.

Fane
Origin: Anglo-Saxon
Meaning 'glad' or 'joyful'.

Faraj
Variants: Farag
Origin: Arabic
Derived from the Arabic *faraj*, meaning 'improvement' or 'remedy'.

Farid
Variants: Fareed (Indian)
Origin: Arabic
Derived from the Arabic *farid*, which means 'unrivalled' or 'unique'.

Farley
Origin: Old English
Derived from the Old English surname meaning 'fair meadow', this has made occasional appearances as a first name.

Farnell
Variants: Farnel
Origin: English
Meaning 'from the fern-covered hill'.

Farold
Origin: Old English
Meaning 'bold traveller'.

Farquhar
Origin: Gaelic
The Scottish Gaelic name Fearchar, derived from the words for 'man' and 'dear', led to the anglicization in the form of Farquhar.

Farr
Variants: Far
Origin: English
Meaning 'traveller'.

Farran m/f
Variants: Farren, Faron
Origin: Old French or Old German
Derived either from the Old French word for 'ferret' or 'pilferer' or as a medieval variant of Ferdinand, this was originally a surname.

Fawaz
Origin: Arabic
Meaning 'victorious'.

Fawzi
Origin: Arabic
This Arabic name is derived from *fawz*, meaning 'triumph' or 'victory'.

Fayad
Origin: Arabic
Meaning 'generous'.

Felix
Variants: Phelim (Irish), Felice (Italian)
Origin: Latin
From the Latin *felix*, meaning 'happy' or 'lucky', this name was in regular use by the nineteenth century. After the mid-twentieth century, its use decline until the 1990s, when it enjoyed a marked revival.

Fenton
Origin: Old English
This English place name is found in several northern counties and has been used as an occasional first name. It is derived from the Old English *fenn* ('fen' or 'marsh') and *tun* ('settlement').

Ferdinand
Diminutives: Ferd, Ferdie, Nandy
Variants: Ferrand, Ferrant (both French)

Origin: Old German
The Old German name Fridenand is itself derived from *fridu*, meaning 'peace', and *nand*, 'bravery'. Alternatively, it could have come from *farth* ('journey') and *nand* ('prepared'). Though it enjoyed a brief peak in the 1550s, it was never popular in England.

Fergal
Variants: Fearghal
Origin: Gaelic
This is an anglicization of the Irish name Fearghal, from the Gaelic *fear* ('man') and *gal*, meaning 'valour'. Well-known bearers of the name include journalist Feargal Keane and musician Feargal Sharkey.

Fergus
Diminutives: Fergie, Fergy
Variants: Feargus
Origin: Gaelic
From the Irish Gaelic *fear* ('man') and *gus* ('strength' or 'force'), this has kept it Celtic associations but is also widespread among other English speakers.

Fernley
Origin: Cornish
This first name comes from Cornwall, but its meaning is uncertain.

Ferrand
Origin: French
Meaning 'with iron-coloured hair'.

Filat
Origin: Greek
This is a Russian name which is derived from the Greek Theophylaktos, from *theo* ('god') and *phylassein*, meaning 'to guard'.

Filbert
Variants: Fulbert, Philbert
Origin: Old German
Derived from the Old German name Filibert (from *fil*, 'much, and *berht*, 'famous' or 'bright'), this is often spelt Fulbert.

Finbar
Variants: Finnbar
Origin: Gaelic
This name is derived from the Irish Gaelic *fionn* ('fair' or 'white') and *barr* ('head') via Fionbarr or Fionbharr.

Fingal
Variants: Fingall
Origin: Gaelic
This name is an anglicized form of the Irish *fionn*, meaning 'white' or 'fair' and *gall* ('stranger'), and translated as meaning 'pale stranger'. It became more widespread after being borne mainly by Norse immigrants.

Finlay m/f
Variants: Finley, Findlay
Origin: Gaelic
Derived from the Scottish Fionnlagh, from *fionn* ('fair' or 'white') and *laogh*, meaning 'warrior'. A famous bearer of the name is musician Finley Quaye.

Finn
Variants: Fionn, Finnegan, Finegan, Finigan
Origin: Gaelic
This Irish name comes from the Gaelic *fionn*, meaning 'fair or 'white'.

Finnegan
See **Finn**

Finnian
Variants: Finian
Origin: Gaelic
From the Gaelic *fionn*, meaning 'fair' or 'white'.

Fitz
See **Fitzroy**

Fitzroy
Diminutives: Fitz
Origin: French
This name means 'son of the king' and was initially used as a nickname for illegitimate sons of English monarchs.

Flannery
Variants: Flann, Flannon, Flanyn
Origin: Irish
Meaning 'red-haired'.

Flavius
Variants: Flavian
Origin: Latin
Meaning 'yellow-haired one'.

Fletcher
Origin: Old French
Derived from the Old French *fleche*, meaning 'arrow', this name means 'arrow-maker'.

Flint
Origin: English
This name means simply 'stream'.

Florian m/f
Origin: Roman
Derived from the Roman Florianus, from *flos* ('flower') this has made occasional appearance since medieval times but has been rare since the mid-nineteenth century.

Floyd
See **Lloyd**

Forbes
Origin: Gaelic
This surname is derived from the Scottish Gaelic *forba* ('district' or 'field'), and is used as a first name chiefly in Scotland.

Ford
Origin: English
This surname refers to a person living next to a river crossing and has made a few appearances as a first name.

Fordel
Origin: Romany
Meaning 'forgiving'.

Forrest
Variants: Forest
Origin: English
This name is derived from the ordinary vocabulary word 'forest' and has made a few appearances as a first name since the nineteenth century. A famous bearer of the name in modern times is the protagonist of the film *Forrest Gump* (1994).

Foster
Origin: Obscure
This is an English surname of uncertain meaning (perhaps 'foster-parent', 'forester' or 'shearer') that has made occasional appearances as a first name.

Francis
Diminutives: Frank, Frankie
Origin: Latin
This comes from the Roman name Franciscus, from the Latin

for 'Frenchman', and it seems the first bearer of the name was St Francis of Assisi, whose father renamed him on his return from France. Notable bearers of the name have included sailor Sir Francis Drake.

Frank
See Francis, Franklin

Franklin
Diminutives: Frank, Frankie
Variants: Franklyn
Origin: Middle English
From the Middle English *frankeleyn*, meaning 'freeman', this was

adopted as a first name in the nineteenth century. Popular in the USA through statesmen Benjamin Franklin and Franklin D. Roosevelt.

Fraser
Variants: Frazer, Frazier, Frasier
Origin: Scottish, from Norman
This is a Scottish place name which has been in use as a first name since the 1930s.

Frayne
Origin: English and French
In English, this means 'foreigner' or 'stranger'; in French, 'from the ash wood'.

Frederick
Diminutives: Fred, Freddie, Freddy
Variants: Frederic
Origin: Old German
Derived from the Old German *fridu* ('peace') and *ric* ('power', 'ruler'), this name came to England with the Normans. Since its peak in the early twentieth century, it has been in decline.

Freeman
Origin: English
From 'free man', this has been adopted as a first name, but it is uncommon.

Frewin
Origin: English
Meaning 'freeman and friend'.

Frith
Origin: Anglo-Saxon
Meaning 'one who lives in the woods'.

Fuller
Origin: Anglo-Saxon
Meaning 'one who works with cloth'.
See also Tucker

Fulton
Origin: Anglo-Saxon
Meaning 'from the field'. Famous bearers of the name have included actor Fulton Mackay.

Babies' Names ☀ Boys

Gabor
Origin: Hungarian
Meaning simply 'my strength is God'.
See also **Gabriel**

Gabriel
Diminutives: Gabe, Gab, Gabby
Variants: Gabor (Hungarian)
Origin: Hebrew
Derived from the Hebrew name Gabriel, meaning 'man of God' or 'my strength is God', this name was popular in the eighteenth and nineteenth centuries; it fell into decline in the twentieth, but was temporarily revived in the 1940s.

Galton
Variants: Galt
Origin: English
Meaning 'from the high town'.

Galvin
Origin: Irish
Meaning 'like a sparrow'.

Gamlyn
Origin: Scandinavian
Meaning 'small and wise'.

Ganesh
Origin: Sanskrit
This Indian name is derived from the Sanskrit *gana*, meaning 'host', 'horde', and *isa* ('lord'), so meaning 'lord of hosts'. This is the name of the Hindu god of wisdom.

Gannon
Origin: Gaelic
Meaning 'little blond one'.

Gar
See **Gareth**

Garbhan
Origin: irish
Meaning 'rough'.

Garek
See **Edgar**

Gareth
Diminutives: Gary, Gar, Gaz
Variants: Garth
Origin: Various, depending on root.
This is a Welsh name which is derived from **Geraint**, but it is also linked with such names as **Garth**, **Gary** and **Gerard**. Interpreted as meaning 'gentle', between the 1930s and 1980s it increased in popularity, but has since declined. Famous bearers of the name include pop star Gareth Gates.

Garfield
Diminutives: Gary, Garry
Origin: Old English
Derived from the Old English *gar*, meaning 'spear', and *feld*, meaning 'open country', this name has been interpreted as 'one living near a triangular field' and has been in use as a first name, mainly in the USA, since the nineteenth century.

Garmond
Variants: Garmon, Garmund
Origin: Anglo-Saxon
Meaning 'spear protector'.

Garner
Diminutives: Gar, Garn
Variants: Garnir
Origin: French
Meaning 'ribboned' or 'wreathed'.

Garnock
Origin: Welsh
Meaning 'from the alder tree by the river'.

Garret
Diminutives: Garry, Gary
Variants: Garrett
Origin: Old German
This name was derived from the surname, itself likely to have come from **Gerald** or **Gerard**, and was adopted as a first name in the seventeenth century, and was especially popular in Ireland.

Garrick

Origin: Old English
From the Old English *gar* ('spear') and *ric* ('ruler'), this has made a few appearances as a first name over time. In the eighteenth century, its use may have been promoted by the actor David Garrick.

Garson

Origin: Old English
Meaning 'son of the spear'.

Garth

Origin: Old Norse
Derived from the Old Norse *garthr*, meaning 'enclosure', this was adopted as a first name by English speakers near the beginning of the twentieth century. Sometimes treated as a variant of Gareth, the 1940s saw a peak in its popularity. Notable bearers of the name include singer Garth Brooks.

Gary

Diminutives: Gaz
Variants: Garey, Garry
Origin: Old German
Ultimately derived from the Old German *gar*, meaning 'spear', the 1930s saw this being adopted as a first name. Between the 1930s and the 1960s, it was popular, but has since been less common.

See also Garfield, Garret, Gareth

Gaston

Origin: Uncertain
This French name may have derived from the German *Gast*, meaning 'guest' or 'stranger', but may also have come from the French *Gascon*, signifying anyone who originates from Gascony.

Gauderic

Origin: Old German
Meaning 'king', 'ruler'.

Gautier

See Walter

Gavin

Origin: Welsh
This is a Scottish name which is derived from the Welsh Gawain and has been in use among English speakers since the beginning of the twentieth century.

Gene m/f

Origin: Greek
This name was developed as a diminutive of such names as Eugene and was especially popular in the USA during the first half of the twentieth century. Notable bearers of the name have included actor Gene Kelly and singer Gene Pitney.

Geoffrey

Diminutives: Geoff, Jeff
Variants: Jeffery
Origin: Old German
The Old German name Gaufrid, itself from *gavja* ('territory') and *fridu*, meaning 'peace', so translated as 'peaceful ruler', developed among English speakers into Geoffrey. Other sources suggest it could have developed from Godfrey. In the nineteenth century it was revived, but it has been much less common since the 1950s.

George

Diminutives: Georgy, Georgie, Geordie, Jody
Variants: Jorge, Goran
Origin: Greek
This name is ultimately derived from the Greek *georgos*, meaning 'farmer', via the Latin Georgius. In the early twentieth century it fell into decline, but was revived again in the 1960s and 1990s. Famous bearers of the name include musician George Harrison and singer Boy George.

Geraint

Origin: Uncertain
It is believed this Welsh name is ultimately derived from the Greek *gerontos*, meaning 'old man', but this is uncertain. In the *Anglo-*

Saxon Chronicle of 705 it appears as Gerente. Geraint was the name of one of the Knights of the Round Table in Arthurian legend.

Gerald
Diminutives: Gerry, Jerry
Variants: Jerold (historical), Gerallt (Welsh)
Origin: Old German
Derived from the Old German *ger* ('spear') and *wald* ('rule'), the Normans brought this name to England. Revived in the nineteenth century, it fell from favour again in the mid-twentieth. Famous bearers of the name have included zoologist and writer Gerald Durrell.

Gerard
Diminutives: Gerry, Jerry
Variants: Gerrard, Jerrard, Gerhard (German)
Origin: Old German
From the Old German *ger* ('spear') and *hardu* ('hardy' or 'brave'), this name was brought to England by the Normans. It was revived in the nineteenth century, declining in the 1950s except among Roman Catholics.

Germaine
Variants: Jermaine
Origin: Roman
This name developed from the

Roman Germanus, meaning 'brother' and it was adopted by English speakers early in the twentieth century.

Gerry m/f
Variants: Gerrie, Jerry
Origin: Old German
This derived from such names as Gerald and Gerard and is now often considered as a name in its own right.

Gervais
Variants: Gervase, Gervaise, Jarvis
Origin: Greek or Old German
Deriving from the Greek *geras*, meaning 'old age', via the Roman name Gervasius, or from the Old German *ger* and *vas* ('spear' and 'servant', respectively). The name was adopted by English Roman Catholics in the sixteenth century.

Gerwyn
Variants: Gerwen
Origin: Welsh
Meaning 'fair love'.

Gethin
Origin: Welsh
Meaning 'dark-skinned'.

Ghassan
Origin: Arabic
Derived from the Arabic *ghassas*,

meaning 'youth', this popular name is also the name of an Arabian tribe.

Gibson
Origin: Old German
Meaning 'son of Gilbert'.

Gideon
Diminutives: Gid
Origin: Hebrew
This name is often interpreted as meaning 'great warrior' and its position in the Bible meant it was adopted by English speakers in the seventeenth century. It is now more common in the USA than in the UK.

Gifford
Variants: Giffard, Gifferd
Origin: Old German
This is derived from the Old German name Gebehard, from *gib* ('give') and *hardu* ('hardy' or 'brave'). It was common as a first name during medieval times, but is now redundant.

Gilbert
Diminutives: Gib, Gil, Gilby, Bert
Origin: Old German and Gaelic
From the Old German name Gisilbert, from *gisil* and *berht* (meaning 'pledge' or hostage and 'bright' or 'famous' respectively),

this is usually translated as 'bright pledge'; in Scotland, it is viewed as an anglicized version of Gilbride (meaning 'servant of St Bridget').

Gilby
See Gilbert

Giles
Origin: Greek
Derived ultimately from the Greek *aigidion*, meaning 'kid', it was often interpreted as referring to kid leather. During the Middle Ages the name was quite common but never became a favourite.

Gillespie
Origin: Gaelic
This is an anglicized version of the Scottish Gaelic Gilleasbaig, meaning 'servant of the bishop'. Its use as a first name is now very rare.
See also Archibald

Gladstone
Origin: Old English
This Scottish place name was derived from the Old English *glaed* ('kite') and *stan* ('rock'), and has been adopted as an occasional first name since the nineteenth century, originally in tribute to Prime Minister William Gladstone.

Glanmor
Origin: Welsh
Meaning 'sea shore'.

Glanville
Variants: Glanvil, Glenvil, Glenville
Origin: Uncertain
This name is derived from either the Norman French place name or from the Old English meaning 'clean field'.

Glasson
Origin: Scottish
Meaning 'from Glasgow'.

Glenn m/f
Variants: Glen
Origin: Gaelic
This name is derived from the Gaelic word *glean*, meaning 'valley', and was adopted as a first name for boys towards the end of the nineteenth century and for girls in the 1940s. In the 1950s and 1960s it enjoyed a peak both in the UK and the USA. Famous bearers of the name include footballer Glenn Hoddle.
See also Glyn

Glenrowan
Origin: Irish
Meaning 'from the valley of rowan trees'.

Glyn
Variants: Glynn
Origin: Welsh
From the Welsh *glyn*, meaning 'valley', its use as a name may have been influenced by such names as Glenn. Popular in Wales, it reached a peak among English speakers in the 1950s and 1960s.
See also Glenn

Glyndwr
Origin: Welsh
From the Welsh *glyn* ('valley') and *dwr*, meaning 'water', this surname was adopted as a first name in the twentieth century.

Godfrey
Variants: Goraidh (Scottish Gaelic), Gottfried (German)
Origin: Old German
Derived from the Old German *god*, meaning 'god', and *fridu* ('peace'), this name has been in decline since the twentieth century.

Godric
Origin: Old English
From the Old English *god* ('god') and *ric* ('powerful'). Used before the Norman invasion, but seems to have disappeared after the fourteenth century.

Godwin

Variants: Goodwin
Origin: Old English
Derived from the Old English *god* ('god') and *wine* ('friend'), eleventh-century Earl of Wessex was named Godwin. Frequent in medieval times, it subsequently became much less common.

Gomer

Origin: Hebrew
This appears in the Bible as the name of Noah's grandson and was adopted by the Puritans in the seventeenth century. In the USA it has continued to be used, but irregularly.

Gomez

Origin: Spanish
Meaning simply 'man'.

Gonzalo

Variants: Gonzalez
Origin: Spanish
Meaning 'wolf'.

Gopal

Origin: Sanskrit
Derived from the Sanskrit *go* ('cow') and *pala*, meaning 'protector', this could mean 'cowherd' or even 'king'. It became popular among Hindus after it appeared in the *Mahabharata* as one of the names of Krishna.

Goran

See **George**

Gordon

Diminutives: Gordie, Gordy
Variants: Gordan, Gorden
Origin: This Scottish place name is said to come from the Scots Gaelic for 'spacious fort'. It is also the name of a famous clan and became popular in the English-speaking world in the late nineteenth century.

Gorhan

Origin: Old English
Meaning 'one who lives in a mud hut'.

Gorman

Origin: Gaelic
Meaning 'small blue-eyed boy'.

Goronwy

Origin: Welsh
The meaning of this name is uncertain. It appeared in the fourth branch of the *Mabinogion* and was subsequently adopted as a first name. Notable bearers of the name have included poet Goronwy Evans.

Govind

Variants: Gobind
Origin: Sanskrit
This name is derived from the Sanskrit *go* ('cow') and *vinda*, meaning 'finding'. It is one of the names borne by Krishna in the *Mahabharata*.

Gower

Origin: Welsh
Meaning 'pure' in Welsh, it is also the name of a local peninsula.

Grady

Origin: Irish
Meaning 'noble', this surname has made occasional appearances as a first name.

Graham

Variants: Graeme
Origin: Old English
This Scottish surname originated in the twelfth century and was adopted as a first name among English speakers. The surname appears to be derived from the town of Grantham, from the Old English *grand* ('gravel') and *ham* ('homestead').

Grant

Origin: Probably Norman French
Thus name is probably derived from the Norman French *grand*, meaning 'big' or 'tall', and was adopted as a first name among English speakers in the nineteenth century. The twentieth century saw a peak in popularity,

perhaps partly due to the character Grant Mitchell in *EastEnders*.

Granville

Variants: Grenville
Origin: Norman French
This baronial surname, based on the French *grand* and *ville* ('big' and 'town', respectively) was adopted as a first name in the nineteenth century. Now little known as a first name apart from the character Granville in the comedy series *Open All Hours*.

Gray

Variants: Grey
Origin: English
From the ordinary vocabulary word 'grey'.

Grayson

Origin: English
Meaning 'son of Gray'.

Greg *See Gregory Gregory*

Diminutives: Greg, Gregg, Greig
Variants: Gregor, Grigor
Origin: Greek
This Latin name is ultimately derived from the Greek *gregorein*,

meaning 'to watch', 'to be vigilant', and has remained fairly popular since the Norman conquest. Famous bearers of the name have included actor Gregory Peck.

Gresham
Origin: Old English
From the place name based on the Old English for 'grazing' and 'hamlet' that was adopted as an occasional first name.

Griffin
Origin: Roman
This Welsh name appears to have developed as a variant of Griffith, from the Roman Griffinus.

Griffith
Diminutives: Griff
Variants: Gruffydd, Gruffudd
Origin: Welsh
This name is derived from the Welsh for 'lord' or 'prince' and records of its use go back to the sixteenth century. Famous bearers of the name include comedian Griff Rhys Jones.
See also Griffin

Gunner
See Gunther

Gunther
Variants: Gunner, Günther
Origin: Old German

Derived from the Old German *gund* ('strife') and *heri* ('army'), this name appears in German mythology and was adopted by English speakers in the Middle Ages, but fell into decline after the fifteenth century.

Gurion
Origin: Hebrew
Meaning 'God's dwelling place'.

Gurpreet
Origin: Indian
Meaning 'love of the teacher'.

Gus
Diminutives: Gussie
Origin: Varies depending on root
This name developed as a diminutive of such names as Angus, Augustus and Gustav and was adopted as a first name in its own right in the nineteenth century.

Gustav
Variants: Gustave
Origin: Swedish
This name is derived from the Swedish name Gotstaf, possibly from *got* ('god') and *stafr*, meaning 'staff'. Records of its use among English speakers date back to the seventeenth century and notable bearers of the name have

included composer Gustav Holst.

Guy
Variants: Gye, Guido (Ital.), Wyatt
Origin: Old German
Ultimately derived from the Old German *wit* ('wide') or *witu* ('wood'), this name came to England with the Normans in the eleventh century and was promoted through the romance of *Guy of Warwick*. It was revived in the nineteenth century. Famous bearers of the name have included conspirator Guy Fawkes

Gwyn
Variants: Gwynn
Origin: Welsh
From the Welsh *gwyn*, meaning 'fair' or 'white', this name has retained its strong Welsh associations, though it has been adopted by people elsewhere since the early twentieth century.

Gwynfor
Variants: Wynfor
Origin: Welsh
From the Welsh *gwyn* ('white', 'blessed' or 'fair') and *mawr*, meaning 'great' or 'large', this has been interpreted as meaning 'great lord' or 'great place' and seems to be a twentieth-century introduction.

Habib
Origin: Arabic
Taken directly from the Arabic *habib*, meaning 'beloved' or 'dear', famous bearers of the name have included Tunisian President Habib Bourguiba.

Habor
Origin: Teutonic
Meaning 'dextrous'.

Hacon
Origin: Old Norse
Meaning 'useful'.

Hadar
Origin: Hebrew
Meaning 'ornament'.

Hadley m/f
Origin: English
Meaning 'heathery hill', this is generally more familiar as a surname.

Hafiz
Variants: Hafeez (Indian)
Origin: Arabic
From the Arabic *hafiz*, meaning 'guardian', this name was once reserved for people who could recite the Koran from memory.

Hagen
See **Hakan**

Haig
Origin: English
Meaning 'from the field which is surrounded by hedges'.

Hakan
Variants: **Hagen**, Hakon, Haakon
Origin: Old Norse
From the Norse name Hakon, which is itself derived from *ha* ('high' or 'horse') and *honr* ('descendant' or 'son').

Hakeem
Variants: Hakim
Origin: Arabic
Derived from the Arabic *hakim*, meaning 'wise'.

Hal
See **Harold**, **Henry**

Halim
Origin: Arabic
Meaning 'patient'.

Hallam
Origin: English
This place name means 'nook' or 'stone' and was later adopted as a first name.

Halsey
Variants: Halsy
Origin: Anglo-Saxon
Meaning 'from Hal's island'.

Hamid
Variants: Hamdi
Origin: Arabic
Meaning 'praising' or 'thankful'.

Hamilton
Origin: English
This place name was originally derived from the Old English *hamel* ('flat-topped') and *dun* ('hill'). It seems to have been adopted by English speakers in the nineteenth century, mainly in the USA.

Hamish
Variants: Seumus
Origin: Latin
This is the Scottish Gaelic Sheumais, a variant of **James**, and was adopted by English speakers about halfway through the nineteenth century.

Hammond
Origin: Old German
This Scottish surname is derived from the Old German *heim*, meaning 'house' or 'home' and has been in occasional use in English-speaking areas since the nineteenth century.

Hamon
Origin: Greek
Meaning simply 'beautiful'.

Hamza
Variants: Hamzah
Origin: Arabic
This name is derived from the Arabic *hamuza*, which means 'steadfast' or 'strong' and is of pre-Islamic origin.

Hanan
Variants: Hani, Haniyya
Origin: Arabic
This name is derived from the Arabic *hanan*, meaning 'tenderness'.

Hanif
Origin: Arabic
Meaning 'orthodox' or 'true', a famous bearer of the name is writer Hanif Kureishi.

Hans
Origin: Scandinavian
See John

Hansel
Origin: Scandinavian
Meaning 'gift from the Lord'.

Hardy
Origin: English
Possibly based on the ordinary vocabulary word 'hardy', this surname has been in use as a first name since the beginning of the twentieth century.

Harlan
Origin: Old English
This place name, from the Old English *hara* and *land* (meaning 'hare' and 'land' respectively) was adopted as a first name in the nineteenth century, mainly confined to the USA. Famous bearers of the name include writer Harlan Coben.

Harland
Variants: Harlan, Harlon, Harland
Origin: Old English
Meaning simply 'army land'.

Harley m/f
Variants: Arley
Origin: English
This surname (of unknown meaning) was adopted as a first name for boys and then girls in the nineteenth century.

Harlon
See Harland

Harold
Diminutives: Hal, Harry
Variants: Errol
Origin: Old English
The Scandinavian Haraldr or Harald, from the Old English *here* ('army') and *wealdan* ('to rule'), thus meaning 'general', influenced the name Harold. The name was revived in the nineteenth century after Byron's poem *Childe Harold's Pilgrimage* was published in 1812. *See also* Herrick

Harris
Variants: Harrison
Origin: Old English
Meaning 'Harold's son'.

Harrison
See Harris

Harry
See Henry, Harold

Hart
Origin: English
Meaning simply 'hart', which is the old word for a stag.

Hartley
Origin: Old English
Usually derived from *heorot* ('hart') and *leah* ('clearing'), this could also mean 'stony meadow'. Notable bearers of the name have included the son of poet Samuel Taylor Coleridge.

Harvey
Diminutives: Harv, Harve
Variants: Hervey, Hervé (French)
Origin: Breton
Derived from the Breton *haer* ('battle') and *vy* ('worthy'), this

name is recorded in the Domesday Book. It was revived in the nineteenth century but has remained irregular since then. Famous bearers of the name include actor Harvey Keitel.

Hasan
Variants: Hassan
Origin: Arabic
This name, derived directly from the Arabic *hasan*, meaning beautiful' or 'good', remains one of the most popular names used in Islamic countries.

Hasani
Origin: Swahili
Meaning 'handsome'.

Hashim
Origin: Arabic
This name, which means 'crushing', is generally understood to refer to someone who breaks bread to eat.

Hasin
Origin: Sanskrit
Meaning 'laughing one'.

Haslett
Origin: English
Meaning 'from the clearing of the hazel trees'.

Hawley
Origin: English
Meaning simply 'from the hedged clearing'.

Haydn m/f
Variants: Haydon, Hayden, Hadyn
Origin: Uncertain
This may be a development of Haddon, meaning 'hill with heather', and may also have derived as a variant of **Aiden**. The music of composer Josef Haydn has been popular in Wales, which may account for the name's popularity.

Heath
Origin: English
Derived from the ordinary vocabulary word, this has been in use as a first name since the nineteenth century. Famous bearers of the name have included actor Heath Ledger.

Heaton
Diminutives: Heat
Variants: Heaten
Origin: English
Meaning 'from the high place'.

Hector
Diminutives: Heck, Heckie
Origin: Greek or Gaelic
Derived from the Greek *ekhein*, meaning 'to hold' or 'to resist', the name appears in Greek mythology but has never been common among English speakers. It has been irregularly used in Scotland since the Middle Ages, sometimes as an equivalent of **Eachan**.

Hedley
Variants: Headley
Origin: Old English
Derived from the Old English *heath* ('heather') and *leah*, meaning 'clearing', this has been adopted as an occasional first name since the nineteenth century.

Heilyn
Origin: Welsh
Derived from the Welsh *heilio*, meaning 'to prepare', this name

was initially reserved for servants who worked as wine-pourers or stewards in large houses.

Helmer
Origin: German
Meaning 'soldier's anger'.

Helmut
Origin: Old German
Derived from the Old German *helm* and *muot* (meaning 'helmet' and 'spirit' respectively), this name seems to have been coined in the Middle Ages and has continued to be used since. Famous bearers of the name have included statesman Helmut Kohl.

Hendry
Origin: Teutonic
Meaning 'manly'.

Henry
Diminutives: Harry, Hank, Hal
Variants: Enrico (Italian), Heinrich (German)
Origin: Old German
An English version of the German Heinrich, itself from *heim* ('home') and *ric* ('owner' or 'ruler'), this was established as a royal name. Less popular in the twentieth century until the Prince and Princess of Wales chose the name for their second son.
See also Iarla

Henson
Origin: English from Old German
Meaning 'son of Henry'.

Herbert
Diminutives: Herb, Herbie
Variants: Heribert (German)
Origin: Old German
This name is derived from the Old German *heri* or *hari* ('army') and *berht*, meaning 'bright'. The original name Herebeorht was replaced by Herbert after the Norman invasion. It was revived in the nineteenth century.

Herman
Variants: Armand
Origin: Old German
Derived from the Old German *hari* ('army') and *man*, meaning 'man', in the mid-nineteenth century, this name was adopted by English speakers, mainly by German immigrants to the USA. Famous bearers of the name have included writer Herman Melville.

Herrick
Origin: Teutonic
Meaning 'army ruler'.
See also Harold

Hesketh
Origin: Old Norse
Derived from the Old Norse *hestr* ('horse') and *skeithr*, meaning

'racecourse', this was originally a place name.

Hezekiah
Origin: Hebrew
This biblical name is based on the Hebrew Hizqiyah, meaning 'Yah is strenth', Yah being an alternative name for God. Adopted by English speakers in the seventeenth century, it has never been common.

Hilary m/f
Diminutives: Hil
Variants: Hillary, Ilar (Welsh), Hilaire (French)
Origin: Latin
This Latin name, from *hilaris*, meaning 'cheerful', developed via the Roman Hilarius. After it was used chiefly for boys in medieval times, the name fell into decline until the nineteenth century, when it was used as a gender-neutral name.

Hilton
Variants: Hylton
Origin: Anglo-Saxon
Meaning 'from the hill farm'.

Hiram
Diminutives: Hi, Hy
Variants: Hyram
Origin: Hebrew
Meaning 'most noble and exalted one'.

Hogan
Origin: Celtic
Meaning simply 'youth'.

Hollis m/f
Origin: English
Meaning 'one who dwells in the holly grove'.

Holmes
Origin: Anglo-Saxon
Meaning 'from the island in the river'.

Holt
Origin: Anglo-Saxon
Meaning 'from the forest'.

Homer
Origin: Uncertain
This name is derived either from the Greek *homeros*, meaning 'hostage' or else from the Old English surname denoting a helmet maker. Mainly associated with the writer of *The Odyssey* and *The Iliad*, more recently it has come to be known as the name of the character in the cartoon series *The Simpsons*.

Horatio
Diminutives: Horry
Origin: Latin
This developed as a variant of Horace from the Latin *hora*, meaning 'time' or 'hour'. In the eighteenth century, it was adopted by English speakers and was common until the end of the nineteenth century, but is now rare.

Horton
Origin: Anglo-Saxon
Meaning 'from the grey farm'.

Hosanna m/f
Origin: Hebrew
Derived from the Hebrew *hosanna*, meaning 'save now' or 'save pray'. In the early thirteenth century, it was adopted by English speakers because of its biblical associations as a name for both boys and girls, though since the seventeenth century, it has been mainly a girls' name.

Hosea
Origin: Hebrew
Meaning simply 'salvation'.
See also Joshua

Hosni
Variants: Husni
Origin: Arabic
Derived from the Arabic *husn*, meaning 'excellence' or 'beauty'.

Houghton
Origin: Anglo-Saxon
Meaning 'from the estate on the cliff'.

Howard
Diminutives: Howie
Origin: Uncertain
With possible Scandinavian, Old French or Old German roots, this name was adopted in the early nineteenth century and enjoyed a peak in the 1960s. Famous bearers of the name include actor Howard Keel.

Howe
Origin: Teutonic
Meaning 'the eminent one', given to a person of high birth.

Howell
Variants: Howel, Hywel
Origin: English or Welsh
Derived either from the Welsh name Hywel or the English surname, this began to be used as a first name in the mid-nineteenth century.

Hubert
Variants: Hobart
Origin: Old German
Derived ultimately from the Old German *hug* ('heart' or 'mind') and *berht*, meaning 'bright', this name has fallen from favour since the early twentieth century.

Hugh
Diminutives: Hughie, Hewie, Huey, Shug, Hugo

Variants: Huw (Welsh)
Origin: Old German
Derived from the Old German *hug*, meaning 'heart' or 'mind', this name revived between the seventeenth and nineteenth centuries and has enjoyed a resurgence since. It is also found as an anglicization of certain Scottish names.
See also **Pugh**

Hugo
Variants: Ugo (Italian)
Origin: Old German
Developed as a diminutive form of **Hugh** in the nineteenth century.

Humphrey
Diminutives: Humph, Huffie
Variants: Humphry

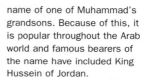

Origin: Old German
From the Old German *hun* and *fridu*, meaning 'Hun' or 'bear cub' and 'peace' respectively, this came to England with the Normans and was common in medieval times, but has since become rare.

Hunter
Origin: English
From the ordinary vocabulary word 'hunter', this has since come to be used as an occasional first name.

Hurley
Origin: Gaelic
Meaning 'sea tide'.

Husam
Origin: Arabic
Derived from the Arabic *husam*, meaning 'sword'.

Hussain
Variants: **Hussein**, Husain, Husayn, Hisein
Origin: Arabic
From the Arabic *hasan*, meaning 'beautiful' or 'good', this was the name of one of Muhammad's grandsons. Because of this, it is popular throughout the Arab world and famous bearers of the name have included King Hussein of Jordan.

Hussein
See **Hussain**

Hutton
Origin: Anglo-Saxon
Meaning 'from the farm on the ridge'.

Huxford
Origin: Anglo-Saxon from Old German
The Anglo-Saxon name meaning 'Hugh's ford'.
See also **Hugh**

Huxley
Origin: Anglo-Saxon from Old German
Meaning 'Hugh's meadow'.

Hyatt
Origin: Anglo-Saxon
Meaning simply 'from the high gate'.

Hyder
Origin: English
Meaning simply 'tanner'.

Hywel
See **Howell**

Ian
See John

Iain
See John

Iarla
Origin: Irish
See Henry

Iarlaith
Variants: Jarlath
Origin: Gaelic
Derived from the Gaelic *ior* (it is not known what this means) and *flaith* ('leader' or 'prince'). The name is rarely found outside of Galway in Ireland.

Ibaad
Origin: Arabic
Meaning 'a believer in God'.

Ibrahim
Variants: Ebrahim, Ibraheem
Origin: Hebrew
This is an Arabic version of the Hebrew name Abraham and is one of the most popular names for boys in the Arab world.

Ibsen
Origin: German
Meaning 'son of the archer'.

Iden
Origin: English

Meaning 'from the pasture in the woods'.

Idris
Origin: Welsh
Meaning 'fiery lord', from *iud* ('lord') and *ris*, meaning 'ardent' or 'fiery'.

Iestyn
See Justin

Ieuan
Origin: Welsh
See John

Ifan
See Evan

Ifor
See Ivor

Ike
See Isaac

Ilias
Origin: Greek
See Elijah

Illian
Origin: Basque
See Julian

Illtyd
Variants: Illtud
Origin: Welsh
Derived from *il*, meaning

'multitude', and *tud* ('land'), translated as meaning 'land of the people', this was the name of a saint in the sixth century but was not adopted as a first name until the nineteenth.

Imala
Origin: Native American
Meaning 'one who imposes disciplne'.

Imam
Origin: Arabic
This name translates directly as 'leader' and has strong Muslim associations.

Imanol
Origin: Hebrew
Meaning 'God is with us', a notable bearer of the name is rugby player Imanol Harinordoquy.

Imbert
Variants: Isambard, Isembert (archaic)
Origin: Old German
This is derived from the Old German name Isenbard, from *isan*, which means 'iron', and the name Bard. As Isambard, probably the most famous bearer of the name was engineer Isambard Kingdom Brunel.

Imran
Origin: Arabic

This means simply 'family of Imran'. Notable bearers of the name include cricketer and politician Imran Khan.

Inderjit
Origin: Sanskrit
Derived from the Indian name Indra (which means 'possessing raindrops') and *jit*, meaning 'to conquer'. The name is often found among Sikhs.

Indiana m/f
Origin: English
This name derived either as a variant of India or from the US state of the same name. In the early twentieth century it was exclusively a girls' name, but became more widespread as a name for boys after the release of the *Indiana Jones* films.

Ingmar
Origin: Norse
This Scandinavian name is a diminutive of Ingemar, which developed from the name of the Norse god Ing with *maerr*, meaning 'famous'. It became famous elsewhere with the actor Ingmar Bergman.

Ingo
Origin: Danish
Meaning 'meadow'.

Ingram
Origin: Probably Old German
This surname is believed to have derived ultimately from the Old German name Ingilrammus, from Engel and *hramn* (meaning 'raven'). It was revived in the nineteenth century.

Innes m/f
See Angus

Ioannis
Origin: Greek
Meaning 'the Lord is gracious'.

Iolo
Variants: Iolyn
Origin: Welsh
This name, which developed as a diminutive of Iorwerth, is sometimes considered to be a variant of Julius. It was adopted as a name in Wales by the eighteenth century.

Ionwyn
Origin: Welsh
Meaning 'fair-skinned ruler'.

Ior
See Ivor

Iorwerth
Diminutives: Iolo
Variants: Yorath
Origin: Welsh
Derived from the Welsh *iôr* ('lord') and *berth* ('beautiful'), this name appears in the *Mabinogion*. Sometimes treated as a Welsh variant of Edward. It appears to have been adopted as a first name in the nineteenth century.

Ipati
Diminutives: Patya
Origin: Greek
From the Greek *hypatos* ('best', 'highest') via Hypatios, this name was fairly common among early Christians.

Iqbal
Origin: Sanskrit
Meaning 'prosperity'.

Ira
Origin: Hebrew
Meaning 'watchful', this biblical name was adopted by English Puritans in the seventeenth century, from where it went to America. Famous bearers of the name have included lyricist Ira Gershwin.

Irving
Variants: Irvin, Irvine
Origin: Scottish
This has been used as a first name since the nineteenth century, from the place name in Dumfriesshire. Perhaps the most famous bearer of the name was songwriter Irving Berlin.

Irwin

Variants: Erwin
Origin: Old English
Derived ultimately from *eofor* ('boar') and *wine*, meaning 'friend', this has made rare appearances as a name since the mid-nineteenth century. Since the middle of the twentieth century, it has become rare.

Isa m/f

Origin: Old German
From the Old German word *isan*, meaning 'iron', suggesting a strong will.

Isaac

Diminutives: Ike, Zac, Zak
Variants: Izaac, Yitzhak
Origin: Hebrew
Derived from the Hebrew name Yitschaq, which seems to mean 'laughter', this was the name of the son of Abraham and Sarah. Famous bearers of the name have included scientist Sir Isaac Newton and writer Isaac Asmiov.

Isas

Origin: Japanese
Meaning 'worthy of praise'.

Isham

Origin: Anglo-Saxon
Meaning 'from the estate of the iron man'.

Isiah

Origin: Hebrew
Derived from the Hebrew name Yeshayah, meaning 'salvation of Yah' (Yah being another name for God). Since the early twentieth century, it has become increasingly rare.

Iskander

Origin: Ethiopian
See Alexander

Ishmael

Variants: Ismail, Esmail (Indian)
Origin: Hebrew
Derived from the Hebrew name Yishmael, meaning 'God will hearken', this biblical name was taken up by English speakers in the nineteenth century.

Isman

Origin: Hebrew
Meaning 'faithful husband'.

Ismat m/f

Origin: Arabic
Derived from the Arabic *isma*, meaning 'infallibility' or 'safeguarding'.

Israel

Diminutives: Issy, Izzy
Variants: Iser (Yiddish), Issur, Sroel
Origin: Hebrew
From the Hebrew name Yisrael, from *sarah* ('to struggle') and *el* ('God'), meaning 'he who struggles with God' or alternatively 'God will prevail'. It now remains confined mainly to Jewish communities throughout the world.

Ivan

Origin: Russian
See John

Ivander

Origin: Hebrew
Meaning 'divine'.

Ives

See Yves

Ivo

See Yves

Ivor

Variants: Ifor, Ior
Origin: Various
This is an English variant of the Scandinavian Ivarr, from *ur* ('yew' or 'bow') and *arr* ('warrior'), and is also (perhaps more) commonly seen as an anglicized version of the Welsh name Ifor. It fell into decline in the 1930s.
See also Yves

Ixara

Origin: Sanskrit
Meaning 'master' or 'prince'.

Jabari
Origin: Swahili
Meaning simply 'valiant'.

Jabez
Origin: Hebrew
This biblical name is derived from the Hebrew Yabets, which means 'he causes sorrow'. Since the end of the nineteenth century, it has more or less disappeared among English speakers.

Jabin
Origin: Hebrew
Meaning 'created by God'.

Jabulani
Variants: Jabulanie, Jabulany, Jabulaney
Origin: African
Meaning 'happy one'.

Jace
Variants: Jaece, Jase, Jayce
Origin: Hebrew
Meaning 'healer'.

Jack
Origin: English.
A diminutive of John. It has evolved from Jan and the Middle English form of Jankin. It is a popular name which has been used in nursery rhymes and fairytales.

Jackie
See John

Jackson
Diminutives: Jack, Jacky
Origin: English, from Hebrew
This means simply 'son of Jack' and was taken up as an occasional first name in the nineteenth century. Famous bearers of the name have included artist Jackson Pollock.

Jacob
Diminutives: Koby, Jake
Origin: Hebrew
From the Hebrew Yaakov or Yakubel via the Latin Jacobus, this means 'may God protect', though it has also been suggested that it means 'supplanter'. Revived in the nineteenth century and rare again in the twentieth, it enjoyed a resurgence in the 1990s.

Jaden m/f
Variants: Jadyn, Jaeden, Jaiden, Jaidyn, Jayden, Jaydin
Origin: Hebrew
Meaning 'Jehovah has heard'.

Jael
Variants: Yael
Origin: Hebrew
Meaning 'to ascend'. Alternatively, it has been suggested it comes from the Hebrew name for a female wild goat.

Jafar
Variants: Gafar, Jaffer, Jaffar
Origin: Arabic
From the Arabic *jafar*, meaning 'stream'.

Jagger
Origin: Old English
From the Old English word for a carter.

Jago
Cornish, see James

Jaheem
Variants: Jaheim
Origin: Hebrew
Meaning simply 'raised up'.

Jahir
Origin: Hindi, meaning 'jewel'.

Jaime m/f
See James

Jake
See Jacob

Jalal
Variants: Galal
Origin: Arabic
From the Arabic *jalal*, meaning 'glory' or 'greatness'.

Jalen
Origin: Greek
Meaning 'healer' or 'tranquil'.

Jalil
Origin: Arabic
Meaning 'exalted and sublime'.

Jamaal
Variants: Jamal, Jamil, Gamal, Gamil, Jameel
Origin: Arabic
Meaning simply 'beauty', this name is popular in the Middle East, some using it only as a boys' name, elsewhere bestowing it on girls as well. It has become popular among English speakers in recent years, especially in America.

James
Diminutives: Jim, Jimi, Jimmie, Jimmy, Jem, Jemmy
Variants: Jago, Jaime, Jay, Hamish, Seamas
Origin: Hebrew
This biblical name is ultimately derived from Jacobus, via Jacomus, and shares the same root as Jacob. It has been popular as a first name since the seventeenth century. As Jaime, it can also be said to be based on the French 'j'aime', meaning 'I like' or 'I love'.

Jamil
See Jamaal

Jamin
Origin: Hebrew
Meaning (rather curiously) 'son of the right hand'.

Jan m/f
Origin: Slavonic
See John

Janesh
Origin: Hindi
Meaning 'leader of people'.

Japheth
Variants: Japhet
Origin: Hebrew
Derived from the Hebrew name Yapheth, meaning 'enlargement' or 'expansion', this biblical name was taken up by Puritans in the seventeenth century.

Jared
Variants: Jarred, Jarod, Jarrod, Yered (Hebrew)
Origin: Hebrew
This biblical name is ultimately derived from the Hebrew *yeredh* (the meaning of which is disputed; it could mean 'descended', 'descent' or possibly 'rose'). In Australia and the USA, it enjoyed a revival in the 1960s.

Jarek
Origin: Polish and Czech
This is a diminutive of such names as Jaroslaw and names beginning with 'Jaro-'.

Jarlath
See Iarlaith

Jaron
Origin: Hebrew
Meaning 'cry out' or 'sing out'.

Jarratt
Origin: Teutonic
Meaning 'strong spear'.

Jarvis
See Gervais

Jason
Origin: Greek
Probably derived ultimately from the Greek *iasthai*, meaning 'to heal', via Iason. Well known from the Greek legend of Jason and the Argonauts, and may also be a variant of Joshua when it appears in the Bible. It was only in the 1970s that it established itself as a favourite name for boys. It has since gone into decline. Famous bearers of the name include actor and singer Jason Donovan.

Jasper
Variants: Caspar, Kasper
Origin: Uncertain
Records of this name go back to the fourteenth century, and it seems to have its origins in the Persian word for 'treasurer', though it is often assumed to relate to the gemstone jasper. Famous bearers of the name include designer Jasper Conran.

Javier
See Xavier

Jay m/f
Origin: Various, depending on the root name.
This is a diminutive of names beginning with 'J', such as James. Often assumed to relate to the bird or to have links with the Roman name Gaius.

Jefferson
Diminutives: Jeff
Origin: English, from Old German
This surname means 'Jeffrey's son' and was adopted as a first name in the nineteenth century, mainly in the USA.

Jem
See James, Jeremy

Jenkin
Variants: Siencyn (Welsh)
Origin: Various
This name is believed to be derived from the medieval first name Jankin (*see also* Jack) and it has strong Welsh connections, partly because a common surname in Wales is Jenkins.

Jensen
Variants: Jenson
Origin: Hebrew
Meaning 'John's son', a famous bearer of this Scandinavian name is racing driver Jenson Button.

Jephthah
Variants: Jephtha, Jeptha
Origin: Hebrew
From the Hebrew name Yiphtah, meaning 'God opens', this biblical name was revived by English speakers in the nineteenth century.

Jerald
See Gerald, Jeremiah, Jeremy

Jeremiah
Diminutives: Jerry, Jem
Origin: Hebrew
From the Hebrew name Yirmeyah, meaning 'exalted by Yah' (Yah is an alternative name for God), this name makes occasional appearances in Ireland, where it is sometimes seen as a variant of Diarmid (*see* Dermot), but is otherwise rare.
See also Jeremy

Jeremy
Diminutives: Jerald, Jerrie, Jerry, Jem, Jez
Origin: Hebrew
Derived from the Hebrew

name Jeremiah, records of the name go back as far as medieval times and it remained popular even after Jeremiah was revived by the Puritans in the seventeenth century. Famous bearers of the name include actor Jeremy Irons. *See also* Jerome

Jermaine
See Germaine

Jerome
Diminutives: Jerry
Variants: Geronimo
Origin: Greek
Derived from the Greek Hieronymus, from *hieros* and *onoma* ('holy' and 'name' respectively), and often confused with Jeremy, to which it bears no relation. The nineteenth century saw a peak in its popularity. *See also* Jeremy

Jerry
See Gerald, Jeremiah, Jeremy, Jerome

Jervis
See Gervais

Jesse
Diminutives: Jess
Origin: Hebrew
Derived from the Hebrew name Yishay, meaning 'Jehovah exists' or 'gift of Jehovah', this is

sometimes spelt Jessie. It was taken up by English speakers in the eighteenth century and one of the most famous bearers of the name was outlaw Jesse James.

Jestin
See Justin

Jesus
See Joshua

Jethro
Origin: Hebrew
From the Hebrew names Ithra or Yitro, meaning 'abundance' or 'excellence', its biblical connections mean it was popular among Puritans in the seventeenth century, and it remained common until the end of the nineteenth. Famous bearers of the name include comedian Jethro.

Jim
See James

Jinan m/f
Origin: Arabic
From the Arabic *jinan*, meaning 'garden' or 'paradise', this is a common name in the Middle East.

Jivin
Origin: Sanskrit
Meaning 'life-giving'.

Joachim
Diminutives: Kim (Scandinavian)
Variants: Joaquin (Spanish), Juaquim (Portuguese)
Origin: Hebrew
This is derived from the Hebrew name meaning 'Jehovah will establish' and appears in the Bible as the name of a king of Judah. The name had fallen out of use by the twentieth century.

Job
Diminutives: Joby, Jobie
Origin: Hebrew
Derived from the Hebrew Iyyobh, meaning 'hated' or 'persecuted', its biblical associations mean this name was popular among Puritans in the seventeenth century. Since the nineteenth century, however, it has almost completely disappeared.

Jocelyn m/f
Diminutives: Jos, Joss
Variants: Jocelin, Joselin, Joselyn
Origin: Disputed
From the Old Norman Joscelin, this was taken up as a name by English speakers. The Norman name may have come from a Germanic tribe, the *Gauts* or *Gautelen* ('little Goths'). Other sources say it comes from the Breton Jedoc or the Old German Josse.

Jock
Origin: Scottish
See John

Jody m/f
Variants: Jodi, Jodie
Origin: Various, depending on root name.
This developed as a diminutive of such names as George, Jude and Joe and increased in popularity as a boys' name in the nineteenth century.

Joe
See Jody, Joseph, Joshua

Joel
Origin: Hebrew
This biblical name is derived from the Hebrew Yeol, meaning 'Yah is god' was in use in medieval times. Since the nineteenth century, it has been mainly confined to the USA.

John
Diminutives: Jack, Jock, Johnny, Jonny, Jonnie
Variants: Ian, Iain, Ieuan, Ivan, Jan, Juan, Jon, Sean, Evan, Yanis
Origin: Hebrew
Ultimately derived from the Hebrew name Yohanan or Johanan, meaning 'Yah is merciful' (Yah being another name for God). It has been

in regular use among English speakers since the sixteenth century. Since a peak in the 1950s, its popularity has declined.
See also Zane

Jolyon
See Julius

Jonah
Variants: Jonas
Origin: Hebrew
From the Hebrew Yonah, meaning 'dove', this biblical name was adopted by the Puritans in the seventeenth century, though some believed it signified bad luck, so its popularity waned.

Jonathan
Diminutives: Jon, Jonty, Nathan
Variants: Jonathon, Johnathan, Johnathon
Origin: Hebrew
From the Hebrew name Yahonathan, meaning 'Yah's gift' or 'Yah has given' (Yah being another name for God), this name is sometimes confused with John. Notable bearers of the name include writer and clergyman Jonathan Swift and actor Jonathan Rhys Meyers.

Jordan m/f
Origin: Hebrew
From the name of the river in the Holy Land, which came from the

Hebrew *hayarden*, which means 'flowing down'. Brought to England by the Crusaders, though it was originally given only to boys who had been baptized in the river Jordan.

Jorens
Origin: Norse
Meaning 'laurel'.

Jorge
See George

Joseph
Diminutives: Joe
Variants: Josiah, Seosaidh, Sepp (German), Seosamh (Gaelic), Yusuf
Origin: Hebrew
From the Hebrew name Yoseph, meaning 'Yah added', translated as 'God gave this son'. It became popular again in the early twentieth century, after which it went into decline before being revived again in the 1990s.

Joshua
Diminutives: Joe, Josh
Variants: Jesus
Origin: Hebrew
This biblical name comes from the Hebrew Yehoshua or Hosea, meaning 'Yah saves' (Yah being another name for God). In the mid-nineteenth century it suffered a decline but the 1950s saw a

revival in the USA and the 1990s in the UK.

Josiah
See Joseph

Joss
See Jocelyn

Joyce m/f
Variants: Jocosa
Origin: Uncertain
Either a surname which was later adopted as a first name or derived from the Norman French Josce, from the Breton name Jodoc or Judoc (meaning 'lord'). Popular in the nineteenth century, this name has been in decline since the 1920s.

Juan
See John

Jude
Diminutives: Jody
Origin: Hebrew
An anglicized variant of Judas via Judah, this name was adopted by English speakers in the seventeenth century. Thomas Hardy used the name in his 1895 novel *Jude the Obscure* and a well-known bearer of the name in more recent times is actor Jude Law.
See also Judith

Jules
See Julian, Julius

Julian
Diminutives: Jules, Jolly, Jules
Variants: Illian, Julien, Julio, Jolyon, Julyan
Origin: Uncertain
Derived from the Roman name Julianus, a variant of Julius, also a medieval variant of the feminine Gillian. It was only in the eighteenth century that it was adopted by English speakers on a significant scale. In the 1960s, it enjoyed a peak but it has since been in decline.

Julio
See Julian

Julius
Diminutives: Jules
Variants: Jolyon, Julio (Spanish), Gyula (Hungarian)
Origin: Uncertain
This Roman name, which possibly has its roots in the Greek word meaning 'downy' or 'hairy', in reference to first beard growth in young men, was adopted by English speakers in the nineteenth century.

Juraj
Origin: Hebrew
Meaning 'God is my judge'.

Juri
Origin: Hebrew
This is a variant of Uriah, which means 'God is my light'.

Justin
Diminutives: Justie, Justy
Variants: Iestyn, Yestin, Jestin, Justyn
Origin: Latin
Descended from the Roman name Justinus, itself from the Latin Justus. It gained in frequency among English speakers in the 1970s.

Justus
Variants: Joost
Origin: Latin
From the Latin meaning 'fair' or 'just', it was used occasionally among English speakers near the end of the nineteenth century.

Juwan
Origin: Hebrew
Meaning 'the Lord is gracious'.

Kabelo
Origin: African
Meaning 'gift'.

Kadar
Origin: Arabic
Meaning 'powerful'.

Kade
Variants: Kayde
Origin: Scottish
Meaning 'from the wetlands'.

Kadeem
Origin: Arabic
Meaning 'one who serves'.

Kahana
Origin: Hawaiian
Meaning 'priest'.

Kai m/f
Diminutives:
Variants: Kaj
Origin: Uncertain
The origins of this name are uncertain. It has been suggested that it is derived from the Roman Caius, but it may also have come from the Old Norse *katha*, meaning 'chicken'.

Kailash m/f
Origin: Sanskrit
Derived from the Sanskrit *kailasa*, the meaning of which is uncertain, this is the name of Shiva's paradise in Indian mythology.

Kaito
Origin: Japanese
Meaning 'ocean and sake dipper'.

Kalea
Origin: Hawaiian
Meaning 'full of happiness'.

Kalyan
Origin: Sanskrit
From the Sanskrit *kalyana*, meaning 'auspicious' or 'beautiful'.

Kamal
Variants: Kamil
Origin: Arabic and Sanskrit
Derived from the Arabic *kamal*, meaning 'complete' or 'perfection', though it is often traced back to the Sanskrit *kamala* among Indians, meaning 'pale red'.

Kamari
Origin: Indian
Meaning 'the enemy of desire'.

Kamil
See Kamal

Kamran
Origin: Sanskrit
Meaning 'successful'.

Kana
Origin: Japanese
Meaning 'powerful'.

Kanaloa
Origin: Hawaiian
This is the name of a Hawaiian god.

Kane
Origin: Gaelic and Welsh
This comes from the Irish Cathán, from *cath*, meaning 'battle' or 'fighter'. It can also be traced to the Welsh word for 'beautiful' and was adopted by English speakers in the 1950s. It is less common in the UK than in Australia and the USA.
See also Kean

Kano
Origin: Japanese
Meaning 'god of waters'.

Kareem
See Karim

Karim
Variants: Kareem
Origin: Arabic
Meaning 'generous' or 'noble', from the Arabic *karim*.

Karl
See Carl

Karsten
Origin: Greek
Meaning 'anointed by God'.

Kashif
Origin: Arabic
This name is from the Arabic, meaning 'discoverer'.

Kasper
See **Jasper**

Kavanagh
Variants: Cavanagh
Origin: Irish
A follower of Kavan.

Kavon
Origin: Gaelic
Meaning 'handsome'.

Kay m/f
Variants: Kaye
Origin: Probably Roman
This name is likely to have been derived from the Roman Caius, meaning 'rejoice', and was originally an exclusively masculine name.

Kean
Variants: Keane, Kane
Origin: Gaelic
This is an anglicization of the Irish name Cian.

Keanu
Variants: Keahnu
Origin: Hawaiian
Meaning 'cool breeze over the mountains', this name has been made famous by actor Keanu Reeves.
See also **Keanna**

Keaton
Origin: English
Meaning 'place of hawks'.

Keefe
Origin: Irish
Meaning simply 'noble'.

Keegan
Origin: Celtic
Meaning 'little fiery one'.

Keenan
Origin: Gaelic
Derived from the Irish Gaelic for 'little ancient one'.

Keir
Origin: Uncertain
It has been suggested the meaning of this name is 'swarthy', from the Scottish Gaelic, but this is uncertain. It was originally taken up as a name in the nineteenth century and is mainly confined to Scotland, though it is known because of the trade unionist Keir Hardie.

Keiran
See **Kieran**

Keith
Origin: Scottish
Originally taken from the Scottish place name, this has been taken up as a first name by English speakers and possibly comes from the Gaelic for 'windy place' or 'wood'. It reached a peak in the 1950s and famous bearers of the name include rock star Keith Richards.

Kelan
Origin: Gaelic
Developed as an anglicization of the Irish Caolan, from *caol*, meaning 'slender'.

Kelby
Diminutives: Kel, Kell
Variants: Kelly, Kelbey
Origin: Scandinavian
Meaning 'from the village of the ships'.

Kell
Origin: Norse
Meaning 'from the well'.

Kellagh
Variants: Celcus
Origin: Gaelic
Meaning 'from the wood'. The anglicized variant, Celcus, was the name of a ninth-century bishop in Armagh.

Keller
Origin: Gaelic
Meaning 'little companion'.

Kelly m/f
Origin: Irish
This surname, spelt Ceallagh in Irish Gaelic (meaning 'strife' or 'war'), having fallen into decline since the 1980s, remains fairly popular as a first name in Australia.

Kelsey m/f
Variants: Kelcey, Kelsie
Origin: Old English
From the Old English name Ceolsige (from *ceol*, meaning 'ship', and *sige*, meaning 'victory'), this has appeared as a name for both boys and girls since the 1870s. Famous bearers of the name include actor Kelsey Grammer.

Kelton
Origin: English and Scandinavian
Meaning 'from the harbour town'.

Kelvin
Origin: English
This name appeared in the 1920s, perhaps under the influence of such names as Calvin and Melvin, and may have its roots in the Old English for 'ship' and 'friend' (*ceol* and

wine). The name is in use throughout the English-speaking world, but is more common in Canada than anywhere else.

Kemp
Origin: English
Derived ultimately from the Middle English *kempe*, meaning 'athlete' or 'wrestler', descended from *kempe*, the Old English.

Ken
See **Kenneth**, **Kendall**, **Kendrick**, **Kenyon**

Kenaz
Origin: Hebrew
Meaning 'the hunter'.

Kendall m/f
Diminutives: Ken
Variants: Kendal
Origin: English
Derived from the place name in Cumbria, meaning 'valley of the River Kent', and taken up as a surname in the mid-nineteenth century. Alternatively, it could be from Kendale, from the Old Norse *keld* ('spring'), or from the Welsh name Cynddelw (though it is not known what this means).

Kendrick
Diminutives: Ken
Variants: Kenrick

Origin: Celtic
This name is derived from the Scottish and Welsh surname, possibly ultimately from the Old Celtic word for 'high summit'; among English speakers, it probably derived from the Old English name Ceneric or Cyneric (*cene*, 'bold', 'keen', and *ric*, 'power'). It has been in use as a first name since the mid-nineteenth century.

Kennedy m/f
Origin: Irish
From the Gaelic *ceann* and *eidigh* ('head' and 'ugly'), via the name Cinneidigh, also as an anglicization of the Scottish Gaelic Uarrig. Popular in the 1960s in the USA in tribute to President John F. Kennedy.

Kenneth
Diminutives: Ken, Kenny, Kennet
Variants: Kennith, Kenith, Cenydd (Welsh)
Origin: Probably Irish
This is believed to have derived from the Irish names Cinead ('born of fire') and Cainneach ('handsome one'). Adopted by English speakers in the nineteenth century, it enjoyed a peak in the 1920s in the UK. Notable bearers of the name have included actor Kenneth Williams.

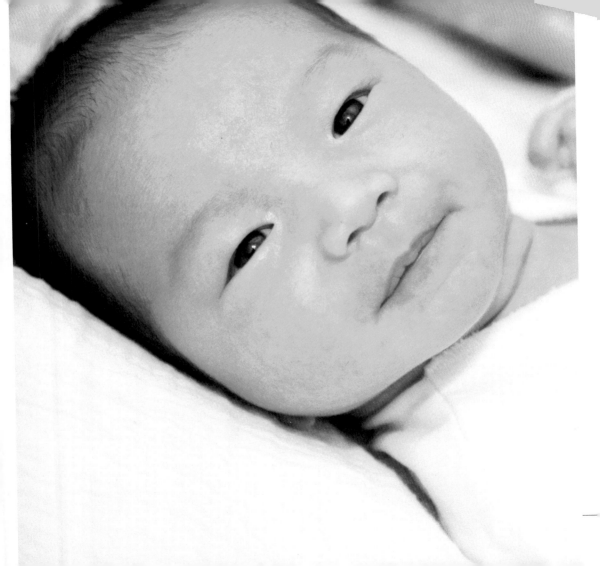

Origin: English
Named for the country of Kent, originally meaning 'border', this appears to have been adopted as a first name in the mid-twentieth century, remaining mostly confined to Canada and the USA. It is sometimes treated as a variant of Kennet (Scandinavian, *see* **Kenneth**).

Kenyon
Diminutives: Ken
Origin: Old English
Meaning 'Ennions' mound', this Lancashire place name has been taken up as a surname and first name.

Kenzo
Origin: Japanese
Meaning simply 'wise'.

Keon
Origin: Irish
See **Evan**

Kerry m/f
Origin: Probably Irish
This name seems to have developed from the name of the county in Ireland, itself meaning 'descendants of Ciar' and was adopted by English speakers in the early twentieth century. Peaking between the 1960s and 1980s, chiefly as a girls' name, it still occasionally appears as a name for boys. Famous bearers of the name include rock star Kelly Jones.

Kester
Origin: Scottish
See **Christopher**

Ketan
Origin: Hindi
Meaning 'home'.

Kevin
Diminutives: Kev
Variants: Kevan
Origin: Gaelic
Derived from the Gaelic Caoimhinn (meaning 'handsome at birth'), from *caomh* ('fair', 'handsome'). Until the twentieth century, it was confined to Ireland and, in the 1960s it enjoyed a peak, though it has since declined. Famous bearers of the name include actors Kevin Kline and Kevin Costner.

Khalid
Variants: Khaled, Khalida (f)
Origin: Arabic
Meaning 'eternal' or 'immortal', this is one of the most popular Arabic names, having been borne by the seventh-century military commander Khalid ibn al-Walid and King Khalid of Saudi Arabia (1913–81).

Khalil
Variants: Khaleel (Indian)
Origin: Arabic
Meaning 'friend'.

Khayrat
Origin: Arabic
Derived from the Arabic *khayra*, meaning 'good deed'.

Kiefer
Origin: German
Meaning 'barrel maker', perhaps the most famous bearer of the name is actor Keifer Sutherland.

Kieran
Variants: Keiran, Kyran, Cieran, Kiaran
Origin: Irish
Derived from the Gaelic Ciaran, this was mainly confined to Ireland until the twentieth century.

Kilby
Origin: Teutonic
Meaning 'farm by the spring'.

Killian
Variants: Kilian
Origin: Irish
From the Irish Cillian, meaning 'church', this is an anglicization of the name.

Kim m/f
Variants: Kym
Origin: Various, depending on the root name.
Developed as a diminutive of Kimberley, it can also be found as a diminutive of Joachim or, according to Rudyard Kipling, Kimball. The name enjoyed a peak both in the UK and the USA in the 1960s.

Kimball m/f
Diminutives: Kim
Origin: Old English
Derived from the Old English *cynebeald* ('kin bold', or 'warrior chief').

Kimberley m/f
Diminutives: Kim
Origin: Old English
Named for the South African town, itself named after John Wodehouse, 1st Earl of Kimberley. This ancestral home was named for the Old English, meaning 'Cyneburga's wood'.

Kincaid
Variants: Kincaide
Origin: Scottish
Meaning 'leader in war'.

King
Origin: English
This developed as a first name in parallel with such names as Duke and Earl in the nineteenth century, though this particular name owes much of its popularity to the civil rights leader Martin Luther King.

Kingsley
Origin: Old English
This place name, which comes from the Old English meaning 'king's wood', was adopted as a first name in the nineteenth century, possibly promoted by writer Charles Kingsley.

Kipp
Diminutives: Kippie
Variants: Kippar
Origin: Anglo-Saxon
Meaning 'one who lives on the pointed hill'.

Kiral
Origin: Turkish
Meaning 'the high king'.

Kiran
Origin: Sanskrit

Derived from the Sanskrit *kirana*, meaning 'dust' or 'thread', usually translated as 'ray of light', the name seems to have invented in medieval times.

Kirby m/f
Origin: Old Norse
Derived from the Old Norse *kirkja*, ('church'), this has been used as a first name since the nineteenth century, but it is not common.
See also Kirk

Kirin
Origin: Latin
Meaning 'spearman'.

Kirk
Origin: Old Norse
Derived from the Old Norse *kirkja* ('church'), this was adopted as a surname before being taken up as a first name in the nineteenth century. It enjoyed a popularity peak in the 1980s. Famous bearers have included actor Kirk Douglas.
See also Kirby

Kit
See Christian, Christopher

Koby
See Jacob

Kofi
Origin: West African

Meaning simply 'born on a Thursday'. Born by Kofi Annan, the former UN Secretary-General.

Kramer
Origin: German
Meaning 'shopkeeper'.

Kris
See Christopher

Krishna m/f
Variants: Kistna, Kishen, Kannan
Origin: Sanskrit
From the Sanskrit *krsna*, meaning 'black' or 'dark', this is the name of the most widely venerated of the Hindu gods and thus has a deep religious significance in India.

Kumar
Origin: Sanskrit
Derived from the Sanskrit *kumara*, meaning 'boy' or 'son', this features in Indian mythology as the name of one of the sons of Shiva.

Kurt
Variants: Curt, Kort (Dutch)
Origin: German
Developed as a diminutive of Konrad, this name was adopted, though not widely, by English speakers in the 1950s. Famous bearers of the name include writer Kurt Vonnegut and rock star Kurt Cobain.

Kushal
Origin: Indian
Meaning simply 'clever'.

Kwame
Origin: Ghanaian
Meaning 'born on a Saturday'.

Kyan
Origin: African-American
Meaning 'little king'.

Kyden
Origin: English
Meaning 'narrow little fire'.

Kyle m/f
Origin: Gaelic
Derived from the name of the place in Ayrshire, from the Gaelic meaning 'narrow', in the 1940s, this was taken up as a first name for boys by English speakers. Famous bearers of the name include actor Kyle MacLachlan.

Kynan
Origin: Welsh
Meaning 'chieftain'.

Kyne
Origin: Anglo-Saxon
Meaning 'royal one'.

Kyran
See Kieran

Lachlan

Diminutives: Lachie, Lockie, Lochlain

Origin: Scottish

Derived originally from the Scottish Lachlann or Lochlann, which was a name for Norwegian settlers, as it means 'land of lochs' or 'land of fjords'. Alternatively, it could be derived from the Gaelic *laochail*, meaning 'warlike'.

Lakshman

Variants: Laxman

Origin: Sanskrit

This Indian name is derived from the Sanskrit *laksmana*, meaning 'having auspicious marks', and it appears in the *Mahabharata* and the *Ramayana*. Other sources claim it has Hindi roots.

Lamar

Origin: Teutonic

Meaning 'famous throughout the land'.

Lambert

Variants: Lambard, Lammert (Dutch)

Origin: Old German

Derived from *lant* ('land') and *berht*, meaning 'bright' or 'famous', this name came to England with the Normans. It was still in use in the twentieth century but has since been in decline.

Lance

See Lancelot

Lancelot

Diminutives: Lance, Launce

Variants: Launcelot

Origin: Uncertain

Derived either from the French *l'ancelle* (meaning 'servant') or an unknown Celtic name, this is famous for being the name of Sir Lancelot of the Round Table in the Arthurian legends.

Landen

Variants: Landyn, Landen, Landon, Landun, Langdon, Langston

Origin: Old English

From the Old English meaning 'the long hill'. One of the characters in writer Jasper Fforde's *Thursday Next* series is named Landen.

Lander

Variants: Landers, Landor, Launder

Origin: Anglo-Saxon

Meaning 'owner of a grassy plain'.

Lando

Origin: Spanish

See Roland

Lane m/f

Variants: Laina, Layne

Origin: Anglo-Saxon

Meaning 'from the narrow road'.

Lanny

See Roland

Larkin

Diminutives: Lark

Variants: Larkan, Larken

Origin: Irish

Meaning 'rough' and 'warlike'.

Larry

See Lawrence

Lars

Origin: Swedish

See Lawrence

Laszlo

Origin: Polish

This is a Polish variant of the Hungarian name Wladyslaw.

Latif

Origin: Arabic

Meaning 'gentle'.

Latimer

Origin: Old French

This English name is derived from the Old French word for 'interpreter'.

Laurence

See Lawrence

Laurent

Origin: French

See Laurence

Lawrence
Diminutives: Larry, Lauri, Laurie, Lawrie, Lori, Laz, Lanty (Irish)
Variants: Laurence, Lorenz, Lorcan
Origin: Latin
Derived from the Latin Laurentius, meaning 'man from Laurentium',

this spelling was adopted in the sixteenth century, and the name itself was revived in the nineteenth century, becoming especially popular in the twentieth.

Lazarus
Variants: Lazare (French), Lazzaro (Italian)

Origin: Hebrew
This biblical name is derived ultimately from the Hebrew name Lazaros and the Aramaic Lazar, from the Hebrew Eleazar or Eliezer (translated as 'God is my help' or 'God has helped'). It is rarely found outside Jewish communities.

Lazhar
Origin: Arabic
Meaning, rather curiously, 'best appearance'.

Leander
Origin: Greek
This is a Latinized version of Leandros, which is derived from the Greek *leon* ('lion') and *andros* ('man'), thus referring to someone strong and brave.

Lee m/f
Origin: Old English
Variants: Leigh
Derived from the Old English *leah*, meaning 'clearing', 'meadow' or 'wood'. This has been a name for boys since the nineteenth century and girls since the twentieth.

Leif
Origin: Old Norse
This Scandinavian name is derived from the Old Norse Leifr (meaning 'heir' or 'descendant').

Leigh m/f
See Lee, Bradley

Leland
Variants: Lealand, Leyland
Origin: Anglo-Saxon
Meaning 'one who lives by the meadow land'.

Lemuel
Diminutives: Lem, Lemmie, Lemmy
Origin: Hebrew
Meaning 'devoted to God', this name was taken up by English speakers in the nineteenth century but seems to have disappeared since the 1930s. Perhaps the most famous bearer of the name is the protagonist Lemuel Gulliver in Jonathan Swift's novel *Gulliver's Travels*.

Len
See Leonard, Lennox

Lennox
Diminutives: Len, Lenny
Variants: Lenox
Origin: Scottish
Adopted as an occasional first name from the surname, which is especially associated with Scotland.

Lenny
See Leonard, Lennox

Leo
Origin: Latin
Derived directly from the Latin *leo*, meaning 'lion', this name peaked in popularity in the nineteenth and twentieth centuries. In 2001, it enjoyed a boost when Prime Minister Tony Blair and his wife Cherie chose the name for their son.
See also Leon

Leon
Origin: Latin
This name is derived from Leo and was common in the nineteenth century, but is now rare outside Jewish communities.
See also Lionel

Leonard
Diminutives: Len, Lennie, Lenny
Variants: Lennard
Origin: Old German
From the Old German *leon* ('lion') and *hard*, meaning 'brave' or 'strong', this name enjoyed a revival in the nineteenth century. In the twentieth century it suffered a marked decline. Notable bearers of the name include actor Leonard Nimoy.

Leopold
Diminutives: Leo
Origin: Old German
This name is derived ultimately from the Old German *liut* ('people') and *bald* ('bold'), this was adopted in the mid-nineteenth century, but was never common and has since become rare.

Leroy
Variants: LeRoy, LeRoi
Origin: Old French
Coming directly from the Old French *le roy*, meaning 'king' or 'the king', it was initially used as a nickname for royal servants and was adopted as a first name in the USA in the nineteenth century and the UK in the 1960s.

Lesley m/f
Diminutives: Les
Variants: Leslie
Origin: Scottish, possibly from Gaelic
Derived from Lesslyn, a place in Aberdeenshire, which may have got its name from the Gaelic *leas cuilinn* ('garden of hollies'). Its use as a first name was recorded in the eighteenth century.

Leslie m/f
See Lesley
Lester
Diminutives: Les
Origin: English
Now known as Leicester (from the

L

Babies' Names ❋ Boys

Old English *Ligora*, a tribal name
of which the meaning is unknown,
and *caster*, meaning 'fort', Lester
was adopted as a first name after
being used as a surname.
Famous bearers of the name
include jockey Lester Piggott.

Levi
Variants: Levy
Origin: Hebrew
This Jewish name comes from
the Hebrew *lewi* ('pledged',
'associated' or 'attached'); in
use among English Jews by
the seventeenth century and
has since been used by non-
Jewish people.

Lewin
Origin: Old English
Derived from the Old English,
meaning 'beloved'.

Lewis
Diminutives: Lou
Variants: Louis, Ludovic,
Lughaidh (Gaelic), Luigi
(Italian), Louie
Origin: Old German
This name has come to English
via the French Louis and
is sometimes seen as an
anglicization of the Welsh
name Llewellyn. Its use was
first recorded in medieval times.

Lex
See Alexander

Liall
See Lyle

Liam
Origin: Old German
This name, which has come to
English via the Gaelic Uilliam, is
an Irish variant of William, has
long been popular in Ireland and
since the 1930s and it has been
spreading throughout the English-
speaking world. Famous bearers
of the name include actor
Liam Neeson.

Lincoln
Origin: Probably Latin
Taken from the place name in
the nineteenth century, this is
more common in the USA than
anywhere else, partly in tribute
to Abraham Lincoln. The original
place name was known as
Lindum colonia.

Lindley
Origin: Anglo-Saxon
Meaning 'by the lime tree
in the meadow'.

Lindsey m/f
Diminutives: Lin, Lyn
Variants: Lindsay
Origin: English, from Latin

From the Lincolnshire place
name Lindsey, meaning 'island
of Lincoln' or 'wetland of
Lincoln'. It was taken as a first
name in the nineteenth century,
initially for boys, but is now rare
among boys.

Linford
Origin: Old English
From the place name in
Berkshire, itself from the Old
English *lin* ('flax') or *lind* ('lime
tree') and *ford* ('ford'), this was
later adopted as a first name.
Arguably the most famous bearer
of the name in recent years is
athlete Linford Christie.

Link
Origin: Anglo-Saxon
Meaning 'from the bank' or
'from the edge'. This name has
gained exposure in recent years,
probably due to the character of
the same name in the *Matrix*
film trilogy.

Linus
Origin: Greek
Probably taken from the Greek
lineos, meaning 'flaxen-haired',
this name is more familiar in the
USA than elsewhere, likely due to
the character of the same name
in the comic strip *Peanuts* by
Charles M. Schultz.

Lionel
Origin: Latin
Meaning 'little lion' from the Latin via French, records of its use go back to medieval times, but it was rare until the early twentieth century. In the 1930s it lost favour again. Famous bearers of the name include singer Lionel Richie.
See also Leon

Llewellyn
Diminutives: Lew, Lyn, Llew
Origin: Probably Old Celtic
Though commonly thought of as a Welsh name, this probably goes back to the Old Celtic name Lugobelinos, the meaning of which has been lost. In Welsh it is taken either to mean 'leader' or to be derived from *llyw*, meaning 'lion', and *eilun* ('likeness'). It was originally spelt Llywelyn.

Lloyd
Variants: Floyd, Loyd
Origin: Welsh
This Welsh surname evolved into a nickname meaning 'grey-haired' and was adopted by English speakers in the twentieth century when it became known through Prime Minister David Lloyd George. Famous bearers of the name include actor Lloyd Bridges.

Lochlain
See Lachlan

Locke
Variants: Lockwood
Origin: Anglo-Saxon
Meaning 'one who lives in the stronghold'.

Logan m/f
Origin: Scottish, probably Gaelic
This Scottish place name from Ayrshire seems to have come from the Gaelic word for 'hollow' and remains mostly confined to Scotland.

Lorcan
See Lawrence

Lorenz
See Lawrence

Lothar
Variants: Lothair (anglicized), Lothario
Origin: Old German
Derived from the Old German *hlud* ('fame') and *hari* ('army' or 'warrior'), as Lothario it has negative connotations as a nickname for any man with a licentious character.
See also Luther

Lou
See Lewis

Loudon
Origin: English
Meaning 'from the low hill'.

Louie
See Lewis

Louis
See Lewis

Lovell
Diminutives: Love
Variants: Lowell, Lovel, Lovet
Origin: Old French
Taken from the Old French nickname Louvel (meaning 'wolf cub' or 'little wolf'), since the fifteenth century it has appeared only infrequently.

Lucan
See Luke

Lucian
See Lucius

Lucius
Diminutives: Lucky
Variants: Lucian, Lucio (Portuguese and Spanish)
Origin: Latin
Derived from the Latin *lux*, meaning 'light', via Roman, it was first used in English in the sixteenth century and was used liberally by Shakespeare in his Roman plays.

Ludovic
See **Lewis**

Ludwig
Diminutives: Lutz
Variants: Lodovico (Italian)
Origin: Old German
Derived from the Old German *hlut* and *wig* ('fame' and 'warrior'), this is also a German version of **Louis**. Probably the most famous bearer of the name was composer Ludwig van Beethoven.

Lugh
Origin: Irish
In Celtic countries, this name is known as Lughnasa; in Celtic mythology, Lugh was the sun god.

Lughaidh
See **Lewis**

Luigi
See **Lewis**

Luka
See **Luke**

Luke
Diminutives: Lucky
Variants: **Luka, Lucan**
Origin: Greek
This name has entered English, via the Roman Lucas, from the Greek name Loukas, meaning 'a man from Lucania (in southern Italy)'. Famous bearers of the name include actor Luke Perry.

Luther
Variants: **Lothar**
Origin: Old German
From the Old German *liut* and *hari* ('people' and 'warrior' respectively), this was adopted as a first name by English speakers in the nineteenth century. Famous bearers of the name include singer Luther Vandross.

Lyle
Variants: **Liall**
Origin: French
Derived from the French *de l'isle*, literally meaning 'of the island' or 'from the island', in the nineteenth century this was adopted as a first name by English speakers. It is popular in Scotland, leading to it becoming confused with the unrelated name Lyall.

Lyndon
Variants: Lindon
Origin: Old English
Derived from the Old English word *linde*, meaning 'lime tree', this place name was later adopted as a first name. It was made popular in the twentieth century in the USA because of President Lyndon Baines Johnson.

Lynfa
Origin: Welsh
Meaning 'from the lake'.

Lynn m/f
Origin: Various root names
Developed as a diminutive of such names as Lynda (*see* **Linda**) and **Lindsey**, it is used as a masculine name in Wales but rarely outside that country.

Lysander
Diminutives: **Sandy**
Variants: Lysand
Origin: Greek
This hero of Greek mythology was known as the liberator of men. Shakespeare used the name for a character in his play *A Midsummer Night's Dream*.

Lytton
Variants: Litton
Origin: English
Originally a surname, this means 'loud torrent' and is best known through the biographer Lytton Strachey.

Mac

Origin: Scottish
Meaning 'son of', this is the prefix for numerous Scottish surnames.

Macauley m/f

This name is gender neutral, but is known mostly as a name for boys, as it was made famous by the actor Macauley Caulkin.

Mackenzie

Origin: Probably Irish
Meaning 'son of Kenneth', this name has close links with Canada, where it is mostly a name for girls, and this is thought to be in reference to the Mackenzie River.

Mackinley

Variants: MacKinlay, McKinlay
Origin: Gaelic
Meaning 'son of the wise one', this is also the name of a mountain in the USA.

Macnair

Origin: Celtic
Meaning simply 'son of the heir'.

Maddox

Variants: Maddock, Madoc, Madog
Origin: Welsh
This Welsh name means 'beneficent'.

Madjid

Origin: Arabic
Meaning 'glorious'.

Madoc

See **Maddox**

Magnus

Variants: Manus (Irish)
Origin: Roman
This Roman name means 'great' and it was revived by English speakers in the early twentieth century. Famous bearers of the name have included TV presenter Magnus Magnusson.

Mahavir

Origin: Sanskrit
This Indian name is derived from the Sanskrit maha ('great') and vira ('hero'). It is popular among Jains as it was the name of the founder of Jainism.

Mahendra

Variants: Mahinder, Mohinder
Origin: Sanskrit
The Sanskrit word maha means 'great, so this name translates as 'the great god Indra'.

Mahfuz

Origin: Arabic
Meaning 'guardian'.

Mahmud

Origin: Arabic
This name is derived from the Arabic hamida, meaning 'to praise', and was made popular by Mahmud of Ghazna, a Muslim commander who conquered India.
See also **Mohammed**

Mahon

Origin: Irish
This is an English version of the Irish name Mathuin, from mathghambain, meaning 'bear'. The eleventh-century Irish king Brian Boru had a brother named Mahon.

Maitland

Origin: Norman French
This was originally a surname, but the meaning of it has been lost.

Makani

Origin: Hawaiian
Meaning simply 'wind'.

Malachi

Origin: Hebrew
This name means 'my messenger' (some sources claim it means 'angel') and was adopted by the Puritans in the seventeenth century, though it is rarely encountered today.

Malcolm
Diminutives: Mal, Malc
Origin: Gaelic
This is English version of the Gaelic name Mael Colum, meaning 'disciple of St Columba'; also an anglicized version of the Scottish name Colum (see Calum). Famous bearers of the name include novelist Malcolm Bradbury.

Maldwyn
Diminutives: Mal
Origin: Welsh, from Old German.
This is a Welsh variant of Baldwin, and is more or less unknown outside Wales.
See also Montgomery

Mali
Origin: Arabic
Meaning 'full and rich'.

Malik
Origin: Arabic
Derived from the Arabic meaning 'king'.

Mallin
Diminutives: Mally
Variants: Malen, Malin, Mallan
Origin: English
Meaning 'small soldier'.

Mallory m/f
Variants: Malory

Origin: Norman French
This was originally a Norman French nickname derived from *malheure*, meaning 'unlucky' or 'unhappy'. This is usually reserved as a name for boys.

Malone
Origin: Irish, from Hebrew
This first name means 'follower of St John' and was originally a surname.

Maloney
Origin: Gaelic
Meaning 'believer in the Sabbath'.

Mander
Origin: Disputed
Meaning simply 'of my own self' in Romany. Other sources claim it is Old French and means 'stable lad'.

Manfred
Origin: Old German
This name is derived from the Old German *mana* ('man') or *magin* ('strength') and *fridu* ('peace'), so means 'man of peace' or 'strong peace'. It disappeared from use until it was revived in the nineteenth century.

Mani
Origin: Sanskrit
This name is taken directly from the Sanskrit word *mani*, which

means 'jewel', and it appears in the *Mahabharata*. It is a common name throughout southern India.

Manik
Origin: Sanskrit
Meaning simply 'precious ruby'.

Manish
Origin: Sanksrit
Meaning 'intelligent'.

Manolo
See Emanuel

Mansur
Variants: Mansoor
Origin: Arabic
This Arabic name means 'victorious' or 'triumphant'.

Manus
See Magnus

Marcel
Variants: Marcellus, Marcella (f)
Origin: Latin and Roman
This French name is derived from Marcellus, which in turn is a diminutive of Marcus (see Mark). Fairly common today in Canada, it has been used occasionally by English speakers since the late nineteenth century.

Marcellus
See Marcel

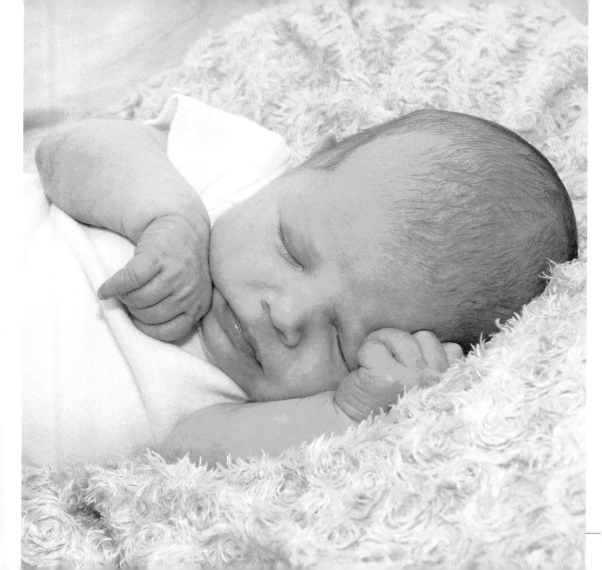

Mario
See **Marius**

Marion m/f
Variants: **Marian** (also f)
Origin: Latin
This name is derived from the Latin **Marius** via the Roman Marianus and has made a few appearances as a first name since the nineteenth century. The real name of actor John Wayne was Marion Michael Morrison.

Marius
Variants: **Mario**, **Marion**, Marcus, **Mark**
Origin: Latin or Roman
Likely to be derived from the Latin *maris* ('male', 'manly') or else as a variant of Mars, the Roman god of war. Another source suggests it comes from *mare*, meaning 'sea' in Latin, but this is not widely accepted.

Mark
Diminutives: Markie, Marky
Variants: Marcus, Marc
Origin: Roman
This name is derived from the Latin Marcus (*see* **Marcel**), and is the name of one of the biblical evangelists. It was not until the 1960s that it became one of the most popular of boys' names. Famous bearers of the name

include writer Mark Twain and guitarist Mark Knopfler.

Marley m/f
Origin: Old English
This name comes from the Old English for 'pleasant wood' and has often appeared recently in tribute to musician Bob Marley.

Marlon
Origin: Uncertain
This name could be derived from **Merlin**, **Mark** or **Marion**, and first appeared among English speakers in the 1950s. Famous bearers of the name include actor Marlon Brando.

Marlow
Variants: Marlowe
Origin: Anglo-Saxon
Meaning 'from the lake on the hill'.

Martin
Diminutives: Marty
Variants: **Morten** (Scandinavian), Martyn
Origin: Roman
Probably derived ultimately from Mars, the Roman god of war, this name enjoyed peaks in the 1960s and 1970s. Famous bearers of the name include writer Martin Amis.

Marvin
See **Mervyn**

Mason
Origin: English
The meaning of this name is fairly self-explanatory, being applied originally to anyone working with stone (masonry). Though it is in use on both sides of the Atlantic, it is more common in the USA than anywhere else.

Masud
Variants: Masood
Origin: Arabic
Meaning 'lucky' or 'fortunate'.

Matthew
Diminutives: Mat, Matt
Variants: Mathieu (French), Mads (Danish), Motya (Russian)
Origin: Hebrew
Derived from the Hebrew name Mattathiah, meaning 'gift of God', in the 1960s and 1970s, this name finally gained a position among the most popular boys' names and it has retained its place there since.
See also **Mattias**

Mattias
Variants: Mathias
Origin: Hebrew
This is a Greek version of Mattathiah (*see also* **Matthew**) and was among the names adopted by the Puritans in the seventeenth century, but it has

never gained particular popularity among English speakers.

Maurice
Diminutives: Mo, Moe, Moss, Maurie, Morrie
Variants: Morris, Merrick/Meurig (Welsh)
Origin: Latin and Gaelic
Ultimately derived from the Latin *maurus* (meaning 'dark-skinned', 'moor' or 'swarthy') via the Roman Mauricius. It can also be found as an anglicized version of the Gaelic Muirgheas, from *muir* ('sea') and *gus*, meaning 'choice'.

Max
See Maximilian, Maxwell

Maxim
Origin: Latin
Derived from the Latin *maximus*, meaning 'greatest', several early Christian saints bore this name. Famous bearers of the name have included writer Maxim Gorki.

Maximilian
Diminutives: Max, Maxie
Origin: Latin
Ultimately derived from the Latin *maximus* ('greatest'), this name seems to go back as far as the third century, but it has been suggested that it was invented in the fifteenth by the Roman Emperor Frederick III for his son.

Maxwell
Diminutives: Max, Maxie
Origin: Scottish
This place name, meaning 'Magnus's well' or 'large spring' was adopted as a surname and in the nineteenth century started being used as a first name.

Mekhi
Origin: African
Meaning 'who is God?'

Melchior
Origin: Persian
Meaning 'king of the city', this is the name of one of the three wise men and is thought to have been developed from a combination of *melk* ('king') and *quart*, meaning 'city'.

Melville
Diminutives: Mel
Origin: Norman French
Originally derived from the Norman French place name Malville, which translates directly as 'bad town' or 'bad settlement', it was a surname in Scotland as early as the twelfth century and in the nineteenth century it was adopted as a first name.

Melvin
Diminutives: Mel
Variants: Melvyn
Origin: Uncertain
The roots of this name are uncertain but it is thought to be derived from the Old English *wine*, meaning 'friend', though another theory suggests it comes from the Gaelic name Malvin, meaning 'smooth brow'.
See also Kelvin

Memphis
Origin: Greek
From the Greek meaning 'beautiful' and 'established', this is also the name of a city in Tennessee, USA.

Mercer
Origin: Anglo-Saxon
Meaning 'merchant'.

Meredith m/f
Diminutives: Merry (f)
Variants: Meridith, Meridyth, Meredyth
Origin: Welsh
Based on the Welsh *mawredd* ('greatness') and *iudd* ('chief' or 'lord'), the name being Maredudd or Meredydd. Sometimes used as a masculine name, but it is far more common among women.

Merle
Origin: Various sources
Often seen as a version of the French *merle*, meaning 'blackbird', it could also be a diminutive of such names as **Muriel** and Meryl (itself a diminutive of Muriel).

Merlin
Variants: Marlin, Merlyn (occ. f)
Origin: Old Celtic
This English version of the Welsh name Myrddin, itself thought to be based on the Old Celtic words for 'fort', 'hill' or 'sea', is most famous for being the name of the magician in the Arthurian legends.

Merrick
Origin: Welsh
See **Maurice**

Mervyn
Variants: Marvin, Mervin
Origin: Old Celtic
The original Welsh name is spelt Merfyn, from the Old Celtic words for 'great and 'sea'. Mainly confined to Wales until the 1930s, famous bearers of the name have included writer Mervyn Peake.

Michael
Diminutives: Midge, Mitch, Mitchell, Mike, Mickey, Micky, Mikey

Origin: Hebrew
Meaning 'who is like God?'. In the 1930s, the name was revived and has remained popular ever since. Famous bearers of the name have included pop star Michael Jackson.

Midge m/f
See **Michael**

Miguel
Origin: Hebrew
This is a Portuguese and Spanish version of **Michael**.

Milan
Variants: Milano
Origin: Slavonic
Meaning 'greatly loved'. It is also sometimes perhaps used in reference to the city in Italy.

Miles
Variants: Myles, Milo
Origin: Uncertain
Links have been made to the Latin *miles*, meaning 'soldier', but also to the Slavonic *mil*, which means 'dear', 'beloved'. Other sources say it comes from the Old German for 'generous' or 'merciful'. Famous bearers of the name have included musician Miles Davis.

Milford
Origin: English
Literally meaning 'mill ford', this name remains relatively rare.

Milhouse
Variants: Milhous
Origin: English
Literally meaning 'from the mill house', this was the middle name of President Richard Nixon but is also famous more recently for being the name of a character in the cartoon series *The Simpsons*.

Milo
See **Miles**

Milton
Diminutives: Milt
Origin: Old English
This place name is derived from the Old English *mylentum*, meaning 'settlement with a mill', and was used as a surname before being taken up as a first name early in the nineteenth century. It is more common now in the USA than anywhere else.

Mitchell
See **Michael**

Mo
See **Maurice**

Mohammed
Variants: Mahmud, Muhammad, Mahomet, Mohammad

Origin: Arabic
Derived from the Arabic *hamida*, meaning 'to praise', this is the name of the founder of Islam and as such has been among the most popular name for Muslim boys globally. Notable bearers of the name include boxer Muhammad Ali.

Mohan

Origin: Sanskrit
This Indian name is derived from the Sanskrit *mohana* ('bewitching') and is featured in Indian mythology as an alternative name for Kama, Krishna and Shiva.

Monroe

Variants: Monro, Munroe, Munro
Origin: Scottish
Believed to have derived from the Scottish place name meaning 'mouth of the Roe', itself a reference to the River Roe in Ireland, from where it is believed the Monroe clan originated.

Montague

Diminutives: Monty, Monte
Origin: Old French
Derived from the Old French *mont* and *aigu* ('hill' or 'mountain' and 'pointed', respectively), via the Norman place name Mont Agigu. The name arrived in England with the Norman invasion and retains its strong aristocratic associations.

Montgomery

Diminutives: Monty
Origin: German and Old French
This name is derived from the French *mont* ('hill' or 'mountain') and the Germanic *gomeric*, meaning 'man power' and translates roughly as 'mountain of the powerful one'. Famous bearers of the name have included actor Montgomery Swift. *See also* Maldwyn

Mordecai

Origin: Probably Persian
This is Hebrew name probably derived from the Persian meaning 'devotee of Marduk' (Marduk was a revered Babylonian god). Today, it is usually only found in Jewish communities.

Mordred

Origin: Welsh
Meaning 'one who takes his own path', Mordred was one of King Arthur's nephews.

Morgan m/f

Origin: Uncertain
The original Welsh Morcant (possibly from *mor*, meaning 'sea', and *cant*, meaning 'edge' or 'circle') gave way to Morgan, but it is of uncertain origin. It is thought to mean 'seabright' and has a long history in Wales.

Famous bearers of the name include actor Morgan Freeman.

Mori

Origin: Ugandan
This literally means 'born before the dowry loan has been paid off'.

Morley

Origin: Old English
From the Old English *mor* ('marsh' or 'moor') and *leah* ('clearing' or 'wood').

Morris

See Maurice

Morten

See Martin

Mortimer

Diminutives: Mort
Origin: Uncertain
Likely to have been derived from the Old French meaning 'dead sea' (referring to a stagnant marsh or lake); in the nineteenth century it was adopted by English speakers as a first name. Alternatively, it could come from the Celtic meaning 'sea warrior'.

Morton

Origin: Old English
From the Old English *mortun*, meaning 'settlement on a moor', this was adopted as a first name

in the mid-nineteenth century. Mostly found within Jewish communities nowadays, as an anglicized version of **Moses**.

Moses
Variants: Moyse, Moss
Origin: Uncertain
Though now seen as a Hebrew name, the origins of Moses are uncertain and it is believed it may have been derived from the Egyptian *mes*, meaning 'child' or 'born of'. In the seventeenth century, it was taken up by Puritans but today it is rare.

Mostyn
Diminutives: Moss
Origin: Old English
Despite its strong Welsh associations, this name is derived from the Old English *mos* and *tun* ('moss' and 'settlement'). It is also a place name in Clwyd.

Muir
Origin: Scottish
This place name, meaning 'moor', was adopted as a surname and occasional first name and notable bearers have included film music director Muir Mathieson.

Mukesh
Origin: Uncertain, probably Sanskrit
This Indian name has obscure origins, but it may be from the Sanskrit *isa*, meaning 'ruler', or it could mean 'conqueror of the demon Muka'.

Mungo
Origin: Welsh
Despite its Scottish links, this name probably comes from the Welsh *mwyn* ('gentle', 'dear', 'kind') though it was the nickname of St Kentigern of Scotland in the sixth century.

Munir
Origin: Arabic
Meaning 'to illuminate', from the Arabic *nawara*, this name means 'bright' or 'shining'.

Murali
Origin: Sanskrit
From the Sanskrit *murali*, meaning 'flute', this is one of the names of **Krishna** in Indian mythology, who himself played the flute.

Murphy
Origin: Irish
A distinctively Irish name, this is derived from Gaelic and means 'sea hound'.

Murray
Variants: Moray, Murry
Origin: Gaelic

Meaning 'sea', *mor* in Gaelic gave its name to the place name Moray, though the name is also an anglicized version of the Gaelic Muireach. Notable bearers of the name include TV sports commentator Murray Walker.

Musad
Variants: Misid
Origin: Arabic
Meaning 'to be lucky' (from the Arabic *saida*).

Mustafa
Variants: Mostafa
Origin: Arabic
This means 'chosen' and is popular among Muslims as one of the titles of the prophet Muhammad.

Mwita
Origin: African
Meaning 'humorous one'.

Myles
See **Miles**

Myron
Origin: Greek
Meaning 'myrrh', this name was taken up by English speakers in the twentieth century and is sometimes thought to mean 'fragrant'. Its biblical links mean it was popular with early Christians.

Nadim

Variants: Nadeem
Origin: Arabic
Meaning 'to drink' from the Arabic *nadama*, this is taken to mean 'confidant' or 'drinking companion'. It is a popular name in Indian communities.

Nadir

Origin: Arabic/Sanskrit
Said to mean 'precious', 'rare' or 'the pinnacle', but has more obvious opposite connotations.

Nahum

Origin: Hebrew
Meaning 'comfort'.

Naim

Origin: Arabic
Meaning 'contented'.

Nairn

Origin: Gaelic
Meaning 'dweller by the alder tree', this is also a seaside town near Inverness.

Najee
Origin: Arabic
Meaning 'dear companion'.

Najib
Variants: Nagib
Origin: Arabic
This name means 'high minded' or 'of noble descent', though a modern derivation suggests it means 'bright' or 'clever'.

Nakia
Origin: Arabic. Meaning 'pure'.

Nakul
Origin: Indian
This name means simply 'mongoose'.

Namid
Origin: Native American
Meaning 'dancer of the stars'.

Nanda
Origin: Sanskrit
Meaning 'joy', this Indian name is also sometimes taken to mean 'son' and was a royal name.

Naphtali
Origin: Hebrew
Meaning, curiously, 'wrestling'.

Narendra
Variants: Narender, Narendhra, Narinder

Origin: Sanskrit
This Indian name is derived from the Sanskrit *nara* and *Indra* ('man' and 'mighty'), though later derivations suggest it may mean 'physician'.

Naseem
Origin: Arabic
Meaning 'benevolent'.
Nash
Origin: English
This is more familiar as a surname, and means 'ash tree'.

Nashif
Origin: Arabic
Meaning 'hard'.

Nasir
Variants: Nasr (Indian)
Origin: Arabic
This name derives from the Arabic *nasara* ('to render victorious'), and has been interpreted to mean 'helper' or 'supporter'.

Nate
See Nathan

Nathan
Diminutives: Nat, Nate
Origin: Hebrew
Meaning 'he has given' or 'gift', around 1900 this name enjoyed a revival in both the UK and the USA. In the 1970s and 1980s, it

became popular once more.
See also Jonathan, Nathaniel

Nathaniel
Diminutives: Nat, Natty
Variants: Nathanael
Origin: Hebrew
Meaning 'God has given' or 'gift of God', this New Testament name was promoted in Shakespeare's *Love's Labours Lost* but is now less common in the UK than in the US. Famous bearers of the name include actor Nathaniel Parker.

Naveen
Origin: Indian
This Indian name means 'new' and a famous bearer of the name is actor Naveen Andrews.

Nayan
Origin: Sanskrit
Meaning 'lovely eyes'.

Nazario
Origin: Hebrew
This name developed from the Hebrew word for 'branch', via the Roman name Nazarius (referencing Nazareth). It was popular among early Christians.

Neacail
See Nicolas

Neal
See Neil

Ned
See Edward, Edwin

Nehemiah
Origin: Hebrew
Meaning 'consoled by Yah' or 'comfort of the Lord', this name's biblical associations meant it was adopted by the Puritans in the seventeenth century, but it has been rare ever since.

Neil
Variants: Neal, Neale, Neill, Neilie/Neillie (Scottish), Niall, Niles
Origin: Gaelic
Derived from the Irish name Niall, this predated the Norman invasion. In the nineteenth century, it began to appear more often and has remained popular ever since. Famous bearers of the name include astronaut Neil Armstrong.
See also Nyle

Neilson
Origin: Irish, from Gaelic
Meaning 'son of Neil'.
See also Nelson

Nelson
Origin: English, from Gaelic
This name, meaning 'son of Neil' or 'son of Nell', was used as a first name in the early years of the nineteenth century as tribute to Admiral Horatio Nelson after he had been killed in the Battle of Trafalgar. A famous bearer of the name is former South African President Nelson Mandela.

Neo
Origin: Greek
Meaning 'new', this name has undoubtedly received an extra boost in recent years due to the popularity of the *Matrix* film trilogy.

Nephi
Origin: Greek
Meaning 'cloud'.

Nero
Origin: Italian
Meaning 'black' or 'dark', this is not a vastly popular name due to its links with the Roman Emperor Nero.

Nessim
Origin: Arabic
Meaning 'breeze'.

Neville
Diminutives: Nev
Variants: Nevil, Nevile, Nevill
Origin: French
Derived from the French place name Neuville, literally translated as 'new town', this name has strong aristocratic associations and was most frequent between the mid-nineteenth century and the 1960s. It has since suffered a decline. Famous bearers of the name include Prime Minister Neville Chamberlain.

Nevin
Variants: Niven
Origin: Gaelic
This Irish name means 'little saint' in Gaelic.

Newton
Diminutives: Newt
Origin: English
This place name, literally meaning 'new town', has been used as an occasional first name since the nineteenth century and is sometimes given in honour of the scientist Sir Isaac Newton.

Niall
See Neil

Nic
See Nicolas, Dominic

Nico
See Nicolas

Nicolas

Diminutives: Nic, Nico
Variants: Neacail, Nicholas, Nickolas, Nichol, Nicol
Origin: Greek
This name is derived from the Greek Nikolaos, from a combination of *nike* ('victory) and *laos* ('people'), and was the name of the fourth-century saint who later gained immortality as Father Christmas. It was revived in the mid-twentieth century and enjoyed a peak in the 1960s and 1970s.

Nigel

Diminutives: Nige
Origin: Probably Latin from Greek
This is believed to be a Latin version of Neil that developed soon after the Norman invasion and used to be written as Nigellus, sometimes wrongly assumed to mean 'black' (from the Latin *niger*). Revived in the nineteenth century, since the 1960s it has been in decline once more.

Nikhil

Origin: Hindi
Meaning 'entire' or 'whole'.

Niles

See Neil

Nixon

Variants: Nickson
Origin: Anglo-Saxon, from Greek
Meaning simply 'Nicolas's son'.

Noah

Origin: Hebrew
Meaning 'long-lived', 'rest' or 'comfort', this name is best known for its biblical associations and was taken up by Puritans in the seventeenth century. Although it is no longer common, the name is still in occasional use.

Noel m/f

Origin: French
Derived from the French word for 'Christmas', this name has been reserved traditionally for children born on or near that day. Since the seventeenth century it has been mostly reserved for boys. Famous bearers of the name include TV presented Noel Edmonds.

Norman

Diminutives: Norm, Norrie
Origin: Old English and Norse
Derived from the Old English *nord* and *man* and meaning 'man from the north', this was the name given to refer to Vikings; it is also an anglicized version of the Norse name Tormod (from Thor and the Old Norse word for 'wrath'). Revived in the nineteenth century, it declined again after the 1950s. *See also* Norris

Norris

Origin: English
This developed as a variant of Norman and was relatively popular in the nineteenth century, but it has since declined. Famous bearers of the name include writer and publisher Norris McWhirter.

Norton

Origin: Old English
From the Old English *nord* and *tun* ('north' and 'settlement'), this name has appeared a few times since the nineteenth century but has never been common.

Nova

Origin: Latin
Meaning simply 'new'.

Nur m/f

Origin: Arabic
Meaning 'light'.

Nyle

Variants: Nyl, Nyles
Origin: English from Gaelic
In English, this means 'from the island', though it is also a variant of Neil.

O

Oakes
Origin: English
Meaning simply 'from the oak trees'.

Obadiah
Variants: Ovadia (modern)
Origin: Hebrew
Meaning 'servant of the Lord', this is one of the many names adopted by Puritans in the seventeenth century, but since then it has been very rare.

Obama
Origin: African
Meaning 'crooked', this name has been made famous in recent years by the American President Barack Obama.

Oberon
See Aubrey

Ocean m/f
Origin: English
Taken from the ordinary vocabulary word 'ocean', this is uncommon and has only recently been adopted as a first name. It may have been inspired by the Greek sea god Oceanus.

Ogden
Origin: Old English
From the Old English meaning 'oak valley', this was adopted as a first name in the nineteenth century. A well-known bearer of the name was poet Ogden Nash.

Ogilvie
Variants: Ogilvy
Origin: Celtic
Meaning 'high peak', this is also a surname.

Oisin
Origin: Irish
Meaning 'small deer', this is also the name of a legendary Irish hero in Irish legend.

Olaf
Variants: Amhlaoibh, Olav, Olen, Olin
Origin: Scandinavian
Meaning 'peaceful reminder' or 'ancestral relic'.
See also Oliver

Olin
See Olaf

Oliver
Variants: Olaf
Origin: Scandinavian or Old German
This is believed either to have developed as a variant of Olaf or to have derived from the Old German *alfihar*, meaning 'elf host'. By the 1980s it was one of the most common of boys' names.

Oman
Origin: Scandinavian
Meaning 'high protector'.

Omar
Origin: Arabic or Hebrew
This biblical name comes either from an anglicized version of the Arabic name Umar (meaning 'flourishing' or 'prosperous') or from the Hebrew meaning 'eloquent'. Famous bearers of the name include actor Omar Sharif.

Omri
Origin: Hebrew
This was the name of a biblical king of Israel and means 'sheaf of grain'.

Onslow
Origin: Anglo-Saxon
Meaning 'hill of the zealous one'.

Oran
Origin: Gaelic
Meaning 'pale-skinned one', the original name is Odhran, from *odhar*, which translates as 'green' or 'sallow'. As Oran, it also means 'song'.

Orban
Origin: Latin
This comes from the Latin via French and means 'globe'.

Orfeo
Origin: Greek
The meaning of this Italian name, which is derived from the Greek Orpheus, has been lost.

Orlando
Origin: Italian *See* Roland

Orson
Origin: Latin
From the Latin *ursus* ('bear') via the French *ourson*, meaning 'bear cub'), perhaps the most famous bearer of the name was actor and director Orson Welles.

Orville
Variants: Orval
Origin: English
This name was invented by writer Fanny Burney for her novel *Evelina* in 1778 and she may have taken it from the French place name. The most famous bearer of the name was flight pioneer Orville Wright.

Osbert
Diminutives: Oz, Ozzie
Variants: Osbart, Osburt, Ozbart, Ozburt
Origin: Old English
Meaning 'famous to God', derived from the Old English *os* and *beorht* ('god' and 'famous'). Records of its use go back to before the Norman invasion and was common until the fifteenth century.

Osborne
Origin: Old English
From the Old English *os* and *beorn* ('god' and 'bear' or 'warrior'

respectively), it has made only infrequent appearances as a first name. Revived in the nineteenth century, it has never been common as a first name.

Oscar
Diminutives: Os, Ossie, Ocky
Origin: Gaelic or Old English
Derived either from the Gaelic *os* and *cara* (meaning 'deer' and 'friend'), or from the Old English *ansfar* ('god-spear').

Osman
See Uthman

Osmond
Diminutives: Ossie
Variants: Osmund (rare)
Origin: Old English
Derived from the Old English *os* and *mund* (meaning 'god' and 'protection' respectively), records of the name go back to before the Norman invasion.

Oswald
Diminutives: Oz, Ozzie
Origin: Old English
Meaning 'divine power' or 'rule of God', from the Old English *os* and *weald* ('god' and 'rule'), this name was revived in the nineteenth century. It suffered in the twentieth century due to the notoriety of fascist leader Oswald Mosley.

Otho
See Otto

Otis
Origin: Old German or Greek
This developed as a variant of Otto, or from the Greek meaning 'keen-eared', this name is rare outside the USA. Famous bearers of the name include singer Otis Redding.

Otto
Variants: Otho, Otis
Origin: Old German
Derived from the Old German *ot* ('riches' or 'possessions'), this name came to England with the Norman invasion and was common until medieval times.

Owen
Variants: Owain, Uaine
Origin: Uncertain
Derived either from Eugene or from the Welsh *oen*, meaning 'lamb'; another theory suggests it may have derived from the Old Celtic, meaning 'born of (Celtic deity) Esos'.

Oz
See Osbert, Oswald

Ozul
Origin: Hebrew
Meaning 'shadow'.

Pablo
Origin: Spanish
See Paul

Pace
Variants: Pacey
Origin: Latin
This is an English version of the French Pascal, meaning 'born at Easter'.

Paco
Variants: Pako
Origin: Italian and Spanish
A Spanish diminutive of Francisco (*see* Francis), or Italian meaning 'pack'.

Paddy
See Patrick

Padma m/f
Origin: Sanskrit
An Indian name derived from the Sanskrit *padma*, which means 'lotus'. Nowadays, it is reserved almost exclusively for girls and is found in ancient Sanskrit literature.

Padraigh
See Patrick

Paine
Variants: Payne
Origin: Latin
Meaning 'a country person', 'a pagan'.

Paolo
See Paul

Paresh
Origin: Indian
Meaning 'supreme standard'.

Paris m/f
Variants: Parris
Origin: Greek
Mainly popular in the USA, Paris was the name of a central character in the story of the Trojan War.

Parker m/f
Origin: English
Meaning 'park keeper', this has been in use as a first name, mainly in the USA, since the nineteenth century.

Parnell
Variants: Parnel
Origin: French, from Greek
Meaning 'little Peter'.

Parry
Origin: Welsh, from Old German
Meaning 'son of Harry' (*ap Harry*), this Welsh surname was adopted as a first name, though it is rarely found anywhere other than Wales.

Pascal
Variants: Paschal, Pascoe
Origin: Latin
This French name is derived from the Latin *paschalis*, meaning 'of Easter'. Popular in medieval Cornwall, it retains its Roman Catholic associations.

Patrick
Diminutives: Paddy, Pat, Packy (rare)
Variants: Padraigh, Padraic (both Gaelic), Patric, Patraic
Origin: Latin
Taken from the Latin *patricius*, meaning 'nobleman', this name is popular in Ireland due to the name of the patron saint, though it seems more likely the saint's name came from Celtic rather than Latin origins.

Patterson
Origin: Irish
Meaning 'son of Patrick'.

Patton
Origin: Old English
Meaning 'from the town of warriors'.

Paul
Variants: Pól (Irish), Paolo (Italian), Pablo (Spanish), Pavel (Eastern European)
Origin: Latin
Taken from the Latin *paulus*, meaning 'small' or 'little', this began as a nickname but was soon seen as a name in its own

right. Since the 1970s it has been in decline. Notable bearers of the name include musician Sir Paul McCartney.

Pavel
Origin: Russian
See Paul

Pax
Origin: Latin
Meaning simply 'peace', though it could also be seen a a diminutive of Paxton.

Paxton m/f
Diminutives: Pax
Origin: English, from Latin
Meaning 'from the peaceful town'.

Peadar
See Peter

Percival
Diminutives: Percy, Perce, Val
Variants: Perceval (French), Parsifal (German)
Origin: Uncertain
This seems to have been invented by poet Chrétien de Troyes in c. 1175; he said it came from perce-val ('one who pierces the valley'). Others seem to have borne this as a surname when they came from Percheval in Normandy. Still others link the name to the Celtic name Peredur, meaning 'hard steel'.

Percy
See Percival

Perry m/f
Origin: Varies depending on root name
Sometimes found as a diminutive of Peregrine or Peter, this name is derived from the Old English pirige ('man who lives by a pear tree'). Since the 1980s it has peaked in popularity. Famous bearers of the name have included singer Perry Como.

Peter
Diminutives: Pete
Variants: Peadar, Piers, Pierce
Origin: Greek
This name comes via the Roman Petrus from the Greek petros, meaning 'stone'. It was revived in the mid-twentieth century but since the 1960s it has been in decline once more.

Phelan
Origin: Gaelic
Derived from the Gaelic word for 'wolf', this is an Irish first name.

Phelim
See Felix

Phelps
Origin: Anglo-Saxon, from Greek
This Anglo-Saxon name means

'son of Philip'.
See also Philip

Philip
Diminutives: Phil, Pip, Flip
Variants: Phillip, Felipe (Spanish)
Origin: Greek
Derived ultimately from the Greek philein and hippos ('to love' and 'horse') via Philippos. This name was revived in the nineteenth century but, since the 1960s, it has been in decline.

Phoenix m/f
Origin: Arabian
Alluding to the Arabian bird of legend, Phoenix appears to have emerged as a first name quite recently.

Pierce
See Peter

Piers
See Peter

Pitt
Origin: English
Meaning simply 'from the pit' or 'from the hollow'.

Prabhu
Origin: Sanskrit
This Indian name is derived from the Sanskrit for 'mighty' (prabhu) and was later interpreted to mean 'king'. It appears in

several classical texts as the name of various gods.

Pradeep
Origin: Sanskrit
Derived from the Sanskrit *pradipa*, meaning 'lantern' or 'light', this name appears in ancient texts but was only adopted as a first name quite recently.

Pranav
Origin: Hindi
Meaning 'spiritual leader'.

Pratik
Origin: Hindi
Meaning simply 'a symbol'.

Pravat
Origin: Thai
Meaning simply 'history'.

Prentice
Origin: Anglo-Saxon
This name means 'apprentice' or 'learner'.

Preston
Origin: Old English
This place name comes from the Old English *preost* ('priest') and *tun* ('enclosure'), meaning 'priest's place', and was first used as a first name in the nineteenth century.

Price
Variants: Pryce
Origin: Welsh
Meaning 'son of Rhys', this surname has been widely accepted as a first name as well.

Primo
Origin: Latin
This name is derived from the Latin *primus*, meaning 'first'. Well-known bearers of the name include writer Primo Levi.

Prince
Origin: Latin
This surname was later accepted as a first name. Derived from the

Latin *princeps*, meaning 'one who takes first place', the name is taken from the royal title.

Priya
Origin: Sanskrit
This Indian name is taken from the Sanskrit *priya*, meaning 'beloved'. It is often used to denote a wife or mistress in ancient texts.

Proctor
Origin: Latin
Meaning 'administrator' or 'official'.

Pryderi
Origin: Welsh
This name means 'anxiety' or 'caring for'. A character with this name is featured in the *Mabinogion*.

Pugh
Origin: Welsh, from Old German
This means 'son of Hugh' and is both a first name and a surname.

Punit
Origin: Hindi
Meaning simply 'pure'.

Qadim
Origin: Arabic
Meaning 'ancient'.

Qasim
Origin: Arabic
From the Arabic meaning 'a distributor', meaning someone who distributes food and money, this is the name of one of the sons of Muhammad.

Quaid
Origin: Irish
Meaning simply 'fourth'.

Quane
Origin: French
Meaning 'intelligent'.

Quentin
Diminutives: Quin, Quinn
Variants: Quintin, Quinton
Origin: Latin
Derived from the Latin for 'fifth', *quintus*, and often bestowed on the fifth son. The name was revived in the nineteenth century, especially in Scotland. Well-known bearers of the name include film director Quentin Tarantino.

Quincy
Variants: Quincey, Quintus
Origin: Latin
Derived from *quintus*, the Latin for 'fifth', this name developed from the Roman Quintus. Popular in the USA as a tribute to President John Quincy Adams. Well-known bearers of the name include musician Quincy Jones.

Quinlan
Origin: Gaelic
Referring to someone who is 'well-formed', with the body of an Adonis.

Quinn m/f
Origin: Gaelic
Meaning 'counsel' or 'wise', this Irish name is derived from a Gaelic surname.
See also Quentin

Qusay
Origin: Arabic
This name predates Islam and is believed to have been borne by an ancestor of Mohammed.

Rab
See **Robert**

Racham
Origin: Hebrew
Meaning 'full of compassion'.

Radha m/f
Origin: Sanskrit
This Indian name is derived from the Sanskrit *radha* ('success') and appears in the *Mahabharata*.

Radley
Variants: Radleigh
Origin: Old English
Meaning 'from the red clearing'.

Rafa
See **Ralph**

Rafferty
Variants: Raferty
Origin: Irish
Meaning 'prosperous'.

Rafiq
Origin: Arabic and Indian
This name has various meanings, including 'friend', 'gentle' and 'companion'.

Raghnall
Origin: Gaelic
This Irish name means 'wise and powerful ruler'.

Raheem
Variants: **Rahim**
Origin: Arabic
Meaning 'kind and merciful'.

Rahim
See **Raheem**

Rahul
See **Raoul**

Raiden
Variants: **Raidon**
Origin: Japanese
Derived from the name of the Japanese god of thunder.

Raidon
See **Raiden**

Raigain
Origin: Gaelic
This Irish name means 'little king'.

Raj
Origin: Sanskrit
This Indian name is derived from the Sanskrit *raja*, meaning 'king' and was the name of several gods.

Rajendra
Origin: Sanskrit
From the Sanskrit *raja* and *indra* and meaning 'king' and 'mighty', in ancient texts this is assumed to mean 'emperor'.

Rajesh
Origin: Sanskrit
From *raja* and *isa* ('king' and 'ruler'), this name seems to have appeared in medieval times.

Rakesh
Origin: Hindi
Meaning 'lord of the night'.

Raleigh
Origin: Old English
Derived from the Old English meaning 'clearing with roe deer', this name is most famous for its links with explorer Sir Walter Raleigh.

Ralph
Diminutives: Ralphie
Variants: **Rafa**, Ralf, Rauf, **Raoul**
Origin: Old Norse
Deriving from the Old Norse name Rathulfr (*raed* and *wulf*, 'counsel' and 'wolf' respectively), thus interpreted as meaning 'wise and strong'. Famous bearers of the name include actor Ralph Fiennes.

Ralston
Origin: English
This place name has been in use as a first name since the nineteenth century.

Rambert
Origin: Teutonic
Meaning 'mighty and brilliant'.

Ramesh
Origin: Sanskrit
Derived from the Sanskrit *isa* combined with the name Rama, this is one of the names borne by Vishnu.

Ramiro
Origin: Old German
Derived from the Old German *ragin* and *mari* ('advice' or 'decision' and 'famous' respectively), this Spanish name was borne by an early Christian martyr.

Ramsay
Variants: Ramsey
Origin: Old English
This English place name comes from the Old English *hramsa* and *eg* ('ram' or 'wild garlic' and 'island'). It was adopted later, especially in Scotland, as a surname and a first name.

Rance
Variants: Ransell
Origin: African
Meaning, rather curiously, 'borrowed all'.

Randall
Diminutives: Rand, Randy, Rolf

Variants: Randal, Randolf, Randolph
Origin: Old English
Meaning 'shield wolf'.

Randolph
Origin: Old English from Scandinavian
From the Old English *rand* (meaning 'shield's edge') and *wulf* ('wolf'), the original Scandinavian name was Ranulfr.
See also Randall

Ranen
Origin: Hebrew
Meaning 'full of God's joy'.

Ranjit
Variants: Ranjeet
Origin: Hindi
Meaning 'victorious in battle'.

Ranulph
Diminutives: Ran
Origin: Old Norse
From the Old Norse name Reginulfr, meaning 'well-counselled and strong', the original English spelling of the name was Ranulf. Famous bearers of the name include explorer Ranulph Fiennes.

Raoul
Variants: Rahul, Raul
Origin: Old Norse

This is a French version of Ralph which is found occasionally among English speakers.

Raphael
Variants: Rafael, Raffaele, Rafaela (f)
Origin: Hebrew
Meaning 'God has healed', this Hebrew name was popular among early Christians and is now frequently found in southern European countries.

Raqib
Origin: Arabic
Derived from the Arabic meaning 'guardian' or 'supervisor', this is a Muslim name.

Rashad
Origin: Arabic
Meaning 'integrity' or 'maturity'.

Rasheed
Variants: Rashid
Origin: Arabic and Indian
This means 'mature' or 'rightly guided'.

Raven m/f
Origin: English
This name has been popular among African-Americans since 1989, when an actress named Raven appeared in *The Cosby Show*.

Ravi

Origin: Sanskrit
From the Sanskrit word *ravi*, meaning 'sun'.

Rawdon

Variants: Rawden, Rawdun
Origin: English
Meaning 'from the rough hill'.

Ray

See **Raymond**

Raymond

Diminutives: Ray
Variants: Redmond, Redmund
Origin: Old German
This name came to England with the Normans as Raimont and means 'well-advised protector'. Famous bearers of the name include writer Raymond Chandler.

Rayner

Variants: Raynor, Rainier, Rainer, Ragnar
Origin: Old German
From the Old German *ragin* and *hari* ('advice' or 'protection' and 'army' or 'warrior' respectively), this name came to England with the Normans. It is now relatively rare.

Reece

See **Rhys**

Reed

Variants: Reid, Read
Origin: Old English
This could come from *read* ('red'), *hroed* ('reeds') or *reod* ('cleared land'). It is most common in the USA.

Reeve

Origin: English
Taken directly from the English vocabulary word 'reeve', meaning 'steward'.

Reginald

Diminutives: Reg, Reggie, Ren, Rex, Reynard
Origin: Old English
Derived from the Old English *regen* ('cousel') and *weald* ('power'). Famous bearers of the name have included politician Reginald Mauling. *See also* **Ronald**

Reid

See **Reed**

Reilly

Variants: Riley, Ryley
Origin: Gaelic
Meaning 'valiant' and 'warlike'.

Ren

See **Reginald**

René

Origin: Latin
This French name is derived from the Latin *renatus*, meaning 'reborn'. Famous bearers of the name have included philosopher René Descartes.

Renfred

Origin: Anglo-Saxon
Meaning 'mighty and peaceful'.

Reno

Origin: Latin. Meaning 'renewed'.

Reuben

Diminutives: Rube, Ruby
Variants: Reuven (Jewish)
Origin: Hebrew
This biblical name was adopted by Puritans in the seventeenth century and means 'behold, a son'.

Rex

Origin: Latin
Taken directly from the Latin *rex*, meaning 'king', though it is also a diminutive of **Reginald**.

Rexford

Origin: Anglo-Saxon, from Latin
This Anglo-Saxon name means 'from the king's ford'.

Reynard

Origin: Old German
Derived from *ragin* and *hard* ('counsel' and 'hard' respectively, thus meaning 'mighty and brave'),

this name was eventually eclipsed by Reynold. It is also found as a variant of Reginald.

Rhain
Origin: Welsh
Meaning 'lance'.

Rhett
See Reece

Rhodri
Origin: Welsh
Taken from the Old Welsh *rhod* ('wheel') and *rhi* ('ruler'), or treated as a Welsh variant of Roderick. Notable bearers of the name include politician Rhodri Morgan.

Rhys
Variants: Reece, Rees
Origin: Welsh
Meaning 'ardour', 'hero' or 'rashness', this Welsh name was adopted by English speakers early on but remains little used outside Wales.

Rian
See Ryan

Ricardo
See Richard

Richard
Diminutives: Dick, Dichon, Dickie, Dixon, Rick, Richie

Variants: Ricardo
Origin: Old German
From the Old German words *ric* ('power') and *hard* ('hard' or 'strong'), thus meaning 'powerful ruler'. Famous bearers of the name have included President Richard Nixon.

Richie
See Richard

Ridley
Origin: Old English
From the Old English *hreod* ('reeds') and *leah* ('clearing' or 'wood'), this place name was later adopted as a first name. Famous bearers of the name include film director Ridley Scott.

Riley
See Reilly

Rio m/f
Origin: Spanish
Meaning simply 'river'.

Riordan
Variants: Rearden
Origin: Irish
This is an English version of the Irish name Rordan, from the Gaelic *riogh* ('king') and *bard* ('poet').

Rip
Origin: Dutch
Meaning 'full-grown' or 'ripe'.

Roald
Origin: Old German
This Norwegian name is derived from the Old German *hrod* and *valdr* ('fame' and 'ruler'), and was adopted by English speakers in the twentieth century. Famous bearers of the name have included writer Roald Dahl.

Robert
Diminutives: Bob, Bobbie, Bobby Rab, Rob, Robbie
Variants: Raibert (Scottish)
Origin: Old German
From the Old German name Hrodebert, meaning 'bright famous one'. Famous bearers of the name have included poet Robert Burns and writer Robert Louis Stevenson.
See also Rupert

Robin m/f
Origin: Old German
This name developed as a diminutive of Robert, but it has been in use as a name in its own right for a significant length of time. It was only in the 1950s that it began to be bestowed on girls, possibly influenced by the garden bird, making it less popular for boys.

Rocco
Variants: Rocky
Origin: Old German

From the Old German *hrok*, meaning 'repose'.

Rockwell
Origin: Anglo-Saxon
Meaning simply 'from the rocky well'.

Roderick
Diminutives: Rod, Roddy, Rory
Variants: Rhodri, Rodrick, Roderic, Rhydderch (Welsh, meaning 'reddish-brown')
Origin: Old German
From the Old German Hrodic, from *hrod* ('fame') and *ric* ('power'), this name has become widespread among English speakers since the nineteenth century.

Rodney
Diminutives: Rod, Roddie, Roddy
Origin: English
This Somerset place name meaning 'reed island' has been used as a first name since the nineteenth century but has been in decline since the 1950s. Famous bearers of the name have included the character Rodney Trotter in the series *Only Fools and Horses*.

Roe
Origin: Anglo-Saxon
Derived from the ordinary word 'roe', meaning 'roe deer'.

Rogan
Origin: Gaelic
Meaning 'the red-haired one'.

Roger
Diminutives: Rodge
Variants: Rodger, Rutger (Dutch), Rory
Origin: Old German
This name came to England via the Norman French from the Old German *hrod* and *gar* ('fame' and 'spear' respectively), thus meaning 'famous warrior'. It has gone into decline since the 1970s. Famous bearers of the name include actor Roger Moore.

Rohan m/f
Variants: Rowan
Origin: Uncertain
This French place name was adopted as a first name, but another derivation links it with the Irish Gaelic for 'red'. Alternatively, in India, it has evolved from the Sanskrit *rohana*, meaning 'ascending'.

Roland
Diminutives: Lando, Lanny, Roly, Rowley, Rollo
Variants: Orlando, Rowland
Origin: Old German
Derived from the Old German *hrod* and *land* ('fame' and 'territory'), this name came to England with the Normans. It has been largely out of favour since a resurgence in the 1920s. Feminie versions and variants include Rolanda and Orlanda.

Rolf
Variants: Rolph, Rollo (Latin), Rudolph
Origin: Old German
This is a variant of Rudolph, from the Old German *hrod* and *wulf* ('fame' and 'wolf') and came to England with the Norman invasion.

Rollo
See Roland, Rolf

Roman
Origin: Latin
Meaning 'man from Rome', this name remains rare among English speakers. Famous bearers of the name include film director Roman Polanski.

Romeo
Origin: Italian
Meaning 'pilgrim to Rome', this name is widely known among English speakers through Shakespeare's play *Romeo and Juliet*. In 2002, it enjoyed a boost afer David and Victoria Beckham chose the name for their second son.

Romero
Origin: Latin
Meaning simply 'wanderer'.

Ronald
Diminutives: Ron, Ronnie
Variants: Ranald, Raghnall (both Scottish)
Origin: Old Norse
This is a version of Reginald, from the Norse name Rognvaldr and has been common among English speakers since the nineteenth century. Famous bearers of the name include President Ronald Reagan.

Ronan
Origin: Gaelic
From the Irish Gaelic word *ron* ('little seal'), famous bearers of the name include pop star Ronan Keating.

Rooney
Variants: Rowney, Ruan
Origin: Gaelic
From the Gaelic meaning 'the red one', someone with a ruddy complexion. The name could also be used today as a tribute to footballer Wayne Rooney.

Rory
Variants: Ruaidhri, Ruairi, Rorie
Origin: Gaelic
From the gaelic *ruadh* ('red') and *ri* ('king'), notable bearers of the name in recent times include comedian Rory Bremner.
See also Roderick, Roger

Roscoe
Origin: Old Norse
This English place name is derived from the Old Norse *ra* ('roe deer') and *skogr* ('copse' or 'wood').

Ross
Origin: Uncertain
Taken from the Gaelic *ros*, meaning 'peninsula' or 'promontory', it can also be traced back to the Old German *hrod* ('fame') or the French *roux* ('red') or *hros* (Anglo-Saxon for 'horse'). Since the 1970s, its popularity has increased.

Rowan m/f
Origin: Gaelic
From the Irish Gaelic name Ruadhan, 'little red-haired one', from the Gaelic *ruadh*, meaning 'red'. Famous bearers of th e name include actor and comedian Rowan Atkinson.

Roy
Origin: Uncertain
This name would seem to come from the Old French *roy* meaning 'king', but it can also be said to have developed from the Gaelic *ruadh*, meaning 'red'. Famous bearers of the name include musician Roy Orbison.

Ruaidhri
See Rory

Rudolph
Diminutives: Rudi, Rudy
Variants: Rudolf
Origin: Old German
From the Old German Hrodulf (*hrod* and *wulf*, meaning 'fame' and 'wolf' respectively), this name has been in use among English speakers since the nineteenth century.

Rufus
Origin: Latin
This biblical name comes from the Latin for 'red-haired' and was a nickname given to William the Conqueror. It was revived in the nineteenth century, but remains rare.

Rune
Origin: Old Norse
Derived from the Old Norse *run*, meaning 'secret lore', this name was revived late in the nineteenth century and has since become popular.

Rupert

Diminutives: Ru
Origin: Old German
Meaning 'bright fame', this name is the English version of the Dutch Rupprecht. Famous bearers of the name include media tycoon Rupert Murdoch and cartoon charcter Rupert Bear.
See also Robert

Russell

Diminutives: Russ, Rusty
Variants: Russel
Origin: French
The French nickname *rousel*, meaning 'little red one', has developed into Russell, which has strong aristocratic associations. Famous bearers of the name include comedian and actor Russell Brand.

Rusty m/f

Origin: American
Referring to someone with red hair, it is also a diminutive of Russell.

Ryan

Variants: Rian
Origin: Uncertain
The origin of this Irish surname is uncertain, though the original Gaelic surname meant 'descendant of Rian'. It could also have come from the name of an ancient sea or river god. Famous bearers of the name include footballer Ryan Giggs.

Ryder

Origin: English
Meaning 'horseman'.

Rylan

Variants: Ryland
Origin: Anglo-Saxon
Meaning 'from the rye land'.

Sadik
Origin: Arabic
Meaning 'truthful'.

Sadler
Origin: English
Taken from the ordinary vocabulary word, this name means 'saddle maker'.

Sa'eed
Variants: Sa'id
Origin: Arabic
Meaning 'happy' or 'lucky'.

Sage m/f
Variants: Saga, Saige
Origin: Latin or English
From the Latin meaning 'wise and healthy', though it is more likely to be named for the herb.

Sahil
Origin: Sanskrit
This name comes from the Sanskrit and means 'guide'.

Sajan
Origin: Sanskrit
This is an Indian name and comes from the Sanskrit meaning 'beloved'.

Saladin
Origin: Arabic
Meaning 'goodness of the faith'.

Salah
Origin: Arabic
This popular Muslim name comes from the Arabic word for 'goodness' or 'righteousness'.

Salim
Origin: Arabic
Meaning 'secure'.

Salman
See **Solomon**

Sam
See **Samson**, **Samuel**

Sama
Origin: Sanskrit
Meaning 'tranquillity'.

Samir
Origin: Arabic
Meaning 'pleasant companion'.

Sampson
Diminutives: Sam, Sammy
Origin: English
This is an English surname that has sometimes been used as a first name.
See **Samson**

Samson
Diminutives: Sam, Sammy
Variants: Sampson
Origin: Hebrew
This is an English version of Shimshon, from *shemesh*, meaning 'sun', and was adopted by the Puritans in the seventeenth century.

Samuel
Diminutives: Sam, Sammy
Variants: Somhairle, Sawyl (Welsh)
Origin: Various depending on root
This is an English version of the Hebrew name Shemuel or Shmuel, meaning 'name of God' or 'God has hearkened'. Another suggestion is that is is derived from *shaul meel* ('asked of God'). In Scotland and Ireland it is considered an anglicized version of **Somhairle**.

Sancho
Origin: Uncertain
This Spanish name may be derived from the Latin *sanctus* ('holy') and was introduced to English speakers in the thirteenth century.

Sandeep
Origin: Indian
This Indian name means 'lighting the way'.

Sanders
Diminutives: Sandy, Sandie
Variants: Sanderson, Saunderson
Origin: Anglo-Saxon from Greek

Meaning 'son of Alexander'.
See also Alexander

Sandon
Origin: Old English
Meaning 'from the sandy hill'.

Sandy
See Alexander, Lysander,
Sanders

Sanjay
Origin: Sanskrit
From the Sanskrit *sanjaya*,
meaning 'triumphant', comes this
name which figures in Indian
mythology and in the
Mahabharata. It was the name of
Gandhi's son.

Santiago
Variants: Diego
Origin: Spanish from Hebrew
This name means 'Saint James'
(Iago is an archaic Spanish
version of James).

Sarid
Origin: Hebrew
Meaning 'survivor'.

Saul
Diminutives: Sonny
Origin: Hebrew
Meaning 'desired' or 'asked for',
this biblical name was adopted
by Puritans in the seventeenth

century and is still found in
Jewish communities. Notable
bearers of the name include
writer Saul Bellow.

Scott
Diminutives: Scottie, Scotty
Variants: Scot
Origin: Scottish and English
This name means 'Scotsman'
or 'Scottish' and was initially
applied to anyone from Scotland.
It became popular in the
twentieth century, perhaps in
tribute to writer F. Scott
Fitzgerald.

Scully
Variants: Scullee, Scullie
Origin: Irish
Meaning 'town crier'.

Seamas
See James

Sean m/f
Diminutives:
Variants: Shane, Shaun, Shawn
Origin: Gaelic, probably from
Hebrew
This is an Irish equivalent of
John and since the 1960s has
been found outside Ireland with
increasing frequency. Famous
bearers of the name include
actors Sean Connery and
Sean Penn.

Sebastian
Diminutives: Seb, Bastian, Baz
Origin: Latin or Greek
Developed from the Roman name
Sebastianus, meaning 'from
Sebasta', a town in Asia Minor.
Alternatively, it could be derived
from the Greek *sebastos*,
meaning 'august' or 'respected'.
Famous bearers of the name
include athlete and politician
Sebastian Coe.

Selby
Origin: English
This place name means 'willow
farm' and has been used as a first
name since the nineteenth century.

Selwyn
Variants: Selwin
Origin: Uncertain
This has been in use as a first
name since medieval times,
possibly being derived from the Old
English *sele* ('prosperity' or 'hall')
and *wine* ('friend'). It could be from
the Latin *silva* ('wood') or from the
Welsh meaning 'ardour' and 'fair'.

Senan
Origin: Irish
This is an English version of
the Irish Seanan, which itself
is derived from *sean*, meaning
'old' or 'wise', and is
pronounced 'Shannon'.

Seosaidh
See **Joseph**

Sepp
Origin: German
See **Joseph**

Sergei
Variants: Serge
Origin: Uncertain
This is a Russian name and is derived from the Latin name Sergius, but the origin of this is unknown.

Seth
Origin: Hebrew and Sanskrit
Derived from the Henrew *sheth* (meaning 'appointed' or 'set'), this biblical name has been in decline since the 1870s. As derived from the Sanskrit *setu* ('bridge') or *sveta* ('white'), it is used by Indian peoples.

Seymour
Variants: Seamor, Seamore, Seamour
Origin: Norman from North African
This surname is derived from the Norman French place name, Saint-Maur, itself taken from St Maurus (maurus meaning 'moor').

Shadwell
Origin: Anglo-Saxon
Meaning 'from the well in the arbour'.

Shafiq
Origin: Arabic
This name comes from *shafiq*, meaning 'compassionate' or 'sympathetic'.

Shahid
Origin: Arabic
This Arabic name means 'martyr' or 'witness'.

Shahin
Origin: Arabic
Meaning 'falcon'.

Shakil
Variants: Shakeel
Origin: Arabic
Meaning 'handsome'.

Shakir
Variants: Shakeel
Origin: Arabic
Meaning 'grateful'.

Shane
See Sean, Shannon

Shannon m/f
Origin: Hebrew
Made up of a combination of Shane (see Sean) and Sharon, though it is often considered to have come from the name of the river in Ireland. Despite the latter theory, the name is little used in Ireland.

Sharif
Variants: Shareef
Origin: Arabic
Derived from the Arabic *sharif*, meaning 'eminent' or 'virtuous', this name is probably best known as the surname of actor Omar Sharif.

Shelby m/f
Origin: Old English
From the Old English, which probably meant 'settlement with willow trees' (other sources say 'from the estate'), it saw its first use as a first name in the USA.

Shem
Origin: Hebrew
Meaning 'name' or 'renown', this biblical name remains rare among English speakers.

Sherman
Origin: Old English
This comes from the Old English *sceara* ('shears') and *mann* ('man') and was initially used as a trade name in the Middle Ages. It is popular in the USA, partly due to the general William Tecumseh Sherman.

Shimon
See Simon

Shiyam
Variants: Sham, Sam
Origin: Sanskrit
This is taken from the Sanskrit *syama*, meaning 'dark' or 'black', and is now understood to mean 'beauty'.

Sholto
Origin: Gaelic
Meaning 'the wild duck'.

Sid
See Sidney

Sidney m/f
Diminutives: Sid, Syd
Variants: Sydney
Origin: Old English or Norman
Possibly from the Norman place name Saint Denis, but more likely from the Old English *sedan* ('wide') and *eg* '(river island'), this name became popular in the nineteenth century. Famous bearers of the name have included actor Sid James.

Siegfried
Origin: Old German
Derived from the Old German *sige* ('victory') and *frid* ('peace'), this name was revived in the nineenth century. Famous bearers of the name have included war poet Siegfriend Sassoon.

Sigmund
Diminutives: Sigi
Variants: Siegmund, Sigismund
Origin: Old German
Derived from the Old German *sige* ('victory') and *mund* ('defender'), so meaning 'victorious defender', perhaps the most famous bearer of this name was psychiatrist Sigmund Freud.

Silas
Origin: Latin
This Hebrew name is derived from the Latin name Silvanus, from *silva*, meaning 'wood'. A famous bearer of the name is the protagonist of George Eliot's 1861 novel *Silas Marner*.

Simon
Diminutives: Si
Variants: Shimon, Ximene
Origin: Hebrew or Greek
This is English version of the Hebrew Shimon, which means 'he who hears' or 'hearkened', can also be traced to the Greek

simos, meaning 'snub-nosed'. It was revived in the twentieth century and remains popular.

Sinclair
Origin: Norman French
Taken from the Norman place name Saint Clair, as a first name this seems to date from the nineteenth century. It is also a Scottish surname.

Solomon
Diminutives: Sol, Solly, Sonny
Variants: Salman, Shlomo, Sulayman
Origin: Hebrew
Derived from the Hebrew *shalom*, this biblical name means 'man of peace'. As Salman, a famous bearer of the name is writer Salman Rushdie.

Somerled
Variants: Summerlad, Somhairle (Gaelic, also Sorley)
Origin: Old Norse
This Scottish surname is derived from the Old Norse meaning 'summer traveller' and is traditionally associated with the Clan Macdonald.

Somerset
Origin: English
This place name means 'summer farmstead'. Perhaps the most

famous bearer of the name was novelist William Somerset Maugham.

Somhairle
See Somerled

Sonny
Variants: Sonnie
Origin: Various, depending on the root name.
Originally developed as a diminutive of such names as Saul and Solomon, this became popular as a name in its own right after it featured in *The Singing Fool* starring Al Jolson in 1928.
See also Tyson

Spencer
Origin: English
Meaning simply 'dispenser', this was originally reserved for stewards who worked in manor houses. Notable bearers of the name have included actor Spencer Tracy.

Stacy
Origin: English, from Greek
This is derived from Eustace and was taken up as a first name in the nineteenth century. Notable bearers of the name have included actor Stacy Keach.
See also Stacey

Stanford
Variants: Stamford
Origin: Old English
Taken from the Old English meaning 'stony ford'. Famous bearers of the name include the *Sex and the City* character Stanford Blatch.

Stanley
Diminutives: Stan
Origin: Old English
Meaning 'stony field' (from the Old English *stan* and *leah*), this has been used as a first name since the eighteenth century. Famous bearers of the name include actor and impressionist Stanley Baxter.

Stanton
Origin: Anglo-Saxon
Meaning 'from the stony farm' or 'from the rocky lake'.

Steadman
Diminutives: Stead
Variants: Steadmann
Origin: English
Meaning 'owner of a farmstead'.

Stephen
Diminutives: Steve, Stevie
Variants: Esteban, Steven, Stephan, Steenie (Scottish)
Origin: Latin and Greek
This name is derived from the Greek name Stephanos ('garland') and the Roman name Stefanus. This biblical name has been consistently popular among English speakers.

Sterling
Variants: Stirling
Origin: Uncertain
This can be traced back to the Middle English *sterrling*, meaning 'little star', but is also derived from the Scottish palce name of uncertain meaning. Famous bearers of the name include racing driver Stirling Moss.

Steven
See Stephen

Storm m/f
Origin: English
Derived from the ordinary vocabulary word 'storm', suggesting a lively and passionate personality, this name does not seem to have appeared until the twentieth century.

Stuart
Diminutives: Stu, Stewie
Variants: Stewart
Origin: Scottish or English
This developed as a French version of Stewart, from either the Old English *stigweard* ('steward') or the Scottish surname.

Suhayl
Variants: Suhail
Origin: Arabic
Derived from *suhayl*, the Arabic name for the star Canopus.

Sumner
Origin: Latin
Meaning 'one who summons', a church official who summoned the congregation to prayer.

Sunil
Origin: Sanskrit
Meaning simply 'very dark blue'.

Suraj
Origin: Hindi
Meaning 'the sun'.

Surinder m/f
Variants: Surendra
Origin: Sanskrit
This Indian name is derived from the Sanskrit and means 'the mightiest of gods' (from *sura*, 'god', and *indra*, 'mighty').

Syed
Variants: Sayyid
Origin: Arabic
This is a common spelling of the name Sayyid and means 'master' or 'noble'.

Sylvester
Diminutives: Sly, Syl
Variants: Silvester
Origin: Latin
This name comes from the Latin for 'of the woods' or 'wood dweller' and was taken up as a first name by English speakers in medieval times. Famous bearers of the name include actor Sylvester Stallone.

Tabib
Origin: Turkish
Meaning 'physician'.

Taffy
Variants: Taff
Origin: Welsh, from Hebrew
This is a Welsh variant of
David and is widely known
as a nickname for anyone who
comes from Wales.

Taine
Origin: Gaelic
Meaning 'river'.

Taj
Origin: Indian
Meaning 'crown'.

Talbot
Variants: Talebot (medieval)
Origin: Uncertain
Derived from either the Old French
taille-botte ('cut-bundle', 'cleave-
faggot') or obscure Germanic
roots, this aristocratic name has
been in use as a first name since
the nineteenth century.

Taliesin
Origin: Welsh
Derived from the Welsh *tal* ('high')
and *iesin* ('shining'), interpreted
as 'shining brow', the most
famous bearer of the name was
the sixth-century poet.

Tamar
Origin: Hebrew and English
This is Hebrew for 'palm tree',
but is also the name of a river
between Cornwall and Devon.

Tamson
Origin: Scandinavian, from
Aramaic
This means 'son of Thomas'.

Tarek
See Tariq

Tariq
Variants: Tari, Tarek
Origin: Arabic
Meaning 'evening caller', 'one
who knocks on the door at night'.
Notable bearers of the name
include political activist Tariq Ali.

Tarquin
Origin: Etruscan
This is a Roman family name and
in Arthurian legend it appears as
the name of a 'recreant knight'.

Tate
Variants: Tait, Teyte
Origin: Old Norse
Coming from the Old Norse
meaning 'cheerful', this is an
English first name and surname.

Tavish
See Thomas

Tay
Origin: Welsh
See David

Tayib
Origin: Indian
Meaning 'delicate' or 'good'.

Taylor m/f
Variants: Tayler
Origin: English
This was originally reserved as a
trade name and given only to
boys. Famous bearers of the
name have included poet Samuel
Taylor Coleridge.

Tearlach
See Charles

Tecwyn
Variants: Tegwen, Tegan
Origin: Welsh
From *tec* ('beautiful', 'fair') and
wen ('blessed', 'white'), this
name seems to be a fairly
modern introduction.

Tennessee
Origin: Native American
The Cherokee word for 'mighty
warrior' and now the name of the
American state.

Terence
Diminutives: Tel, Terry
Variants: Terance, Terrance,

Terrence, Terrell
Origin: Uncertain
It has been suggested this is derived from the Latin meaning 'gracious', but it is known it developed from the Roman name Terentius. It was adopted by English speakers in the late nineteenth century and famous bearers of the name include actor Terence Stamp.

Terry
Diminutives: Tel
Variants: Thierry (French)
Origin: Various, depending on the root name
Derived from Germanic words meaning 'power' and 'tribe', this is also a diminutive of names such as Terence and Theodore. Famous bearers of the name include TV presenter Terry Wogan.

Tex
Origin: English
This is a fairly frequent nickname for people hailing from the state of Texas in the USA and it is mostly confined to America. Famous bearers of the name have included cartoon director Tex Avery.

Thabo
Origin: African
Meaning 'filled with happiness'.

Thaddeus
Diminutives: Tad, Thad, Thadis
Origin: Various, depending on the root name
From the Hebrew meaning 'valiant' or 'wise' or derived from Theodore, this biblical name has been in use among English speakers since the nineteenth century.

Thane
Origin: Anglo-Saxon
This was originally a title for a noble who held land with the king's permission, and was a chief title in Scotland. In the nineteenth century it was adopted as a first name.

Theobald
Diminutives: Theo
Variants: Thibaut, Tybalt
Origin: Old German
From the Old German name Theudobald, from *theud* and *bald* ('people' and 'brave').

Theodore
Diminutives: Theo, Ted, Teddy
Variants: Fyodor (Russian)
Origin: Greek
Derived from the Greek *theos* and *doron* ('god' and 'gift'), this name was revived in the nineteenth century. A famous bearer of the name was

President Theodore Roosevelt, after whom the teddy bear was named.

Theron
Variants: Theyron
Origin: Greek
Meaning simply 'hunter'.

Thibaut
See Theobald

Thierry
French, see Terry

Thomas
Diminutives: Tam, Tammy (both Scottish), Thom, Tom, Tommy
Variants: Tavish
Origin: Aramaic
This biblical name is derived via the Greek Didymos from the Aramaic word meaning 'twin'. One of the most famous bearers of the name was St Thomas Becket.

Thorley
Origin: Old English
From the Old English meaning 'thorn wood', this has been in use as an occasional first name since the nineteenth century.

Thorne
Origin: Anglo-Saxon
Meaning 'from the thorn bush'.

Thornton
Origin: English, probably from Anglo-Saxon
This name means 'settlement among the thorns' and was originally a place name. Since the nineteenth century, it has been used occasionally as a first name.

Thorpe
Variants: Thorp
Origin: Anglo-Saxon
Meaning 'from the small village'.

Thurman
Origin: Scandinavian
Meaning 'servant of Thor'.

Tiernan
Variants: Tiarnan, Tierney
Origin: Gaelic
This Irish name is derived from the Gaelic word for 'lord'.

Timothy
Diminutives: Tim, Timmy
Origin: Greek
From the Greek *time* ('honour') and *theos* ('god') via Timotheos, this name enjoyed a peak between 1950 and 1980 but has since gone into decline. Famous bearers of the name include tennis player Tim Henman.

Tobias
See Toby

Toby
Variants: Tobias, Tobin
Origin: Hebrew
This is an English version of the Hebrew name Tobias, meaning 'the Lord is good' and enjoyed a revival in the 1980s and 1990s.

Todd
Variants: Tod
Origin: English
This comes from a dialect word meaning 'fox' and has made a few appearances as a first name. Famous bearers of the name include actor Todd Carty.

Tracy m/f
Origin: French
Meaning 'place of Thracius', this was first adopted as a surname and, from the nineteenth century, it was used as a first name among English speakers. Also possibly a diminutive of Teresa, this name was originally bestowed on boys as well as girls.

Travis
Variants: Travers
Origin: French
This surname meaning 'crossing' or 'toll keeper' has been used as a first name since the twentieth century. It is derived from the French *traverser*, 'to cross'.

Tremaine
Variants: Tremayne
Origin: Cornish
This Cornish name means 'homestead on the rock'.

Trent
Origin: English
Meaning 'trespasser', a Celtic word referring to a river's tendency to flood, this name comes from the name of the river and is more common in the USA and Canada than the UK. A famous bearer of the name is rock star Trent Reznor.

Trevelyan
Origin: Cornish
Derived from a combination of the Cornish name Elian and the dialect word *tref*, meaning 'settlement', this translates as 'Elian's place'. It is still mostly confined to Cornwall.

Trevor
Diminutives: Trev
Variants: Trefor
Origin: Welsh
This is derived from the Welsh words *tref* ('homestead') and *mawr* ('great') and has been used as a first name since the 1860s. It enjoyed a peak in the mid-twentieth century and well-known bearers of the name include newsreader Trevor McDonald.

Trey
Origin: English
Meaning 'the third son', as 'trey' is an old word for 'three'.

Tristan
See Tristram

Tristram
Diminutives: Tris
Variants: Tristan, Tristran, Trysan
Origin: Uncertain
Possibly from the Celtic word *drest* or *drust* (meaning 'din', 'tumult'), or from the Latin *tristis* ('sad') via French. Records of the name go back as far as the twelfth century.

Troy
Origin: Uncertain
Derived from the city of Troyes, or from the Irish for 'foot soldier' (or from a saying meaning 'from the place of people with curly hair'). The name is rare in the UK but is popular in Australia and the USA.

Truman
Origin: Old English
From *treowe* and *mann* ('true' or 'trusty' and 'man'), this name is rarely used outside the USA. Notable bearers of the name have included writer Truman Capote.

Tucker
Origin: Old English
Meaning 'a fuller of cloth'.
See also Fuller

Tully
Origin: Varies depending on root name
From the Roman name Tullis (meaning 'one who bears a title' or from the Irish meaning 'at peace with God'.

Tyler m/f
Variants: Tylar
Origin: English
From the surname used to denote someone who tiled roofs, this has made occasional appearances as a first name.

Tyrell
Origin: German
Meaning 'thunder ruler'.

Tyrone
Diminutives: Ty, Tye
Variants: Tyrus
Origin: Various, depending on the root name
Either from the Irish meaning 'from Owen's land', or from Greek, meaning 'monarch', this is an occasional first name mostly confined to Ireland and the USA.

Tyson
Diminutives: Ty
Variants: Sonny
Origin: Teutonic
Meaning 'son of the German'.

Uaine
See Owen

Udo
Origin: German
Meaning 'prosperous'.

Udolf
Origin: Anglo-Saxon
Meaning 'prosperous wolf'.

Ulric
Variants: Ulrich
Origin: German
Meaning either 'ruler of the wolves' or 'fortune and power', depending on the source.

Uri
Origin: Hebrew
Meaning 'light', the most famous bearers of the name in recent years are illusionist Uri Geller and astronaut Uri Gagarin.

Usher
Origin: English
Derived from the ordinary vocabulary word 'usher', this name has been made famous by the American R&B star.

Uthman
Variants: Osman
Origin: Arabic
This Arabic name for 'baby bustard' is found frequently throughout the Islamic world, being the name of Mohammed's son-in-law.

Uziel
Origin: Hebrew
Meaning 'God is my strength' or 'a mighty force'.

Vadin
Origin: Hindi
Meaning 'good with words'.

Valente
Origin: Latin
Meaning simply 'valiant'.

Vallis
Origin: French
Meaning 'Welshman'.

Vance
Diminutives: Van
Origin: Old English or Anglo-Saxon
Either from the Anglo-Saxon for 'from the grain barn' or from the Old English meaning 'fen-dweller' or 'marshland', depending on the source.

Vasilis
Variants: Vasileior, Vasos
Origin: Greek
Meaning 'knightly' or 'magnificent'.

Vaughn
Variants: Vaughan

Origin: Welsh
Taken from the Welsh *fychan*, meaning 'little one' or 'small', this has been used as a first name since the nineteenth century.

Verner
See Werner

Vernon
Diminutives: Verne, Vern
Origin: French
Derived from the French place name meaning 'alder grove' or 'place of alders', this is widespread as a first name among English speakers.

Victor
Diminutives: Vic
Origin: Latin
From the Latin meaning 'conqueror' via the Roman name Victorius, this ancient name was revived in the nineteenth century. Well-known bearers of the name have included writer Victor Hugo.

Vidal
Variants: Vitale
Origin: Hebrew
This Spanish name is derived from the Hebrew *hayyim* ('life') and famous bearers of the name include celebrated hairdresser Vidal Sassoon.

Vijay

Variants: Bijay, Bijoy
Origin: Sanskrit
From the Sanskrit *vijaya*, meaning 'booty' or 'victory', this Indian name has been popular for several centuries and is also found as a component of longer names.

Vikesh

Origin: Hindi
This Hindi name means simply 'the moon'.

Vikram

Origin: Sanskrit
From the Sanskrit *vikrama* ('pace' or 'stride') and interpreted to mean 'heroism' or 'strength', this name is found in the *Mahabharata*. Well-known bearers of the name include novelist Vikram Seth.

Ville

Origin: Varies depending on root name
This name literally means 'town' in French, but it is also the Finnish equivalent of William (with the final 'e' pronounced).

Vinay

Variants: Vinayak
Origin: Sanskrit
From the Sanskrit *vinaya*, meaning 'guidance' or 'leading

asunder', this name denotes a code of behaviour for Buddhists.

Vincent

Diminutives: Vince, Vin
Variants: Vinnie, Vinny
Origin: Latin
Derived from the Latin *vincens*, meaning 'conquering', this name was revived in the nineteenth century. Notable bearers of the name have included artist Vincent Van Gogh.

Vishal

Origin: Indian
This Indian name means 'immense', 'spacious'.
See also Vishala

Vivian m/f

Diminutives: Viv
Variants: Vyvyan, Vivyan
Origin: Latin
Derived from the Latin *vivus* ('alive', 'lively'), records of this name go back to the twelfth century and it was originally given only to boys.

Wade

Origin: English
Meaning 'ford' or 'dweller by the ford', this English surname has been used as a surname only since the nineteenth century, mainly in the USA.

Wakeley

Origin: Anglo-Saxon
Meaning 'from the wet meadow'.

Walcott

Origin: Anglo-Saxon
Meaning 'cottage dweller'.

Wallace

Diminutives: Wal, Wally
Variants: Walsh, Wallis, Welsh
Origin: Old French
This Scottish surname means 'Welshman' or 'Welsh' (from the Old French *waleis* meaning 'foreigner' or 'stranger'). It has strong Scottish connections, particularly with freedom fighter William Wallace.

Waller

Origin: German
Pronounced 'valler', this means simply 'powerful'.

Walsh

See Wallace

Walter

Diminutives: Wally, Walt, Wat
Variants: Watkin
Origin: Old German
Derived from the Old German *waldhar*, meaning 'army ruler' or 'folk ruler', the Old English version was Wealdhere. Famous bearers of the name include poet Walt Whitman and cartoonist and film-maker Walt Disney.

Warren
Variants: Waring
Origin: Uncertain
Derived either from the Norman French *La Varenne* (meaning 'game park') or the Old German *Warin* ('to protect', a tribal name). Other sources suggest it is Teutonic. Revived in the nineteenth century, famous bearers of the name include actor Warren Beatty.
See also Werner

Warwick
Origin: English
This place name from Warwickshire means 'farm by the weir' and was adopted as a first name in the nineteenth century and is particularly popular in Australia.

Wasim
Variants: Waseem (Indian)
Origin: Arabic and Indian
This name means 'good-looking' or 'handsome'.

Waylon
Origin: English
Meaning 'land by the road', a famous bearer of the name is country singer Waylon Jennings.

Wayne
Origin: English
This means 'carter' or 'cart-maker' and became popular as a first name in the 1940s and in the 1970s was common, though it has since declined. Famous bearers of the name include dancer Wayne Sleep.

Werner
Variants: Verner, Wernher
Origin: Old German
Derived from the Old German tribal name Warin (*see* Warren), famous bearers of the name include film director Werner Herzog.

Wesley
Diminutives: Wes
Origin: Old English
Meaning 'west meadow', many Methodists chose the name in tribute to John Wesley. Famous bearers of the name include actor Wesley Snipes.

Wickham
Origin: English
Meaning 'from the village enclosure'.

Wilbur
Origin: Obscure
Possibly from the Old English *will* ('will') and *burh* ('defence'), this name is rarely encountered outside the USA. Famous bearers of the name include novelist Wilbur Smith.

Wilder
Diminutives: Will
Variants: Wild
Origin: English
Meaning 'wild and free'.

Wiley
See William

Wilford
Origin: Anglo-Saxon
Meaning 'from the willow ford'.

Wilfred
Diminutives: Wil, Wilf
Origin: Old German
From the Old German *will* and *frid* ('desire' or 'will' and 'peace' respectively), this has declined since the mid-twentieth century. Famous bearers of the name include war poet Wilfred Owen.
See also Wilkie

Wilkie
See William, Wilfred

William
Diminutives: Wilkie, Wiley, Liam, Will, Willie, Bill, Billy
Variants: Uilleam (Gaelic), Guillaume (French)
Origin: Old German
Derived from *wil* and *helm* ('will' and 'helmet' or 'protection' respectively), usually translated as 'defender'. Famous bearers of

the name include playwright William Shakespeare.
See also Wilmot

Willis
Origin: English (from Old German?)
Meaning 'son of Will', this was adopted as a first name in the nineteenth century, but has never been popular.

Willoughby
Origin: Old English and Old Norse
From *welig* (Old English for 'willow' and *byr* ('settlement' in Old Norse), this has been a first name only since the nineteenth century and had practically disappeared from use by the early twentieth.

Wilmot
Origin: Uncertain
Derived either from William or from the Old German *wil* and *muot* ('desire' or 'will' and 'courage' or 'mind' respectively), this name was revived in the nineteenth century but remains rare.

Winston
Diminutives: Win, Winnie
Origin: English
Derived from the name of the Gloucestershire village of Winestone ('Wynna's [boundary] stone' or 'friend's settlement').

Winter m/f
Origin: English
From the ordinary vocabulary word 'winter'.

Wolfgang
Origin: Old German
From the Old German *wolf* ('wolf') and *gang* ('going'), the most famous bearer of the name was composer Wolfgang Amadeus Mozart.

Worral
Variants: Worrell, Worrill
Origin: Anglo-Saxon
Meaning 'from the manor of the loyal man'.

Wyatt
See Guy

Wyclef
See Wycliff

Wycliff
Variants: Wyclef, Wycliffe
Origin: Anglo-Saxon
Meaning 'from the white cliff'.

Wymer
Origin: Anglo-Saxon
Meaning 'renowned in battle'.

Xander
See Alexander

Xavier
Variants: Javier, Zavier
Origin: Uncertain
Derived either from the Arabic for 'bright' or from the Basque place name Etchberria ('new house'), this name is popular in Catholic France and Spain.

Ximene
See Simon

Yadid
Origin: Hebrew
Meaning 'loving friend'.

Yahir
Origin: Spanish
Meaning 'handsome one'.

Yanis
Variants: Yannis
Origin: Greek
This is a variant of John.

Yasin
Origin: Arabic
This name is formed by a sequence of Arabic letters from a passage in the Koran.

Yestin
See Justin

Yitzhak
Origin: Hebrew
This is a modern Hebrew version of Isaac and notable bearers of the name include Israeli Prime Minister Yitzhak Shamir.
See also Isaac

York
Origin: Old English
Derived from the Old English word for 'yew', this place name has been adopted as a surname and first name.

Yosu
Origin: Hebrew
See Jesus

Yusuf
See Joseph

Yves
Variants: Ives (Cornish), Ivo (German), Ivor
Origin: Old Norse
This name is derived from the Old Norse *yr*, meaning 'yew', and famous bearers of the name include fashion designer Yves Saint Laurent.

Zac
See Isaac, Zachary

Zachary
Diminutives: Zac, Zack, Zak
Variants: Zachariah, Zachaeus (rare)
Origin: Hebrew
This is an anglicized version of the Hebrew name Zachariah, meaning 'Jehovah has remembered' and was adopted by the Puritans in the seventeenth century.

Zahid
Origin: Arabic
Meaning simply 'abstinent'.

Zahir
Origin: Arabic
Meaning 'shining bright'.

Zain
See Zane

Zaire
Origin: African
Meaning 'river from Zaire'.

Zane
Variants: Zain
Origin: Uncertain
This may be derived from a place name of obscure origin or a Danish variant of John.

Zared
Origin: Hebrew
Meaning 'the ambush', the significance of bestowing this name on a baby is unclear.

Zarek
Variants: Zarec
Origin: Polish
Meaning 'God save the king'.

Zeb
Origin: Varies depending on root name
Derived as a diminutive of either Zebedee or Zebuwn (meaning 'exaltation').

Zachariah
See Zachary

Zephyr
Diminutives: Zeph
Origin: Greek, meaning 'west wind'.

Aasta
Origin: Teutonic
Means 'love'.

Abia
Diminutives: Abi
Origin: Arabic
Means 'great'.

Abigail
Diminutives: Abi, Abbie, Abby, Gael, Gail
Variants: Abagail
Origin: Biblical
Means 'father's joy', 'my father rejoices'. Previously popular for working class women, it fell out of favour until its recent comeback.

Abijah
Origin: Hebrew
Means 'God is my father'.

Acacia
Origin: Greek
Means 'immortality' or 'resurrection', best known as the name of a shrub, use as a first name is a recent development.

Acantha
Origin: Greek
Meaning: 'thorny' or 'spiny'.

Ada
Diminutives: Ad, Addie, Adie
Origin: English (German?)

Possibly from German *adal*, meaning 'noble', now less popular as a first name. Lord Byron's daughter was named Ada.

Adabelle
Origin: Latin
Means 'Joyous, happy and beautiful'.

Adamina
Diminutives: Addy, Addie, Mina
Origin: Latin
Feminine form of Adam; also meaning 'mortal' or 'from the red earth'.

Adara
Origin: Greek
Means 'beauty'.

Adelaide
Diminutives: Addi, Della
Variants: Adele, Edeline, Adelaida
Origin: Teutonic
Meaning 'gracious lady of noble birth'; the wife of William IV made the name popular and the Australian city is named after her.

Adelpha
Origin: Greek
Means 'sisterly', 'friend of mankind'.

Adina
Diminutives: Dena, Deena
Variants: Adeen

Origin: Hebrew
Suggests fertility; 'voluptuous', 'mature'.

Adilah
Origin: Arabic
Means 'just and fair'.

Adele
See **Adelaide**

Adione
Origin: Latin
Means 'goddess of travellers'.

Adnette
Origin: French, from Old German
Means 'noble'.

Adora
Variants: Adorée
Origin: Latin
Means 'beloved' or 'adored gift'.

Adorna
Origin: Latin
Means 'adorned with jewels'.

Adrienne
Diminutives: Drena, Drina
Variants: Adriane, Adrianne, Adriana, Adrianna
Origin: French
First came into use as a feminine version of **Adrian**, in use by English speakers since the early sixteenth century.

Aelwen
Variants: Aylwen
Origin: Welsh
Means 'fair-browed', developed as a feminine version of Aelwyn.

Aeronwen
Variants: Aeronwy
Origin: Welsh
Means 'berry stream'.

Africa
Origin: English
Named after the continent; popular among African-Americans.

Agatha
Origin: English
From Greek Agathe, from *agathos*, meaning 'good'.

Agave
Origin: Greek
Means 'illustrious and noble'.

Agnes
Diminutives: Aggie, Nessie, Nesta
Variants: Agnethe, Inez, Agneta
Origin: Greek
From the Greek Hagne, from *hagnos* ('chaste', 'pure').

Ahuda
Origin: Hebrew
Means 'praise' or 'sympathetic'.

Aidan m/f
See **Edana**

Aiko
Origin: Japanese
Means 'beloved' 'little loved one'.

Aileen
Variants: Eileen
Origin: English
From the Irish Eibhlin, from Aveline, from *avos*, meaning 'struggle'.

Ailsa
Diminutives: Ailie
Origin: Scottish, from Ailsa Craig in the Firth of Clyde
Originally from Norse Alfsigesy ('island of Alfsigr'), possibly gained popularity due to similarity to Elsa.

Ainsley m/f
Variants: Ainslee, Ainslie
Origin: English
Named after a place common to Nottinghamshire and Warwickshire, from Old English *an* and *leah* (meaning 'one' and 'clearing' or 'wood'). A famous bearer of the name is the popular TV chef Ainsley Harriot.

Aisha
Variants: Ayesha, Asia
Origin: Arabic
Means 'alive'.

Aisling
Variants: Aisleen, Aislin, Isleen, Ashing
Origin: Irish
From the Gaelic for 'dream' or 'vision'.

Akasuki
Origin: Japanese
Means 'bright helper'.

Akili
Variants: Akela, Akeyla, Akeylah
Origin: Tanzanian
Means 'wisdom'.

Alana
Variants: Alanis
Origin: English and Scottish
From the Celtic *alun*, 'harmony'; otherwise interpreted as 'rock' or 'shining'; Alanis made famous by Canadian rocker Alanis Morissette.

Alberta
Variants: Albertine, Albertina
Origin: English
First developed as a feminine form of Albert.

Alcina
Variants: Alsena
Origin: Greek
Means 'sorceress'.

Aldara
Origin: Greek
Means 'winged gift'.

Aldena *See* **Helen**

Aletta
Origin: Greek, means 'carefree'.

Alexandra
Diminutives: Alex, Lexi, Zandra
Variants: Alexandria, Alexandrina
Origin: Greek
A feminine form of Alexander, in frequent use in medieval times, enjoyed a significant revival in the 1970s.

Alice
Diminutives: Ali
Variants: Alys, Alis, Ailis, Ailish
Origin: Old German
From the Old German *adelheit*, meaning 'noble woman'; famous as the name of Lewis Carroll's heroine; famous names include rock star Alice Cooper.

Alida
See **Adelaide**

Alima
Variants: Alimah
Origin: Arabic
Means 'skilled in dancing and music'.

Alisa
Variants: Aleesha, Alesha, Alecia, Alisha
Origin: Hebrew

Means 'happiness'; also a derivative of Elizabeth.

Alison
Diminutives: Ali, Allie, Ally
Variants: Alyson, Allison
Origin: English
From the Old English, meaning 'the light of the sun'.
See also **Louise**

Aliya
Variants: Aliyah (Arabic)
Origin: Hebrew
Means ascend; the Arabic form means 'sublime' or 'exalted'.

Aliza
Variants: Aleeza, Alieza, Aliezah, Alitza, Alizah
Origin: Hebrew
Means 'joyful'.

Allegra
Origin: Italian
From the Italian *allegro*, meaning 'happy', 'lively'; possibly invented by Lord Byron for his illegitimate daughter.

Almira
Origin: English
Meaning: probably derives from Arabic *amiri*, meaning 'princess'; in use as a first name since the early sixteenth century but chiefly confined to the USA.

Althea
Origin: English, from Greek
From the Greek Althaia, from Greek *althein*, meaning 'to heal'.

Alvira
Variants: Alvirra
Origin: Latin
Means 'the fair one'.

Alysia
Origin: Greek
Means 'unbroken chain'.
See also **Alice**

Ama
Origin: African
Means 'born on a Saturday'.

Amanda
Diminutives: Mandy, Manda
Origin: English
From the Latin *amanda*, meaning 'lovable'.

Amber
Variants: Ambretta, Amberly
Origin: English
Derived from the gemstone amber; used as a name since the sixteenth century, revived popularity in the 1970s.

Amelia
Diminutives: Millie, Milly
Variants: Amélie
Origin: Roman

From the Roman Aemilia, meaning 'striving' or 'eager', influenced by Old German *amal*, meaning 'labour'.

Amena
Variants: Amina, Amine
Origin: Celtic
Means 'honest' or 'incorruptible truth'.

Aminta
Variants: Amintha, Aminthe
Origin: Greek
From the name of a shepherdess in Greek mythology, thus meaning 'protector'.

Amy
Variants: Amie, Amey
Origin: possibly Roman
From the Old French *amee,* 'loved' and Latin *amare,* 'to love'; possibly originating from pre-Roman times.

Anaïs
Origin: French
From the Greek, meaing 'fruitful'; writer Anaïs Nin is a famous bearer of the name.

Anastasia
Diminutives: Stacey, Tansy
Origin: Greek
From the Greek *anastasios*, meaing 'resurrection'; Princess Anastasia was the youngest daughter of Tsar Nicholas II.

Andrea
Diminutives: Andie, Andi
Origin: English, possibly from Greek
Developed from the masculine Andrew, possibly influenced by the Greek Andreas; writer Andrea Newman and tennis player Andrea Jaeger are famous bearers of the name.

Aneira
Origin: Welsh
Means 'golden' or 'honourable'.

Anemone
Origin: Greek
Means 'wind flower'; in Greek mythology, a nymph was chased by the wind and turned into an anemone flower.

Angela
Diminutives: Ange, Angie
Origin: English and Italian
The feminine form of Angel, used in the sixteenth century until the 1960s, when its popularity began to decline.

Angelica
Diminutives: Ange, Angie
Variants: Angelina, Angeline, Anjelica, Angelique
Origin: Latin
From the Latin *angelica*, its popularity as a first name has diminished since the 1950s.

Angharad
Origin: Welsh
From the Welsh language *an* ('more') and *car* ('love'), thus being interpreted as meaning 'much loved'. Mostly confined to Wales, but gained popularity after the actress Angharad Rees starred in *Poldark*.

Angwen
Origin: Welsh
From the Welsh, meaning 'very beautiful'.

Anita
Diminutives: Nita
Origin: Hebrew
A Spanish variant of Ann.

Annabel
Diminutives: Belle, Bel
Variants: Annabelle, Annabella
Origin: Scottish
As early as the twelfth century, this name appeared as Annaple; did not gain popularity among English speakers until the sixteenth century.

Ann
Diminutives: Annie, Nan, Nana, Nancy, Nina

Origin: English, from Hebrew
Evolved as a variant of the
Hebrew name **Hannah**, usually
interpreted as meaning 'grace'.

Anna
Origin: Hebrew
First evolved as the Greek or
Latin form of **Hannah**, thus
meaning 'grace' or 'favour'.
Famous bearers of the name
have included actress Anna
Massey and newsreader Anna
Ford.

Anne
Origin: French
Used by English speakers as a
variant of **Ann**; famous bearers
of the name include Anne of
Cleves and Anne Boleyn, wives
of Henry VIII.

Anneka
Variants: Anneke
Origin: Swedish
A variant of **Ann**. A famous
bearer of the name is TV
presenter Anneka Rice.

Annette
Diminutives: Annie, Nettie
Variants: Annetta, Annett
Origin: French
A diminutive of **Anne** which
peaked in popularity around the
middle of the sixteenth century.

Annette Crosby and Annette
Bening are famous bearers
of the name.

Anthea
Origin: Greek
From the Greek Antheia, from
antheios, meaning 'flowery', it
first appeared as a name in the
sixteenth century but did not gain
much popularity until the
sixteenth century. Since its peak
in the 1950s, it has suffered a
decline. Anthea Turner, a TV
presenter, is one famous bearer
of the name.
See also **Thea**

Antonia
Diminutives: Toni, Nettie
Variants: Antonina, Antoinette,
Tonya (*see also* **Tanya**)
Origin: Latin
Meaning 'beyond price', the
name originally developed as a
form of Antony (*see* **Anthony**);
established as a first name
in continental Europe long
before being adopted by
English speakers in the
early sixteenth century.

Anya
Variants: Ania, Annia
Origin: Hebrew
Means 'grace' or 'mercy'.

Apple
Origin: English
The name of the well-known
fruit, chosen by Chris Martin
and Gwyneth Paltrow for their
baby daughter.

April
Variants: **Avril**
Origin: English
Inspired by its associations with
new birth, it seems to have been
only in the early sixteenth century
that it gained popularity as a first
name and reached a peak in the
1960s and 1970s.

Arabella
Diminutives: **Bella, Belle**
Variants: Arabelle, Arabel
Origin: English or Latin
Thought to have evolved from
Annabella (see **Annabel**);
alternatively, possibly derived
from Latin *orabilis*, meaning
'entreatable', 'obliging' or
'yielding to prayer'.

Aradhana
Origin: Sanskrit
Meaning 'worship'.

Aria
Origin: Italian
Meaning 'melody'.

Ariadne
Variants: Arianne, Arianna
Origin: Greek
Possibly from the Greek *ari* ('more') and *agnos* ('chaste', 'pure'), thus interpreted as 'holy'. In Greek mythology, Ariadne, the daughter of King Minos, showed Theseus how to find the way out of the Labyrinth.

Ariana
Diminutives: Ari
Variants: Ariane, Arianna, Arienne
Origin: Greek, Welsh or Latin
The Greek translation means 'the very holy one', though there are different versions of where the names originates. Some say it is Welsh, meaning 'silver'; others say it is from the Latin meaning 'beautiful melody'. It seems likely that it was originally from the Latin.

Arlene
Variants: Arline, Arleen, Arlena
Origin: English
The name seems to have evolved from names such as **Charlene** and **Marlene**.

Arvinda
Variants: Arabinda
Origin: Sanskrit
Meaning 'lotus blossom'.

Asha
Origin: Sanskrit
Meaning 'hope' or 'desire'.

Ashley m/f
Diminutives: Ash
Variants: Ashleigh, Ashlee, Ashlea
Origin: English
Derived from a place name from the Old English *aesc* ('ash') and *leah* ('wood' or 'clearing'). First used as a first name in the sixteenth century. Margaret Mitchell helped it gain popularity in *Gone With The Wind* with the character Ashley Wilkes.
See also **Scarlett**

Ashlyn
Diminutives: Ash
Origin: English
Means 'pool by the ash tree'.

Asia
Origin: Assyrian or Greek
Named after the continent. Also a diminutive of the Polish name Joasia, which means 'God is gracious'.
See also **Aisha**

Astrid
Diminutives: Asta, Sassa
Origin: Scandinavian
From the Old Norse Astrithr, from *ans* ('god') and *frithr* ('fair'), and interpreted as meaning 'divinely beautiful'. In the eleventh century, Queen Astrid was the wife of St Olaf of Norway.

Athena
Variants: Athene, Athenee
Origin: Greek
Means 'immortal' and 'wise', the name comes from the Greek goddess Athena and the city of Athens also came from the same source.

Aubrey m/f
Diminutives: Aub
Origin: German
From the old German Alberic, from *alb* ('elf') and *richi* ('power' or 'riches').

Audrey
Diminutives: Aud, Audie, Audi
Variants: Audrie, Audry
Origin: English
From the Old English Aethelthryth, from *aethel* ('noble') and *thryth* ('strength').

Augusta
Diminutives: Gus, Gussie
Variants: Augustine, Augustina
Origin: Roman
Originally evolved from the Roman name Augustus, it became popular in Britain because of Princess Augusta of Saxe-Coburg-Gotha, the wife of Frederick, Prince of Wales, in the sixteenth century.

Aura
Variants: Aurea
Origin: Latin or Greek
Meaning 'gold' or 'soft breeze'.

Aurelia
Variants: Aurelie, Auriol, Auriel, Oriole
Origin: Latin
From *aurelius*, which means 'gold', this has been used as a first name since the sixteenth century.

Autumn
Origin: English
Derived from the season of the same name.

Avonwy
Origin: Welsh
From the Welsh language, meaning 'someone who lives by the river'.

Avril
Variants: Averil
Origin: English or French
Derived either from the French *avril* after the month, or the Old English Eoforhild, from *eofor* ('boar') and *hild* ('battle'), suggesting strength in battle.
See also April

Aya
Origin: Japanese
This name means 'colourful' in Japanese.

Ayanna
Variants: Ayana
Origin: American
This name means simply 'grace'.

Ayesha
Variants: Ayisha
Origin: Persian
This name seems to have gained in popularity in recent years, and means 'happy one'.
See also Aisha

Azura
Origin: English
Evolved from the colour azure, though the original source may be the Persian word for 'blue sky'.

Babette
Variants: Babetta (rare)
Origin: French
First developed as a diminutive of **Elizabeth**, though English speakers also use it as a diminutive of **Barbara**.

Badia
Variants: Badea, Badiyn
Origin: Arabic
This name means simply 'elegant'.

Bahiyya
Origin: Arabic
Arabic for 'beautiful', this name is also a feminine form of **Baha**. Bahiyya was a character in Egyptian folklore, who is now seen as a personification of Egypt.

Bailey m/f
Variants: Baeli, Bailee
Origin: English
Means 'enforcer of the law'.

Bala m/f
Variants: Balu, Balan
Origin: Sanskrit
From the Sanskrit word for 'young'. The name is sometimes used to refer to the young Krishna.

Bambi
Origin: Italian
Short for *bambino*, which is the Italian word for 'child'.

Barbara
Diminutives: Babs, Barbie, Bobbie
Origin: English, German, Polish
Ultimately derived from the Greek *barbaros*, meaning 'strange' or 'foreign', the name was popular in medieval times until it fell out of favour during the Reformation because it was not used in the Bible. The early sixteenth century saw a rise in popularity once more, but it fell out of favour again after the 1950s.

Barrie
Origin: Gaelic
From the Gaelic word for 'markswoman'.

Bathsheba
Diminutives: Sheba
Origin: Hebrew
Means 'seventh daughter' or alternatively 'daughter of the oath', depending on the source. In the Bible, Bathsheba was the wife of Uriah, who became the lover and then wife of King David.

Beata
Variants: Beatha
Origin: Latin
From the Latin word *beatus*, meaning 'blessed' or 'happy', the name was popular among Roman Catholics in Europe as a tribute to the African martyr St Beata. In occasional use as a diminutive of **Beatrice**.

Beatrice
Diminutives: Bee, Bea, Beattie, Tris, Triss, Trissie
Origin: Latin
Derived from the Latin *beatus*, meaning 'happy'. Became well known in the sixteenth century as the name of the youngest daughter of Queen Victoria and Prince Albert. More recently, the Duke and Duchess of York chose the name for their youngest daughter.

Beatrix
Diminutives: Trix, Trixie
Origin: Latin
Like Beatrice, this name is derived from the Latin *beatus* and was the name of a fourth-century Christian martyr and subsequently became popular among Christians. Queen Beatrix of the Netherlands and the children's writer Beatrix Potter are well-known examples.

Belinda
Diminutives:
Variants:
Origin: Italian or German
The name derives either from the Italian *bella*, meaning 'beautiful',

or the Old German *lint*, which means 'snake', but the former seems more likely. Common in medieval Europe but not used among English speakers until the sixteenth century, reaching its peak in the 1950s.

Bella
Variants: Belle
Origin: English and Italian
First originated as a diminutive form of names such as **Isabella** and **Arabella**, this has been used as a name since the sixteenth century and has remained popular ever since.

Benita
Variants: Bernita
Origin: Spanish
This name means simply 'blessed'.

Berenice
See **Bernice**

Berit
Variants: Beret
Origin: Scandinavian
Means 'splendid' or 'gorgeous'.

Bernadette
Diminutives: Bernie, Detta
Variants: Bernardette, Bernadine, Bernadetta
Origin: French
Means 'courageous'; also the feminine form of **Bernard**. Well-known bearers of the name include Irish political activist Bernadette Devlin.

Bernice
Diminutives: Bernie, Berry, Binnie, Bunny
Variants: **Berenice** (older version of the name)
Origin: Greek
Derived from the Greek Pherenike, meaning 'bringer of victory'.
See also **Veronica**

Bertha
Diminutives: Bert, Bertie
Variants: Berta, Bertina, Berthe
Origin: Old German
The name derives ultimately from the Old German *beraht*, meaning 'bright' or 'famous'.

Beryl
Diminutives: Berry
Origin: English
Name derived from the stone of the same name. Famous Beryls have included writer Beryl Bainbridge and actress Beryl Reid.

Bess
Origin: English
Queen Elizabeth I became known as Good Queen **Bess**, though it was only in the sixteenth century that the name came into common use. It remained popular for a couple of hundred years but is now rare.

Bethany
Diminutives: Beth
Variants: Bethanie
Origin: English
Derived from a Hebrew word meaning 'house of figs', it appears in the New Testament as a village near Jerusalem. Because of Mary of Bethany, sister of Lazarus, it has remained popular among Roman Catholics.

Bethesda
Origin: Hebrew
Mentioned as a name in the Bible, it also means 'from the house of mercy'.

Betsy
Variants: Betsey
Origin: English
First developed as a diminutive of **Elizabeth**, but its popularity has now decreased and use of the name has become rare.

Betty
See **Elizabeth**

Beverley
Diminutives: Bev
Variants: Beverly
Origin: English
Meaning 'from the beaver's clearing'; often used as a boys' name in mainland Europe.

Bevin
Variants: Bebhinn, Bethinn
Origin: Gaelic
Meaning 'melodious lady', one whose voice stops even the birds from singing, it's so beautiful.

Beyoncé
Origin: American
Made popular by the singer Beyoncé Knowles, originally of the girl band Destiny's Child.

Bhavna
Variants: Bhavana
Origin: Indian
From the Sanskrit word meaning 'wish', 'thought' or 'desire'.

Bianca
Diminutives: Biancha, Biancia
Origin: Italian
Meaning 'bleached' or 'white'.

Bibi
Origin: Arabic
This name means simply 'lady' in Arabic.

Bibiana
See **Vivian**

Billie m/f
Origin: English, from Old German
A pet form of the boys' name **William** which is being used increasingly as a name for girls. Billie Jean King was one famous example of a Billie.

Bina
Origin: Hebrew
This Hebrew name means simply 'knowledge'.

Birgit
Variants: Birgitta
Origin: Norwegian
Means 'splendid'. **Birkita**
Origin: Celtic
This Celtic name means 'strong'.

Blaine m/f
Origin: Scottish
A surname, now used occasionally as a first name for both boys and girls.

Blake m/f
Origin: English
Possibly from the Old English *blaec* ('black') or *blac* ('white' or 'pale'); this has been used as a first name since at least the sixteenth century.

Blanche
See **Bianca**

Bly
Variants: Blye
Origin: Native American
Meaning 'tall'.

Blythe
Origin: English
From the ordinary word 'blithe', this has been used as a first name since the 1940s but remains rare.

Bobbie
Origin: English, from the Old German
First developed as a diminutive of **Roberta**, now used as a name in its own right.

Bonita
Variants: Bonitta
Origin: Spanish
The Spanish word for 'pretty' has developed into a first name for girls.

Bonnie
Variants: Bonny
Origin: Scottish
From the local word 'bonnie', which means 'pretty' or 'good'. Famous bearers of the name have included the dancer Bonnie Langford.

Brandy
Variants: Brandie, Brandee
Origin: English
A feminine form of **Brandon**; also named after the drink.

Branwen
Variants: **Bronwen**, Branwin, Branwyn
Origin: Welsh
From the Welsh language *bran* ('raven') and *gwyn* ('white' or 'blessed'); the daughter of Llyr in Arthurian legend bore the name.

Breana
Variants: Breanna (Irish)
Origin: English, from Celtic
A feminine form of **Brian**.

Brenda
Diminutives: Bren
Origin: English
Derived from the Old Norse word for 'sword' or 'torch' (*brandr*), the name enjoyed its peak in the mid-sixteenth century, though its use has since gone into decline.

Brianna
Variants: Bryanna, Brianta
Origin: Celtic
Meaning 'honourable' and 'noble'; also a feminine version of **Brian**.

Bridget
Diminutives: Gita, Bridie, Biddy
Variants: **Brighid**, Brigitte, Brigitta, Britt
Origin: English
From the original Gaelic Brighid, from the Celtic word for 'strength' or 'power' (*brigh*). Popular in Scotland and Ireland due to its associations with the Celtic fire goddess. Less popular since the 1950s.

Brighid
See **Bridget**

Brittany
Variants: Britney, Britani, Britanee

Origin: English
Derived from the French Bretagne and anglicized, this name became popular as a first name for girls in the USA in the 1960s, but the reasons for this are unclear and perhaps it is the sound of the name which is important. Since the 1980s, the UK has begun to take up the trend. Famous bearers of the name include US pop singer Britney Spears.

Bronwen *See* Branwen

Brooke
Origin: English
Meaning 'dweller by a stream', this was taken up as a first name near the end of the sixteenth century. The masculine form is Brook.

Brooklyn m/f
Variants: Brooklynn, Brooklyr
Origin: English
Named after the area of New this name enjoyed significant increase in popularity in 1999 when David and Victoria Beckh chose this as a name, as they were in New York when they discovered Victoria was pregna

Bryher
Origin: Cornish
The name of one of the Isles of Scilly, which are located off the Cornish coast.

Brynn
Origin: Welsh
Meaning 'hopeful'; the masculine form is Bryn.

Bryony
Variants: Briony
Origin: English
From the Old English word meaning 'twining vine'; also seen as a feminine form of Brian. Seems to have been used as a first name for girls from around the middle of the sixteenth century.

Bryssa
Variants: Brisa, Brissa
Origin: Spanish
Meaning simply 'beloved'.

Buena
Variants: Buona
Origin: Spanish
Meaning 'the good one'.

Buffy
Origin: American
Meaning 'buffalo', 'from the plains'; also a diminutive form of Elizabeth.

Bunty
Origin: English
Became popular after a 1911 play called *Bunty Pulls the Strings*, but is more commonly used as a nickname than a first name.

Caitlin
See **Catherine**

Caja
Variants: Caya
Origin: Cornish
Originally the name of a
daisy-like flower.

Calida
Variants: Calyda, Kalida, Kalyda
Origin: Latin
Meaning 'warm and loving'.

Calista
Variants: Callista
Origin: Greek
From the Italian Calisto, from
the Roman Calistos, which
itself came from the Greek
kalistos, meaning 'most
beautiful' or 'best'.

Calla
Variants: Calli, Cala, Kala
Origin: Greek
Meaning 'beautiful'; or from the
English, named after the cala lily.

Cameron m/f
Diminutives: Cam
Origin: Scottish
From the Gaelic *cam shron*,
meaning 'crooked nose', this has
been in use as a first name for
both boys and girls since the early
sixteenth century and retains its

Scottish connections, though it
has gained purchase elsewhere in
the English-speaking world since
around the 1990s. Famous
bearers of the name have included
the actress Cameron Diaz.

Camilla
Origin: English
A version of the Roman Camillus
which has been in used since the
thirteenth century; famous
bearers of the name have
included Camilla Parker-Bowles,
the Duchess of Cornwall.

Candice
Diminutives: Candy, Caddy
Variants: Candis
Origin: Unverified
Used as a first name since at
least the sixteenth century,
derived from the original
name Candace.

Candida
Diminutives: Candi, Candia,
Candie, Candy
Variants: Candide (French)
Origin: Roman
From the Latin *candidus*, which
means 'white'.

Candra
Variants: Chandra
Origin: Latin
Meaning 'luminescent'.

Caoimhe
Origin: Irish
Meaning 'gentle' or 'graceful'.

Caprice
Origin: Italian
Meaning literally 'on a whim',
famous bearers of the name have
included supermodel Caprice.

Cara
Variants: Caragh (Irish)
Origin: Italian and Irish
Meaning 'dear friend' in
both languages.

Caron
Origin: Welsh
Meaning simply 'love'.

Carey m/f
Variants: Cary
Origin: English
The rivers Cary and Carey in
Somerset and Devon respectively,
subsequently adopted as a first
name for both boys and girls.

Carla
Variants: Carly
Origin: English
Originally a feminine form of **Carl**, it
gained popularity both in the UK and
the USA in the 1940s and enjoyed
a boost in popularity in the 1980s.
Famous bearers of the name have
included singer Carly Simon.

Carmel

Variants: Carmela, Carmelina, Carmelita, Carmencita
Origin: Hebrew
A place name meaning 'garden' or 'vineyard'; appeared in the Bible as the name of a sacred mountain.

Carmen

Origin: Spanish
Derived originally from **Carmel**, but because of Bizet's opera of the same name it has links with dancing. Famous Carmens have included the Portuguese singer and actress Carmen Miranda.

Carol

Variants: Carole
Origin: English, from Old German
First developed as a diminutive of **Caroline** and is sometimes given as a name to girls born at Christmas. It has become less common in recent years and is now relatively rare.

Caroline

Diminutives: Caddy, Caro, Lina
Variants: Carolyn, Carolyne
Origin: English, from Old German
Derived from the Italian Carolina, from the masculine Carlo (*see* Charles). Princess Caroline of Monaco is one famous bearer of the name.

Cassandra

Diminutives: Cass, Cassie,

Sandra

Origin: Greek
Meaning 'ensnaring men'; one famous bearer of the name was the sister of celebrated novelist Jane Austen.

Cat m/f

Origin: English
Originally, anyone with a fiery character may have been nicknamed Cat. Famous bearers of the name have included musician Cat Stevens. More often used as a diminutive of **Catherine**, for example TV presenter Cat Deeley.

Catherine

Diminutives: **Cat**, Cath, **Kate**, Katy, Kit, **Kitty**, **Kay**
Variants: **Katherine**, Kathryn, Cathleen, **Kathleen**, **Catriona**, **Katrina**
Origin: Greek
Goes as far back as the Greek Aikaterina (probably from *katharos*, meaning 'pure', though it has been linked with *aikia*, meaning 'torture') and has links with St Catherine, who was tortured on a spiked wheel before being beheaded. Emily Brontë's *Wuthering Heights* included the famous character Catherine Earnshaw who was in love with Heathcliff.

Cecilia

Diminutives: Cecil, **Celia**, Ciss, Cissie, Sissy
Origin: Latin
From *caecus*, meaning 'blind', this was taken up as a name during the Middle Ages and reached a peak in the sixteenth century, though it has since become far less common.

Celeste

Origin: Latin
From the original Latin *caelestis*, meaning 'heavenly', it was adapted for girls from the French boys' name Céleste.

Celia

Origin: Latin
From the Roman name Caelia, itself probably from the Latin *caelum* (meaning 'heaven'). Also treated as a diminutive of **Cecilia**, records of its use go back to the sixteenth century, but it was not taken up widely until the nineteenth. It enjoyed a slight peak in the 1950s and famous bearers of the name include actress Celia Imrie.
See also **Sheila**

Celine
Variants: Célina
Origin: French
From the original Roman Caelina, probably derived from the Latin *caelum*, meaning 'heaven'.
See also **Selina**, **Celia**

Ceridwen
Diminutives: Ceri
Variants: Ceridwin
Origin: Welsh
From the Welsh *cerdd* ('poetry') and *gwen* ('blessed', 'white').

Famous for being the name of a Celtic goddess of poetry; also the name of the poet Taliesin's mother. Rare outside Wales.

Cerise
Origin: French
Referring to both the name of the fruit and the colour cherry-red.

Cerys
Variants: Carys, Ceris
Origin: Welsh
Meaning simply 'love'.

Chantal
Variants: Chantelle
Origin: French
From the Old Provençal word for 'rock' or 'boulder', but also associated with the word *chant*, which means 'song'. This name has become popular since the sixteenth century, particularly among French-Canadians.

Charis
Variants: Charissa
Origin: English

From the Greek *kharis* meaning 'grace'.

Charity
Diminutives: Cherry, Chattie
Origin: English
After the Reformation, many names alluding to Christian virtues were taken for use as first names. Charles Dickens created the character Charity Pecksniff in *Martin Chuzzlewit*.

Charlene
Diminutives: Charlie
Variants: Sharleen, Charleen, Sharlene
Origin: English
Became popular in the 1980s with the popularity of the TV soap opera *Neighbours*, where Kylie Minogue's character was named Charlene.
See also **Caroline**

Charlotte
Diminutives: Charlie, Charley, Lottie, Tottie
Origin: Italian
Related to the masculine **Charles**, derived from the Italian Carlotta; the name was adopted by English speakers around the sixteenth century and enjoyed a surge of popularity in the 1970s.

Charmaine
Variants: Charmain, Sharmain, Sharmane, Sharmaine
Origin: English
Stories vary as to its origin; in the mid-sixteenth century it became popular, partly due to the song 'Charmaine' which was released in 1926.
See also **Carmen**

Chastity
Origin: English
Adopted as a 'virtue' name by the Puritans after the Reformation, it remains in use as a first name, though it is relatively rare.

Chelsea
Variants: Chelsey, Chelsie
Origin: English
From the place in London, meaning 'landing place for limestone', the 1950s saw this used as a first name, first in Australia and the USA but later it became more widespread and has remained popular.

Cherie
Origin: French
From the French *chérie*, meaning 'darling' or 'dear'; famous names have included actress Cherie Lunghi and Tony Blair's wife Cherie Booth.

Cherry
Origin: English
Originally a diminutive of such names as **Charity**, **Cherie** and **Cheryl**, but now seen as a name in its own right, and retains its links with the fruit of the same name.

Cheryl
Variants: Sheryl, Sherill, Cheryll
Origin: English
Thought to have come from a combination of Cherry and Beryl, it came into use in the early sixteenth century but did not become popular until the 1940s and 1950s. A famous bearer of the name is TV presenter and pop star Cheryl Baker (Rita Crudgington).

Cheyenne
Origin: Native American
Named after the tribe. Marlon Brando named his daughter Cheyenne.

Chloe
Variants: Chlöe
Origin: Greek
Derived from the Greek Khloe, meaning 'young, green shoot', it has been a regular fixture as a name since the sixteenth century.

Christabel
Diminutives: Chris, Chrissie, Chrissy, Christie, Christy,

Bella, Belle
Variants: Christobel, Christabelle, Christabella
Origin: English
From the Latin *christus* ('Christ') and *bella* ('beautiful'), this was in use as a name from at least the sixteenth century.

Christine
Diminutives: Chrissie, Chris, Christa, Kirsty, Chrissy
Variants: Christen, Kristin, Kristine, Kirsten, Crystin, Crystyn
Origin: English and French
From Christiana via Christina, this variant of the name became popular in the sixteenth century.

Cilla
Origin: English
Developed as a diminutive of Priscilla (and also Druscilla), this appeared as a name in its own right in the mid-sixteenth century. In the UK, the name is known through the TV presenter and singer Cilla Black.

Cindy
See Cynthia

Claire
See Clara

Clara
Diminutives: Clarrie

Variants: Klara (German), Claire
Origin: Latin
Developed from the Latin *clarus*, meaning 'clear' or 'pure'. It is sometimes considered in Scotland to be an anglicized version of Sorcha.

Clarabella
Diminutives: Bella, Clara
Variants: Clarabelle
Origin: Latin and French
Meaning 'bright, shining beauty'.

Claramae
Variants: Chlarinda, Clarinda
Origin: English
Meaning simply 'brilliant beauty'.

Clarice
Variants: Clarissa, Chlaris
Origin: Latin
From the original Clara, adapted into French form.

Claudia
Variants: Claudette, Claudine
Origin: English, French and German
From the Roman Claudius, itself derived from the Latin *claudus*, meaning 'lame'. Famous names include supermodel Claudia Schiffer.

Clodagh
Origin: Irish
Named for the river in County Tipperary; sometimes treated as an Irish form of Claudia, this remains rare outside of Ireland.

Coco
Origin: Spanish, a diminutive of the name Socorro; also the root word for 'chocolate'. Made famous by Coco Chanel, and David Bowie's PA Coco Schwab.

Cody m/f
Variants: Codey, Kody
Origin: English
Thought to have derived from an Irish name meaning 'descendent of a helpful person', this is more popular in the USA than the UK.

Colette
Variants: Collette
Origin: French
Derived from the French name Nicolette (*see* Nicola). Recorded as a name as far back as the thirteenth century. In the early sixteenth century, the novelist Colette popularized the name.

Colleen
Origin: Irish
Derived from the Gaelic *cailin*, meaning simply 'girl'; also sometimes considered to be a feminine form of Colin. Despite its Irish roots, it is unusual in Ireland.

Comfort m/f
Origin: English
Fairly popular after the Reformation, it seems likely it is now defunct as a first name.

Constance
Diminutives: Con, Connie
Variants: Constancy, Constantina
Origin: Roman
From the Roman Constantia, this was a popular name in the Middle Ages and after the Reformation, but has seen a decline in recent years.

Consuela
Diminutives: Connie
Variants: Consuelo (m)
Origin: Spanish
Meaning simply 'consolation', a friend in need; also attributed to the Spanish name for the Virgin Mary ('Our Lady of Consolation').

Contessa
Variants: Contesa
Origin: Italian
Meaning 'pretty'; also Italian for Countess.

Cora
Variants: Coretta
Origin: English
From the Greek *kore*, meaning 'girl', the name has been suffering a decline since the early sixteenth century.

Coral
Diminutives: Cory
Variants: Coraline
Origin: English
Apparently adopted as part of the fashion for naming children after gemstones in the sixteenth century, but can also be seen as a variant of Cora.

Cordelia
Diminutives: Cordy, Delia
Origin: English or Latin
Altered from the original Cordeilla to Cordelia by Shakespeare for *King Lear*; alternatively, a variant of the Celtic Cordula, itself from the Latin *cor*, meaning 'heart'.

Corey m/f
Variants: Cory
Origin: English
The origin of this surname is uncertain, but it has been in favour chiefly in Black American communities since the 1960s.

Corinne
See Cora

Courtney m/f
Variants: Courtenay
Origin: English, from Norman
From the Norman place name, meaning 'domain of Curtius', this has been a name for boys since the mid-sixteenth century, but the sixteenth century saw a rise in its popularity as a name for girls. Famous bearers of the name have included rock star Courtney Love.

Cristin
See Christine

Crystal
Variants: Chrystal, Krystal
Origin: English
Apart from the obvious connection with the jewel, the popularity of this name may lie with its connections with Christel, the German variant of Christine.

Cyan
Origin: Greek
Meaning 'light blue', also the name of a nymph in Greek mythology.

Cynthia
Diminutives: Cimmie, Cindy
Variants: Cinzia (Italian)
Origin: Greek
After Mount Kynthos in Greece, where Artemis was born. Taken as a name in the sixteenth century, its popularity increased until the middle of the sixteenth century, when it started to become rare.

Dagna
Origin: Scandinavian
Meaning simply 'new day'.

Dahlia
Variants: Dalia, Dalya
Origin: English
Named after Dahl, the Swedish botanist.

Daisy
Origin: English
Named after the flower, itself named from the Old English *daegeseage*, meaning 'day's eye', because it opens its petals at daybreak. Also seen as a diminutive of Margaret through its associations with the French *marguerite*, which means 'daisy'.

Dakota
Origin: Native American
Meaning 'allies', 'friend' or 'partner'; also the name of a Native American tribe, now a state.

Dale m/f
Origin: English
Simply means 'dale' or 'valley', and was taken up for use as a first name mainly in the USA in the sixteenth century.

Damara
Origin: Greek
Meaning 'gentle girl'.

Damaris
Origin: Greek
The name of a woman who was converted by St Paul to Christianity; subsequently used by Puritans as a first name in the sixteenth century, it has since become much less popular.

Dana m/f
Variants: Danuta (Polish)
Origin: English and Hebrew
Originally a diminutive of Daniel, but can also be linked to the surname Dana. Nowadays, it is far more likely to be a girl's name than a boy's, however, from names such as Donna and Danielle. Famous bearers of the name have included the winner of the 1970 Eurovision Song Contest.

Danae
Origin: Greek
Meaning 'bright and pure'.

Danala
Variants: Danalla
Origin: English
Meaning simply 'happy'.

Dandy m/f
Origin: English
Diminutive of such names as Danielle and Andrew, but also named for the ordinary vocabulary word 'dandy'.

Danielle
Diminutives: Dan, Dannie, Danny, Dani
Variants: Daniella, Daniela, Danniella
Origin: French, from Hebrew
Feminine equivalent of Daniel which has become popular among English speakers since the 1940s. A famous bearer of the name is US writer Danielle Steel.

Danika
Origin: Slavonic
From the name of the morning star, this remains only an occasional choice of name for English speakers.

Danu
Origin: Welsh
In Celtic mythology, Danu was the mother of the gods.

Danuta
See Donna

Daphne
Diminutives: Daff, Daffy, Daph
Origin: Greek
From the Greek *daphne*, 'laurel tree'. First popular among English speakers in the sixteenth century, it enjoyed a peak in the late sixteenth century and the 1930s, when it was fashionable to name children after flowers or plants.

The name of the writer of *Rebecca*, Daphne du Maurier.

Dara m/f
Variants: Darach
Origin: Irish
Derived from the Gaelic Mac Dara; popular among Jewish people because it is the Hebrew word for 'pearl of wisdom'.

Darcey
See Darcy (m)

Darel
See Darlene

Daria
Diminutives: Dasha
Variants: Darya (Russian)
Origin: Italian, from Persian
The feminine equivalent of Darius; also the name of a third-century Greek martyr.

Darina
Variants: Daireann, Doirend, Doirenn
Origin: Irish
From the Irish Gaelic *daireann*, meaning 'fruitful'.

Darla
Origin: English
Meaning simply 'darling'.

Darlene
Variants: Darline, Darleen
Origin: English
Thought to have derived from 'darling' under the influence of such names as Charlene. In the 1980s, this name was especially popular in Australia.

Darryl m/f
Variants: Daryl, Darel, Darrell, Darell
Origin: Norman or English
From the Norman d'Airelle, a baronial surname, this has been in use as a name for both girls and boys sicne the early twentieth century. Other sources suggest the name comes from the Old English *deorling*, meaning 'darling'. A famous female bearer of the name is actress Daryl Hannah.

Davina
Variants: Davida, Davinia, Davena
Origin: Scottish, from Hebrew
Feminine equivalent of David, this name appears to be a fairly recent invention. A famous bearer of the name is TV presenter Davina McCall.

Dawn
Variants: Dawna
Origin: English
Named for the vocabulary word 'dawn', which is likely to have been coined by William Shakespeare, although the name is also thought to date to Anglo-Saxon times. Popular in the 1960s, it is now much less common. Famous bearers of the name have included actress and comedienne Dawn French.

Dea
Origin: Latin
Based on the Latin word for goddess.

Deborah
Diminutives: Debbie, Debs
Variants: Debra
Origin: Hebrew
From the Hebrew word meaning 'bee', suggesting an industrious, hard-working nature. Has become relatively uncommon since its peak in the 1960s.

Dee
Variants: DeeDee, Didi
Origin: English
First used as a diminutive of such names as Deirdre and Dorothy, now sometimes used as a first name in its own right.

Deirbhaile
See Dervla

Deirdre
Variants: Deidre, Diedre, Deidra
Origin: Irish

From the Irish *deardan*, meaning 'storm', therefore suggesting a tempestuous nature, the name was adopted in the 1930s and gained in popularity in the 1950s but is now very rare among young people.

Delia
Origin: English, from Greek
Derived from the name of the Greek island of Delos, the mythological home of Artemis and Apollo. Also found as a diminutive of such names as Cordelia.

Della
Diminutives: Dell
Origin: English
Originally taken as a name near the end of the sixteenth century, it developed as a diminutive of such names as **Adela** and **Delia**. It became quite popular in the sixteenth century.

Delphine
Variants: Delfina, Delphina, Delvene, Delfine
Origin: Roman or Greek
From the Roman Delphina, 'woman of Delphi'; this town was famous for its oracle, so the name has links with fortune telling. Also said to be from the Greek word for 'dolphin', or to have links with the delphinium flower.

Delta
Origin: Greek
Meaning 'the fourth child', this is also the fourth letter of the Greek alphabet.

Delyth
Origin: Welsh
From the Welsh word 'del', which means 'pretty'.

Demeter
Origin: Greek
The goddess of fertility and harvests, the Earth Mother celebrated by pagans.

Demi
Origin: English, from Greek
From Demetra, related to Demeter. Also the literal French word for 'half', this name was made famous in recent times by the actress Demi Moore.

Dena See Dinah

Denise
Diminutives: Dennie
Variants: Deneice, Denice, Deniece
Origin: French
First evolved as a feminine equivalent of Denis (*see* **Dennis**), it enjoyed a peak in popularity in the mid-sixteenth century.

Derry
Origin: Irish
Meaning 'red-haired girl'; also obvious links with the Irish town of the same name.

Derryth
Origin: Welsh
Meaning 'of the oak'.

Dervla
Variants: Deirbhail(e), Deirbhile, Dervila, Derval, Dervilia
Origin: Irish
Possibly meaning 'daughter of a poet', from the old Irish *dear* and *file*, the second syllable may instead derive from *Fal* (Ireland or a figure from legened), so 'daughter of Ireland'. Notable bearers are actress Dervla Kirwan (b. 1971) and cyclist and travel writer Dervla Murphy (b. 1931).

Désirée
Origin: French.
Meaning 'desired' or 'wanted'; ultimately from Roman name *Desiderata*, from the Latin. Sometimes also written with no accents.

Desma
Origin: Greek
Meaning 'pledge', 'oath'.

Deva
Origin: Sanskrit
The name for the Moon Goddess; divine.

Devi
Origin: Hindu
The name of a Hindu goddess.

Devnet
Variants: Daimhnait (Irish)
Origin: Celtic
Meaning 'white wave'.

Devon m/f
Origin: English
From the county of the same name.

Dew
Origin: English
Meaning simply 'dew'.

Dia
Origin: Greek
Meaning 'like a goddess'; sometimes used as an alternative name for Hera, the queen of the Greek gods.

Diana
Diminutives: Di
Variants: Diane, Dianne
Origin: English, from Roman
Named for the Roman goddess of the moon and the hunt; pagan links did not prevent the name being popular after the Reformation and it enjoyed a peak in the mid-sixteenth century. Popular bearers of the name have included actress Diana Rigg.

Diantha
Variants: Dianthia
Origin: Greek
The divine flower of Zeus.

Dido
Origin: Phoenician
Meaning 'bold'. This name has been made famous by the singer Dido.

Dielle
Origin: Latin
Meaning 'a person who worships God'.

Dilys
Diminutives: Dil, Dill, Dilly
Variants: Dylis, Dyllis
Origin: Welsh
Meaning 'steadfast', genuine' and 'sincere'. Seems to have found favour as a name in the sixteenth century, but has since become less common.

Dimona
Origin: Hebrew
Uncertain meaning, but likely to mean simply 'south'.

Dinah
Origin: Hebrew
Meaning 'judged', 'revenged' or 'lawsuit'.
See also **Dyna**

Divine
Origin: Italian
Meaning 'heavenly', 'divine'

Divya
Origin: Sanskrit
Meaning 'the divine'.

Dixie
Origin: French
Meaning 'tenth'; also a Scandinavian word for 'sprite'.

Dolores
Origin: Spanish
Meaning 'sorrows', this name became popular in the sixteenth century when many people came to the UK from Spain.

Donna
Origin: Italian
Meaning simply 'girl' or 'woman', this name was widespread in the 1960s and became popular again in the 1980s.

Dora
Diminutives: Dorry, Dorita, Dorette, **Dorinda**
Origin: English
Developed as a diminutive of such names as **Dorothy**, **Isadora**,

Theodora, then became an accepted name in its own right. Since the early sixteenth century, it has seen a decline in popularity and is now rare.

Dorcas
Origin: Greek
From Greek *dorkas* ('doe or gazelle'). It appears in the bible as a translation of the Aramaic **Tabitha**.

Dorian m/f
Variants: Dorien, Dorrien
Origin: English
As a name, it is believed Dorian made its first appearance in Oscar Wilde's book *The Picture of Dorian Gray*, but it has since been used as a girls' name as well.

Dorinda
See **Dora**

Doris
Origin: English or Greek
From the Greek for 'bountiful' or as a combination of **Dorothy** and **Phyllis**. It is now much less common. A famous bearer of the name is the writer Doris Lessing.

Dorleta
Origin: Basque
The name for the Virgin Mary in the Basque Country.

Dorothy
Diminutives: Dot, Dottie, **Thea**, **Dee**, Dodie, **Dora**
Variants: Dorothea
Origin: Greek
Originally derived from Dorothea from the Greek *doron* ('gift') and *theos* ('god'), the name is now much less common. Dorothy L Sayers is one famous bearer of the name.

Drew m/f
Origin: Uncertain
From **Andrew** or possibly from the Old German 'Drogo'. Was established in Scotland before becoming well-known elsewhere, and one famous bearer of the name is the actress Drew Barrymore.

Duana
Origin: Celtic
Means simply 'a song'.

Dulcie
Variants: Dulcea, Dulce
Origin: Latin
Meaning simply 'sweet'.

Durene
Origin: Latin
Meaning 'enduring one', suggesting a wish for a long life.

Dusana
Variants: Dusa, Dusanka, Dusicka, Duska
Origin: Czech
Meaning 'soul' or 'spirit'.

Dusty
Origin: English
Either a feminine version of **Dustin** or simply from the ordinary vocabulary word 'dusty'.

Dylana
Origin: Sanskrit
Meaning 'meditation'; perhaps also used as a feminine form of **Dylan**.

Dyna
Origin: Greek
Meaning 'powerful'.
See also **Dinah**

Dysis
Origin: Greek
Meaning simply 'sunset'.

Eadan
Variants: Etan
Origin: Irish
Features in Irish mythology as the name of a sun goddess and is possibly derived from the Old Irish *et*, which means 'jealousy'. Became popular after the 1914 opera *The Immortal Hour*.

Earla
Origin: English
Meaning 'leader'.

Earlene
Variants: Earley, Earlie, Earline, Erline, Erlene
Origin: Anglo-Saxon
The Anglo-Saxon word for a noble woman; also feminine equivalent of Earl.

Eartha
Variants: Ertha, Erthel
Origin: English
From the ordinary vocabulary word 'earth'; links with Mother Earth. It has never been a common name and is most closely associated with the jazz singer Eartha Kitt.

Ebba
See **Eve**

Ebony
Variants: Ebbony, Ebonnee, Eboni, Ebonie
Origin: English
The name of a black wood, making this name popular among African-Americans and reaching a particular peak in popularity in the 1970s. After the 1980s, when it reached another peak due to the song 'Ebony and Ivory', its popularity began to fade.

Echo
Origin: Greek
The name of a nymph who annoyed the queen of the gods by talking a lot.

Eda
Variants: Eada, Edda
Origin: Anglo-Saxon and Greek
Meaning 'poetry' in Anglo-Saxon and in Greek, 'prosperous' and 'loving mother of many'.

Edana
Variants: Aidan, Aiden, Eidann
Origin: Gaelic
Meaning 'little fiery one', suggesting warmth, a loving nature and perhaps a quick temper.

Eden m/f
Origin: English
From Old English Edun or Edon, from *ead* ('riches') and *hun* ('bearcub'). In the sixteenth century, this name was used by Puritans but it has always been uncommon.

Edia
Origin: Hebrew
Meaning 'mighty'.

Edie
See **Edith**

Edina
See **Edna**

Edith
Diminutives: Edie, Eda
Variants: Edyth, Edythe, Editha
Origin: English, French, German, Scandinavian
Based on the Old English *ead* ('riches') and *gyth* ('strife'), the name was revived in the sixteenth century after enjoying massive popularity in the Middle Ages. Over the sixteenth century, it suffered a decline and is now rare.

Edmee
Origin: Anglo-Saxon
Meaning 'fortunate protector'.

Edna
Variants: Edina
Origin: Hebrew or Irish
Derived either from the Hebrew *ednah*, meaning 'pleasure' or 'rejuvenation', or from the Irish Eithne. Most common between the late sixteenth century and the 1920s, but is now rare.

Famous bearers of the name have included Edna Purviance, Charlie Chaplin's favourite leading lady.

Edra
Origin: Hebrew
Meaning 'mighty'.

Edrea
Diminutives:
Variants:
Origin: Anglo-Saxon
Meaning 'powerful and prosperous'.
See also **Andrea**

Edwina
Variants: Edwena, Edwyna
Origin: English
Evolved as a feminine form of **Edwin**; probably first appeared in the sixteenth century when the name Edwin became popular again. Famous bearers of the name include politician, writer and broadcaster Edwina Currie.

Effie
Origin: Greek
Meaning 'famous beauty'.
See also **Euphemia**

Eileen
Diminutives: Eily
Variants: Aileen, Eilean, Ilene
Origin: English and Celtic
Derived from the Irish Eibhlin; also treated as an Irish form of **Helen**. In the sixteenth century, it was spread widely by Irish emigrants and its peak came in the 1920s, since when it has been in severe decline.

Eilwen
Variants: Eilwyn
Origin: Welsh
Meaning simply 'fair of brow'.

Eithne
Origin: Irish
Often treated as a feminine version of **Aidan**, this could also have derived from the Gaelic *eithne*, meaning 'kernel'. Rare outside Ireland, the name, in its phonetic form, has been made famous by the Irish singer Enya.

Ekata
Origin: Sanskrit
Meaning 'unity'.

Elaine
Origin: English
From the French Hélène; from the late sixteenth century, it enjoyed increasing popularity. The mother of Sir Galahad was named Elaine. A famous bearer of the name is singer Elaine Paige.

Eldora
Origin: Spanish
Meaning 'the gilded one'; derives from El Dorado, the land of gold.

Eldreda
Variants: Eldrida
Origin: Anglo-Saxon
Meaning 'wise companion'.

Eleanor
Diminutives: Nelly, Ellie, **Nell**, **Nora**, Norah
Variants: Elenora, Lenore, Elinor
Origin: English
The origin of this name is uncertain, but it seems likely to have derived from Helen.

Electra
Origin: English
Anglicized version of the Italian name Elettra, from the Latin *elector*, meaning 'brilliant'.

Elen
Variants: Elin
Origin: Welsh
The Welsh form of Helen, though perhaps derived from the Welsh *elen*, which means 'nymph', rather than coming directly from Helen.

Eleri
Origin: Welsh
The meaning of this name is uncertain, though it appears in Welsh mythology as the name of Chief Brychan's daughter.

Elga
Variants: Olga
Origin: Slavic
Meaning 'consecrated'.

Eliane
Variants: Eliana
Origin: French
From the Roman Aeliana via the Greek *helios*, meaning 'sun'.

Elinel
Origin: Celtic
Meaning simply 'shapely'.

Eliora
Variants: Eleora
Origin: Hebrew
Meaning 'God is my light'.
Elise
See Elizabeth

Eliza
Origin: English, from Hebrew
Derived from Elizabeth, now considered a name in its own right. Famous bearers of the name include the folk musician Eliza Carthy.

Elizabeth
Diminutives: Beth, Betty, Elise, Elyse, Eliza, Libby, Lisbeth, Liz, Lizzie, Betsy, Bess
Variants: Bethan (Welsh)
Origin: Hebrew
Derived from the Greek Elisabet from the Hebrew Elisheba, meaning 'God has sworn'. Enjoyed a peak in the sixteenth century due to tributes to Queen Elizabeth I and has remained popular in various forms ever since.

Elke
Variants: Elkie
Origin: German
German form of 'Alice'. One famous bearer of the name is singer Elkie Brooks. *See also* Alice.

Ella
Origin: English
Derived from the Old German Alia, from Old German *al*, meaning 'all'. Though it came to Britain with the Normans, it was not until the sixteenth century that it was taken up as a name in both the UK and the USA. Can be a diminutive of such names as Eleanor and Ellen.

Elle
Origin: French
The French for 'her' and 'she'.

Ellema
Variants: Ellemah, Elema
Origin: African
Meaning 'dairy farmer'.

Ellen
Diminutives: Ellie, Nell, Nelly
Origin: English
Used as a variant of Helen in the sixteenth century, the name became popular at the end of the sixteenth century but suffered a decline in the sixteenth.

Ellice
Variants: Elyse
Origin: Greek
Meaning 'Jehovah is God'; also the feminine form of Elias.

Ellis
Origin: English
Evolved from Isabel or Alice; alternatively, derived from the identical surname. Possibly from the Irish Eilis, the Welsh Elisud, from *elus*, meaning 'kind'. One famous bearer of the name is novelist Ellis Peters.

Ellora
Origin: Greek
Meaning simply 'light'.

Elma
Origin: Greek
From the Greek, meaning 'pleasant and amiable'.

Elodie
Origin: Greek
Meaning 'fragile flower'.

Eloise
Origin: French
German roots, though with uncertain origin, this name has made occasional appearances among English speakers over time.

Elrica
See **Ulrica**

Elsa
Diminutives: Ellie
Origin: English, German and Swedish
Derived from **Elizabeth**, this name became popular in the sixteenth century. A well-known bearer of the name was Elsa the lioness, featured in Joy Adamson's book *Born Free*.

Elsie
Diminutives: Else
Origin: Hebrew
Derived from Elspie from **Elspeth**, sometimes encountered as a diminutive of **Elizabeth**. Popular among English speakers in the nineteenth and twentieth centuries, it has been less common since the 1920s. A famous bearer of the name was Elsie Tanner, from the soap opera *Coronation Street*.

Elspeth
Origin: Hebrew
Derived as a diminutive of **Elizabeth** in the nineteenth century, one famous bearer of the name was writer Elspeth Huxley.

Elva
Origin: Old English
Meaning 'of the elves'.

Elvina
Variants: Elvyna
Origin: Old English
With an obvious relation to **Elva**, this name means 'friend of the elves'.

Elvira
Origin: Spanish, possibly Old German
Possibly derived from the Old German *al* ('all') and *wer* ('true'), thus meaning 'true to all'. Likely taken up in the nineteenth century, it has remained uncommon. Famous bearers of the name have included the fictional film critic Elvira and the wife of Don Juan in the Mozart opera *Don Giovanni*.

Elyse
See **Elizabeth** and **Ellice**

Elysia
Origin: Greek
A feminine version of the Greek

name Elysium, which is the name of heaven in Greek mythology; it means 'blissful'.

Ember
Origin: English
A name based on the literal meaning of the smouldering remains of a fire.

Emer
Variants: Emir (rare)
Origin: Irish
Famous in Ireland as the name of Chuchulain's lover.

Emiko
Variants: Emuko
Origin: Japanese
Meaning simply 'pretty child'.

Emilia
Origin: Roman
First used in the Middle Ages in England as a variant of **Amelia**, one famous bearer of this name is Iago's wife in Shakespeare's *Othello*.

Emily
Diminutives: Em, Emmie, Emmy, Milly
Variants: Emilie (French)
Origin: Roman
From the Latin for 'eager' or 'striving', adopted as a first name among English speakers in the eighteenth century, it reached its peak in the nineteenth century but suffered a decline in the twentieth; however, it has seen a revival since the 1970s.

Emma
Diminutives: Em, Emmie, Emmy
Origin: Old German
From the Old German word *ermen*, meaning 'entire' or 'universal'; it came into use in the Middle Ages and was popular during the nineteenth century, reaching its more recent peak in the 1980s. A famous bearer of the name is British actress Emma Thompson.

Emmeline
Diminutives: Emeline, Emelyn, Emblem, Emblyn
Origin: Old German
This name developed as a variant of **Emma**, but also has links with the Old German *amal* via the Old French name Ameline. In medieval times, it was taken up by English speakers as a first name, but its popularity declined until its revival in the eighteenth century. Perhaps the most famous bearer of this name was the suffragette leader Emmeline Pankhurst.

Emmeranne
Origin: French, Old German
Meaning simply 'raven'.

Emogene
See **Imogen**

Ena
See **Eithne**

Enid
Origin: Welsh
The roots of this name are uncertain, but may come from the Welsh *enaid*, meaning 'soul' or 'life', or alternatively, from *enit*, which means 'woodlark'. Towards the end of the nineteenth century, it became popular and was in frequent use during the 1920s, but, since then, it has suffered a severe decline. One of the famous bearers of the name was children's writer Enid Blyton.

Ennata
Origin: French or Greek
Meaning simply 'goddess'.

Enola
Origin: Probably English, though uncertain
Introduced as a name in the latter part of the nineteenth century, it was the notoriety gained by the Superfortress bomber, nicknamed the 'Enola Gay' after the pilot's mother, which was used to drop the first atomic bomb on Hiroshima. A famous use of the name was in

the song 'Enola Gay', released in 1980 by Orchestral Manoeuvres in the Dark.

Eostre
Variants: Easter, Eastra
Origin: Old English
The name for the goddess of spring in pre-Christian times, Eostre lent its name to what we now know as Easter, thus suggesting new life.

Ephratah
Variants: Efrata, Efrat
Origin: Hebrew
Meaning 'fruitful'.

Erica
Diminutives: Rikki, Rica, Ricki
Variants:Erika (Scandinavian)
Origin: Old Norse
Developed as the feminine form of Eric, it is possible that the name comes from *Erica*, which means 'heather'; it is treated in Scotland as an anglicization of Oighrig. Early use began at the end of the eighteenth century and the 1960s saw a significant peak in its popularity.

Erin
Variants: Errin, Eryn
Origin: Irish
From the Irish name for Ireland itself (*Éireann*) and has been used as a first name, not only in Ireland,

since the end of the nineteenth century. One famous bearer of the name is Erin Brockovich in the film of the same name.

Eris
Origin: Greek
From the name of the mythological character.

Erlinda
Origin: Hebrew
Meaning simply 'spirited'.

Erma
See Irma

Erna
Origin: English
Meaning simply 'sincere'.

Esha
Variants: Eshe
Origin: Hindi
Meaning 'desire'.

Esme
Variants: Esmée, Edmé (Scottish)
Origin: Old French
From the Old French *esme*, meaning 'esteemed' or 'loved', this name seems to have been imported from France to England in the sixteenth century and its feminine spelling of Esmée appeared in the eighteenth century; it is actually a gender-

neutral name but is now almost exclusively used as a feminine. Sometimes treated as a diminutive of **Esmerelda**.

Esmerelda
Diminutives: Esme
Variants: Esmeralda, Esmaralda
Origin: Spanish
From *esmeralda*, which is Spanish for 'emerald'; famous as the name of Quasimodo's great love in Victor Hugo's book *The Hunchback of Notre Dame*.

Essylt
Origin: Welsh
Meaning 'beautiful to behold'.
See also Isolde

Estelle
Diminutives: Essie
Variants: Estella
Origin: Latin
This French name comes from the Latin word for 'star' and is derived from **Stella**. Used as a name since the nineteenth century, it became popular in the 1970s. Estella was the name of a central character in *Great Expectations* by Charles Dickens.

Esther
Diminutives: Ess, Essa, Esta, Hettie

Variants: Ester (Scandinavian), Eszter (Hungarian)
Origin: Persian or Hebrew
Can possibly be traced back to the Persian *stara*, meaning 'star', but also linked with the Hebrew name Hadassah, meaning 'myrtle' or 'bride'. Alternatively, it could be a Hebrew version of the Persian goddess of love, Ishtar. Used by English speakers since the seventeenth century, its peak was the nineteenth century, but is now quite rare. A famous bearer of the name is TV presenter Esther Rantzen.

Estra
Diminutives:
Variants:
Origin: Angla-Saxon
The goddess of spring.
See also **Eostre**

Etain
Origin: Irish
Meaning simply 'shining'.

Ethel
Diminutives: Eth, Thel (rare)
Origin: Old German
Derives ultimately from the Old German *ethel*, meaning 'noble'; believed to represent a shortened version of many Anglo-Saxon names, including Ethelburgha, Ethelthryth and Ethelgive. It became popular in its own right in the nineteenth century and remained common into the twentieth, but is now virtually defunct. Famous bearers of the name have included actress Ethel Barrymore.

Etsu
Origin: Japanese
Meaning simply 'delight'.

Eudora
Diminutives: Eudore
Variants: **Dora**
Origin: Greek
Meaning 'generous gift'.

Eugenie
Diminutives: Gene, Genie
Variants: Eugenia (rare)
Origin: Greek
Developed first as a feminine equivalent of **Eugene**, it was used occasionally in the nineteenth century and continues to be used every so often. Most recently, a notable bearer of the name is Princess Eugenie, the second daughter of the Duke and Duchess of York.

Eunice
Variants: Unice
Origin: Biblical, from Greek
From the Greek *eu* ('well') and *nike* ('victory'). In the Bible, Eunice is the mother of Timothy and it was thus used by Puritans in the seventeenth century (usually with a three-syllable sound). It reached a peak in the 1920s but has since become rare.

Euphemia
Diminutives: Effie, Phemie, Eppie, **Fanny**
Variants: Eufemia (Spanish and Portuguese), Euphémie (French)
Origin: Greek
Meaning 'well regarded', 'of good repute', the name comes from the Greek *eu* ('well') and *phenai* ('to speak'). Seems to have appeared as a name in the twelfth century, it reached a peak in the nineteenth, especially in Scotland (as an anglicized Oighrig).

Eustacia
Diminutives: Stacy, **Stacey**
Origin: Greek
Evolved from the masculine form of the name, **Eustace**, this has never been a common name. One famous bearer is the character in Thomas Hardy's *The Return of the Native*.

Eva
Diminutives: Evita
Variants: **Eve**, Ewa (Polish)
Origin: Hebrew
Derived from the Hebrew name

Havvah, which means 'living';
English speakers adopted it as an
alternative to Eve in the mid-
nineteenth century and it enjoyed
a peak in the early twentieth.
See also **Eve**

Evadne
Origin: Greek
From the Greek *eu* ('well'), but
the other root is unknown, the
name was used sporadically
in the seventeenth century.
In the nineteenth century,
it became quite fashionable
but is now rare.

Evangeline
Diminutives: **Eva**, Evie
Origin: Latin
From the Latin *evangelium*, the
name became popular among
African-Americans due to its use
in the Henry Wadsworth
Longfellow narrative poem
Evangeline. Evangeline Booth,
a Salvation Army leader, was one
well-known bearer of the name.

Evania
Variants: Evanne
Origin: Greek
Meaning 'tranquil' and 'untroubled'.

Evanthe
Origin: Greek
Meaning simply 'lovely flower'.

Eve
Diminutives: Evie
Origin: Hebrew
From the Hebrew Havvah, from
hayyah, which means 'living', this
name has always been popular
with Christians because of its
biblical associations with Adam.
It has been in use among English
speakers since at least the
Middle Ages and has remained
popular, rising in frequency since
the 1960s.
See also **Eva**, **Eveleen**, **Evelyn**

Eveleen
Variants: Eibhlin (Gaelic)
Origin: Gaelic
Meaning simply 'pleasant'.

Evelyn m/f
Diminutives: Evie, **Eve**.
Variants: Evaline, Eibhlin, Evalina
Origin: English
Possibly influenced by **Eve**
and **Lynn** in the nineteenth
century and likely influenced by
the French Aveline. Since its
peak in the 1920s, it has
suffered a decline. Famous
bearers of the name include
Scottish percussionist Evelyn
Glennie.

Evette
See **Yvonne**

Evonne
See **Yvonne**

Fabia
Origin: Latin
Derived from the Roman Fabius, from the Latin *faba*, meaning 'bean', this name has never been in frequent use since its adoption by English speakers in the nineteenth century. Actress Fabia Drake was one notable bearer of the name.

Fahari
Origin: Swahili
Meaning 'splendour'.

Fahimah
Origin: Arabic
A Muslim name meaning 'intelligent' or 'discerning'.

Faith
Diminutives: Faithie, Fay
Origin: English
Popular among English Puritans in the seventeenth century, this was originally a gender-neutral name, but has since been used exclusively for girls. Unlike other 'virtue' names, Faith has remained common.

Faiza
Origin: Arabic
Meaning 'victorious'.

Faline
Origin: Latin
Meaning 'cat-like'.

Fallon
Origin: Gaelic
Meaning 'the grandchild of the ruler'.

Fanny
Diminutives: Fan
Variants: Fannie
Origin: English
Originally a derivative of such names as Euphemia, Frances, and Myfanwy, this has since been used as a name in its own right, though it is less popular today than it once was due to some unfortunate connections. A notable bearer of the name includes Fanny Price, the heroine of Jane Austen's novel *Mansfield Park*.

Farah
Variants: Farrah
Origin: Middle English
Meaning 'beautiful'.

Farica
Origin: Teutonic
Meaning 'peaceful rule'.
See also Frederica

Farideh
Origin: Persian
Meaning 'glorious'.

Fariha
Origin: Arabic
Meaning 'happy'.

Farran m/f
Variants: Faren
Origin: Old English
Meaning simply 'traveller'.

Fatima
Variants: Fatma
Origin: Arabic
Derived from the Arabic word *fatima*, which means 'abstaining', or 'weaning', often translated as meaning 'motherly' or 'chaste'. A favourite daughter of Mohammed was named Fatima in the seventh century and has long been popular among Muslims because of its implication of chastity and being a 'good woman'. Many British know the name through the athlete Fatima Whitbread.

Faustine
Variants: Faustina (rare)
Origin: Latin
This French name is derived from the Latin *faustus*, meaning 'fortunate'.

Fawn
Origin: English
Seems to derive from a combination of such names as Fay and Dawn, or from the ordinary vocabulary word. It first appeared in the nineteenth century and is still in use, but it is quite rare.

Fay

Variants: Fae, Faye
Origin: English
From the traditional word for 'fairy', also used as a diminutive of **Faith**. Instances of the name appeared early; Morgan le Fay was King Arthur's treacherous sister. It was not until the nineteenth century that it was used widely as a first name, but it still remains rare.

Fayola

Origin: Nigerian
Meaing 'lucky'.

Fayre

Origin: Old English
Meaning simply 'beautiful'.

Fe

Origin: Spanish
The Spanish word for 'faith'.
See also **Faith**

Feige

Variants: Fayge
Origin: Yiddish
The Yiddish *Feygl*, meaning 'bird', is the origin of this name

Felicity

Diminutives: Flick, Lis, Lissie, Lucky, **Lecia**
Variants: Felicia (rare)
Origin: Latin
From the Latin word meaning 'good fortune' or 'luck' and often used as a feminine form of **Felix**. A 'virtue' name, it was popular among Puritans in the seventeenth century and enjoyed a peak in the 1980s and 1990s. One famous bearer of the name is actress Felicity Kendall.

Fenella

Diminutives: Nella, Nola, **Nuala**
Variants: Finella, Finola, **Fionola**
Origin: Irish
From the Irish Gaelic *fionn* ('white' or 'pure') and *guala* ('shoulder'). In the nineteenth century, it became popular when Sir Walter Scott's novel *Peril of the Peak* contained a character called Fenella. Actress Fenella Fielding is one famous bearer of the name.

Fenia

Origin: Scandinavian
The name of a giantess in Scandinavian mythology.

Feodora

See **Theodora**

Fern

Origin: English
Derived from the name of the plant, *fearn* in Old English. It seems likely it was coined as a name in the nineteenth century, when it was fashionable to use the names of plants and flowers as names, but it has never been common. One notable bearer of the name is TV presenter Fern Britton.

Fernanda

Origin: German
'Born with an adventurous spirit'.

Fia

Origin: Italian
The meaning of this name, 'flame', may suggest a fiery spirit.

Fiala

Origin: Czech
Meaning 'violet flower'.

Fidelity

Variants: Fidelitee
Origin: Latin
Meaning 'faithful' and 'true', this name is self-explanatory.

Fifi

Origin: French from Hebrew or Old Norse (depending on the root name).
A diminutive of such names as **Josephine** and **Yvonne**, this name is rarely used for girls since it gained popularity as a name for poodles.

Filippa

See **Philippa**

Filomena
See **Philomena**

Finette
Origin: Hebrew
Meaning 'little addition'.

Finlay m/f
Diminutives: Fin
Variants: Finley, Findlay
Origin: Gaelic
Derived from the Gaelic Fionnlagh, formed from *fionn* ('fair', 'white') and *laogh* ('warrior').

Finna
Origin: Celtic
Meaning simply 'white', with its inherent suggestion of purity.

Finola
See **Fenella**

Ffion
Variants: Fion
Origin: Welsh
The Welsh name for a foxglove and used in poetry to describe the cheek of a beautiful girl.

Fiona
Diminutives: Fi
Variants: Fina, Triona
Origin: Gaelic
Derived from the Scottish Gaelic *fionn*, meaning 'white', thought to have first been used by James Macpherson in his Ossian poems in the eighteenth century. A well-known bearer of the name is actress Fiona Shaw.

Fiora
Origin: Irish
From the Gaelic, meaing 'pale and fair'.

Flavia
Diminutives: Flave, Flavie
Origin: Latin
From the Latin *flavus*, which means 'golden' or 'yellow' comes this Roman name that has been in use among English speakers since at least the sixteenth century.

Fleur
Diminutives: Fleurette
Origin: French
Meaning simply 'flower' in French, the early twentieth century saw English speakers start using this as a first name for girls, though its recorded use in France dates back to the Middle Ages.
See also **Flora**

Flo
See **Florence**

Floella
Diminutives: Flo
Origin: English
Likely to have derived from combinations of such names as **Flora** and **Ella**, this name seems to have first appeared in the 1950s, and a famous bearer of the name is TV presenter Floella Benjamin.

Flora
Diminutives: **Flo**, Florrie, Floss
Variants: Florinda, Floretta
Origin: Latin
From the Latin for 'flower' or 'blossoming' (*flos*), this was used by English speakers from the eighteenth century. A famous bearer of the name was Flora (Fionnaghal) Macdonald, who helped Bonnie Prince Charlie to escape after the Battle of Culloden in 1746.

Floramaria
Origin: Italian
Meaning 'flower of Mary', this is a literal combination of **Flora** and **Maria**.

Florence
Diminutives: **Flo**, Florrie, Flossie, Floy
Variants: Florenz (German), Floris (Dutch)
Origin: Latin
From the Latin *florens*, which means 'blossoming' or 'flourishing', this was a name

for girls and boys alike in medieval times; its peak was the nineteenth century but it has since suffered a decline.

Florian m/f
Origin: Latin
From the Latin *flos*, meaning 'flower' or 'blossoming'; the name is derived from the Roman Florius.

Florimel
Diminutives: Flo
Origin: Greek
The Greek word for 'nectar', suggesting a honey-sweet nature.

Fonda
Origin: English
Meaning 'affectionate'.

Fossetta
Origin: French
Meaning simply 'dimpled'.

Frances
Diminutives: Fran, Francie, Frankie
Variants: Francine
Origin: Latin
First used by English speakers in the seventeenth century, this name enjoyed a peak in the nineteenth, but has gone into decline since then.
See also **Francesca**

Francesca
Diminutives: Fran, Franny
Variants: Franziska (German), Francisca (Spanish)
Origin: Latin
From the Latin for 'Frenchman', this has been in infrequent use among English speakers since the mid-twentieth century.

Francine
See **Frances**

Freda
Origin: Old German
Developed as a diminutive of such names as **Frederica** and **Winifred**, often also treated as a feminine equivalent of **Frederick**.

Frederica
See **Frederick**

Freya
Variants: Freja
Origin: Old Norse or German
Named for the Norse goddess of love, but is also believed to come from the German *Frau* ('woman'). Since the nineteenth century, it has been in use among English speakers, mainly popular in Scotland and the Shetland Isles.

Frieda
See **Frederick**

Fritzi
See **Frederica**

Fuchsia
Origin: German
Named after the flower. A famous bearer of the name was Lady Fuchsia in Mervyn Peake's *Gormenghast* trilogy.

Gabby
See **Gabrielle**

Gabinia
Origin: Latin
The name of a famous Roman family from central Italy.

Gabrielle
Diminutives: Gaby, **Gabby**
Origin: Latin
Meaning 'woman of God'.

Gaerwen
Origin: Welsh
Meaning 'white castle'.

Gael
See **Abigail**

Gaia
Variants: Gaea
Origin: Greek
Derived from the Greek *ge*, meaning 'Earth', this is the name of the Earth Goddess and gave its name to the Gaia Theory.

Gail
See **Abigail**

Gala
See **Galina**

Galane
Variants: Galliane
Origin: French
The French name of *Chelone obliqua*, a flower native to the US.

Galia
Origin: Hebrew
Meaning 'God has redeemed'.

Galilah
Origin: Hebrew
Named for a place in Galilee.

Galina
Diminutives: Gala
Origin: Russian
May derive from the Greek *galene* which means 'calm'.

Ganya
Variants: Ganyah
Origin: Hebrew
Meaning 'garden'.

Gardenia
Origin: Latin
Named after the genus of flowers.

Gauri
Variants: Gowri
Origin: Sanskrit
An Indian name from the Sanskrit meaning 'white', implying purity.
The wife of Shiva was named Gauri.
See also **Kamala**

Gavra
Origin: Hebrew
Meaning 'God is my rock'.

Gay
Variants: Gaye
Origin: French
From the French, meaning 'cheerful', this became popular among English speakers in the 1930s, originally in the USA, but went into a sudden decline in the 1960s when it came to be used as a slang word for homosexual men.

Gayle
See **Gail**

Gaynor
Variants: Gaenor
Origin: Welsh
Derived from **Guinevere** in medieval times.

Gemma
Diminutives: Gem
Variants: **Jemma**
Origin: Italian
From the Italian for 'jewel' or 'gem', this has become a relatively common name, possibly under the influence of **Emma**, and it reached a peak in popularity from the 1960s to the 1980s.

Gene m/f
Origin: Greek
Developed as a variant of **Eugenia**, this name was

especially popular in the USA during the first half of the twentieth century. One famous bearer of the name is actress Gene Tierney.

Geneva
Origin: English
This may simply be derived from the name of the Swiss city, but could also have developed from **Genevieve** or **Jennifer**.

Genevieve
Diminutives: Ginny, Gina, Veva
Variants: Genoveffa, Ginevra
Origin: Old German
From the Old German *geno* ('people' or 'race') and *wefa* ('woman' or 'wife'), interpreted as meaning 'lady of the people'. After being established in France, English speakers adopted it in the nineteenth century and it became popular after the release of the film of the same name in 1953.

Genista
Origin: Latin
Derived from the Latin *genista*, the plant also known as broom, the name was introduced to English speakers by the Plantagenet (*planta genista*), whose founder Geoffrey Plantagenet would wear a sprig of broom into battle.

Genoveffa
See **Genevieve**

Georgette
See **Georgina**

Georgia
See **Georgina**

Georgiana
See **Georgina**

Georgina
Diminutives: Gina, Georgie, George
Variants: Georgene, Georgiana, Georgine
Origin: English (from Greek via Latin) One of the most common feminie versions of **George**, taking precedence over Georgiana and now popular throughout the English-speaking world and beyond, although Georgia is more popular in the USA.

Geraldine
Diminutives: Gerrie, Gerry
Origin: Old German
First used as a feminine form of **Gerald**, from the Old German *ger* ('spear') and *wald* ('rule'). Records of the use of this as a first name go back as far as the sixteenth century and enjoyed a peak in popularity in the 1950s. Famous bearers of the name have included actress Geraldine McEwan.

Gerlinde
Origin: Old German
From the Old German *ger* ('spear') and *lind* ('soft' or 'weak').

Germaine
Variants: Jermaine
Origin: Roman
From the Roman name Germanus ('brother'), this name came into use among English speakers in the early part of the twentieth century.

Gerry m/f
Variants: Gerrie, Jerry
Origin: Old German
First used as a diminutive of such names as **Geraldine**, now often considered to be a name in its own right.

Gertrude
Diminutives: Gert, Gertie, Trudy
Variants: Gertrud (German)
Origin: Old German
From the Old German *ger* ('spear') and *traut* ('strength') and was taken up as a name among English speakers in medieval times, but then its popularity waned until the nineteenth century when it was revived.

Ghada
Origin: Arabic
Meaning 'graceful lady'.

Ghadir
Origin: Arabic
Meaning 'stream' or 'brook'.

Ghislaine
Diminutives: Gigi
Variants: Ghislane, Ghislain
Origin: Old German
Developed as a variant of **Giselle**, this name has appeared among English speakers on an irregular basis since the 1920s.

Ghufran
Origin: Arabic
Meaning 'forgiveness'.

Giacinta
See **Hyacinth**

Gianna
Diminutives: Gia
Origin: Italian
Meaning 'God is gracious'.

Gigi
Origin: French
Meaning 'girl from the farm'; also a feminine form of **George**.

Gilah
Variants: Gila
Origin: Hebrew
Meaning 'joy'.

Gilbertine
See **Gilbert**

Gilda
Origin: Irish
Meaning 'servant of God'.

Gillian
Diminutives: Gill, Gilly, Gillie
Variants: Jillian
Origin: English
Thought to be either an elaboration of Jill or as a feminine version of Julian; also thought to be derived from the Scottish Gaelic for 'servant of St John'.

Gina
See **Georgina**

Ginette
See **Genevieve**

Ginny
See **Virginia**

Giselle
Variants: Gisela (Dutch)
Origin: Old German
From the Old German *gisil*, meaning 'pledge'. Possibly came about as a name in medieval times via the practice of handing over children as a promise or pledge. Long popular in France, it was not until the nineteenth century that it made its way to English speakers.
See also **Ghislaine**

Gita
Variants: Geeta
Origin: Sanskrit
An Indian name form the Sanskrit word for 'song'.
See also **Bridget**

Gitana
Variants: Gipsy
Origin: Spanish
From the Spanish word for 'gypsy'.
See also **Gypsy**

Gladys
Diminutives: Glad, Gladdie
Variants: Gwladys
Origin: Welsh
Possibly from the Welsh *gwledig*, which means 'princess' or 'ruler over territory'.

Glenda
Diminutives: Glen
Origin: Welsh
From the Welsh *glan* ('holy', clean') and *da* ('good'). English speakers outside Wales took up the name in the 1930s but was never common. Actress and politician Glenda Jackson is perhaps the most famous bearer of the name.

Glenn m/f
Variants: Glen, Glenna (rare)
Origin: Gaelic
From the Gaelic *gleann* ('valley'), at the end of the nineteenth

century, it was taken as a name for boys before being used for girls in the 1940s. Sometimes treated as a diminutive of **Glenda** or **Glenys**. Actress Glenn Close is one famous bearer of the name.

Glenys
Diminutives: Glen, **Glenn**
Variants: Glenis, Glenice
Origin: Welsh
This has been used by English speakers since the 1940s and may have started as a combination of such names as **Gladys** and **Glenda**.

Gloria
Variants: Glory
Origin: Latin
From the Latin *gloria*, this name was taken up at the beginning of the twentieth century and is

thought to have first appeared in the George Bernard Shaw play *You Never Can Tell*. Singer Gloria Gaynor and TV presenter Gloria Hunniford are two famous bearers of the name.

Glynis
Variants: Glynn
Origin: Welsh
Thought to have developed from *glyn* ('valley'), possibly due to influence from such names as **Glen** and **Gwyn**.

Godiva
Origin: Old English
From the Old English *god* ('god') and *gyfu* ('gift'), the name is linked with Lady Godiva, who famously rode naked through the streets of Coventry. It has made only infrequent appearances since then.

Golda
Variants: Golde, **Goldie**
Origin: Yiddish
A Jewish name derived from a Yiddish nickname meaning 'gold'.

Goldie
Origin: English
This name has uncertain origins, but probably derives from the ordinary vocabulary word 'gold'; it may have been taken from the

surname or used as a name or nickname for anyone with blond hair. Perhaps the most famous bearer of the name is actress Goldie Hawn.

Goretti
Origin: Italian
A tribute to St Maria Goretti, who forgave her own murderer before she died.

Gormlaith
Variants: Gormla, Gormelia
Origin: Gaelic
From the Gaelic *gorm* ('illustrious') and *flaith* ('lady').

Grace
Origin: English
From the vocabulary word 'grace', this was popular among Puritans in the seventeenth century but suffered a decline in the eighteenth, reviving in the nineteenth century. It enjoyed a peak in the 1990s.

Grainne
Variants: Grania, Granya, Grace (anglicism)
Origin: Irish
Arguably deriving variously from the Gaelic for 'grain' (*gran*), 'disgust' (*grain*) or 'love' (*graidhne*). In Irish legend Grainne was the tragic daughter of King Cormac.

Greer
Variants: Grear, Greir
Origin: Latin
A Scottish name derived from the Latin Gregor (*see* **Gregory**), this has been a first name since the Middle Ages.

Greta
Origin: Greek
Originally a diminutive of Margareta (*see* **Margaret**).

Gretchen
See **Margaret**

Griselda
Diminutives: Grizzle, **Zelda**
Variants: Grizel, Grizzel (Scottish)
Origin: Old German
From *gris* ('grey') and *hild* ('battle'), so can be interpreted as meaning 'grey warrior'. It has become very rare since its popularity in the Middle Ages.
See also **Zelda**

Gudrun
Origin: German and Scandinavian
Meaning 'wily in battle', this name has made only occasional appearances among English speakers since the nineteenth century.

Guenevere or Guinevere
See **Jennifer**

Gunnhild
Variants: Gunhild, Gunhilda
Origin: Old Norse
This has always been rare among English speakers but has been popular among Scandinavians since Viking times.

Gwenda
Diminutives: Gwen **Origin**: Welsh
From the Welsh *gwen* ('white', 'fair') and *da* ('good'), this name was not taken up by English speakers until the twentieth century.

Gwendolyn
Diminutives: Gwen, Gwenda
Variants: Gwendolin(e), Gwendolen, Guendolen
Origin: Welsh
From the Welsh *gwen* ('white', 'fair') and *dolen* ('ring' or 'bow'), this is often interpreted as referring to the moon (a 'white circle'). The wives of legendary Welsh King Locrine and Arthurian sorcerer Merlin bore this name.

Gwenfrewi
See **Winifred**

Gwenhwyfar
See **Jennifer**

Gwenllian
Origin: Welsh
Confined mostly to Wales, this comes from the Welsh *gwen* ('white') and *lliant* ('flow', 'flood') and means 'foamy white' and is taken to refer to a pale complexion.

Gwyneth
Diminutives: Gwen
Variants: Gwenyth, Gwynedd, Gweneth
Origin: Welsh
From *gwynaeth*, meaning 'happiness' or 'luck', this name travelled from Wales in the nineteenth century and has remained in use in the UK since, though it is rare outside the UK.

Gypsy
Variants: Gipsy
Origin: English
This was taken up as a name in the nineteenth century, not only by gypsies but also by people attracted by the romanticism of the idea. A famous bearer of the name was actress Gypsy Rose Lee.

Gytha
Variants: Githa
Origin: Old English or Norse
From the Old English *gyth* ('strife') or the Norse *guthr* ('war'), either way suggesting hardship and adversity. Records of its use go back to before 1066; revived in the nineteenth century, but has been rare since.

Hadara
Origin: Hebrew
Meaning 'beautiful ornament'.

Hadassah
Diminutives: Dassah
Origin: Hebrew
In the Bible as an alternative form of **Esther**, this is still found among modern Jews in its ancient Hebrew form.

Hadil
Origin: Arabic
Meaning 'cooing', this name can be traced back to the time of Noah as the name of a bird which went extinct when it was killed by a hawk.

Hadley m/f
Origin: English
Meaning simply 'heathery hill'.

Hafsa
Variants: Hafza
Origin: Uncertain, probably Arabic
An Arabic name which is usually translated to mean 'motherliness', this was the name of one of the wives of Mohammed.

Hafwen
Variants: Hafwyn
Origin: Welsh
Meaning 'summer'.

Haidee
Variants: Haydee, Haydie
Origin: Greek
Meaning 'modesty'.

Hala
Variants: Halah
Origin: Arabic
From the Arabic, meaning 'the aura around the moon'.

Halcyon
Variants: Halcyone
Origin: Greek
From Greek mythology, in which Halcyon was saved from drowning herself by Aphrodite.

Halfrida
Diminutives: Frida, Freida, Hallie
Variants: Halfrieda
Origin: Teutonic
Meaning 'peaceful heroine', someone who uses diplomacy rather than war. *See also* **Freda**

Halima
Origin: Arabic
Meaning 'kind' and 'humane'.

Halla
Origin: African
Meaning 'an unexpected gift'.

Halle
Origin: Uncertain
An English name, possibly derived from the Scandinavian names Halsten and Halvard. The most famous bearer of the name in recent times is actress Halle Berry, who was reputedly named after Halle Brothers, a US department store.

Hallie
Variants: Halette, Halley, Hali
Origin: Greek
Meaning 'thinking of the sea'.
See also **Halfrida**

Hanan
Variants: Hani, Haniyya
Origin: Arabic
From the Arabic, meaning 'tenderness'.

Hanele
Variants: Hanaleh
Origin: Hebrew
Meaning 'full of compassion'.

Hannah
Diminutives: Han, Hannie, Nancy
Variants: Hanna
Origin: Hebrew
Meaning 'grace' or 'favour'; can be interpreted as meaning 'God has favoured me'. The name of the mother of **Samuel** in the Bible, it was popular among English Puritans in the seventeenth century and

remained common until the last years of the nineteenth century, but then suffered a decline until it enjoyed a surge in the 1970s. *See also* **Anna**

Hanu
Origin: Hawaiian
Meaning 'the breath of the spirit'.

Haralda
Variants: Haraldine, Harolda, Haroldina
Origin: Norse
A feminine form of Harold.

Harika
Origin: Turkish
Meaning 'the most beautiful'.

Harley m/f
Origin: English
A surname that was used as a first name for boys in the nineteenth century and which has since been extended to girls. Possibly meaning 'from the clearing of the army'.

Harlinne
Variants: Harlene, Harleen
Origin: English
Meaning is said to come from the clearing of the army.

Harmony
Variants: Harmonie, Harmonia

Origin: Greek
From Greek via Latin, meaning 'unity' or 'concord'. This is relatively recent name, coming into use in English in the twentieth century and has so far remained quite rare. *See also* **Melody**

Harriet
Diminutives: Hattie, Harrie, Harry
Variants: Harriett, Harrietta
Origin: Old German
First developed as a feminine equivalent of Harry in the seventeenth century and remained popular until the early twentieth, when it suffered a sharp decline until its revival in the 1990s. Famous bearers of the name have included novelist Harriet Beecher Stowe.
See also **Henrietta**

Hasana
Origin: Swahili
Meaning 'the first born of female twins'.

Hasna
Variants: Hasnah
Origin: Arabic
Meaning simply 'beautiful'.

Hatsu
Origin: Japanese
Meaning 'first born'.

Hattie
See **Henrietta**

Haven
Variants: Heaven
Origin: English
From the ordinary vocabulary word 'haven', meaning 'sanctuary'.

Hayden m/f
Origin: English
Meaning 'a hedged valley'.

Hayley
Variants: Haley, Hailey, Haylie
Origin: Old English
From the place name Halley, from the Old English *heg* ('hay') and *leah* ('clearing').

Hazel
Diminutives: Haze
Origin: English
Derives from the name of the tree, but also refers to the colour of a person's eyes; taken up as a first name in the late nineteenth century as part of the trend for naming children after plants and flowers. Fell into decline after its peak in the 1930s.

Heather
Diminutives: Hev, Hevs
Origin: English
From the name of the plant, this name was taken up in the

nineteenth century, especially in Scotland, where the plant grows in abundance. Enjoyed a peak in the middle of the twentieth century but has since suffered a decline.

Hebe
Origin: Greek
From the Greek *hebos*, meaning 'young', this appeared among English speakers at the tail end of the nineteenth century. Hebe was a daughter of Zeus and was revered as a cupbearer to the gods and a goddess of youth.

Hedda
Variants: Edda (Italian)
Origin: German
From the German name Hedwig, itself from the Old German *hadu*, meaning 'struggle' or 'contention', and *wig* ('war'). The name has made occasional appearances among English speakers since the nineteenth century and a well-known bearer of the name was actress Hedda Hopper (Elda Flurry).

Hedia
Origin: Greek
Meaning 'pleasing'.

Hedva
Origin: Greek
Meaning 'an industrious worker'.

Heera
Origin: Sanskrit
Meaning 'diamond'.

Heidi
Variants: Haidee
Origin: Swiss
From the Swiss Adelheit, this name was popular among English speakers in the 1960s as a consequence of the successful TV series *Heidi*.
See also **Hilda**

Helanna
Origin: American
A combination of **Helen** ('bright') and **Anna** ('graceful', 'merciful').

Helen
Variants: **Eileen, Eleanor, Ella, Ilona, Nell,** Helena and more
Origin: Greek
Possibly from the Greek *helios*, meaning 'sun', therefore translating as 'shining one' or 'bright one'. Usually associated with Helen of Troy, the name was in use among English speakers as early as the sixteenth century. Notable bearers of the name include actress Helen Mirren and singer Helen Shapiro.

Helga
Variants: Hella
Origin: Old Norse

From the Old Norse *heill*, meaning 'hearty', though it has since been interpreted as meaning 'holy' or 'blessed'.
See also **Olga**

Helia
Origin: Greek
From the Greek word for 'sun'.

Helianthe
Origin: Greek
Meaning 'sunflower' or 'bright flower'.

Helice
Variants: Helixa
Origin: Greek
Meaning 'spiral'.

Heloise
See **Louise**

Helsa
Origin: Scandinavian
See **Elizabeth**

Henrietta
Diminutives: Etty, Etta, Hennie, **Hattie,** Netty, **Minette**
Variants: Henriette (French)
Origin: Old German
Charles I's French wife Henriette-Marie made the name popular among English speakers in the seventeenth century. Overtaken by **Harriet**, it enjoyed a resurgence at the end of the nineteenth

century, but suffered a further slump in the twentieth century.

Henrika
Variants: Henrike
Origin: German
A feminine form of Henry.

Hera
Origin: Greek
Meaning 'lady', Hera was the queen of the Greek gods and is linked with marriages.

Hermia
Variants: Hermina, Hermine, Herminia
Origin: Greek
Meaning 'a messenger'.

Hermione
Origin: Greek
From Hermes, the Greek messenger of the gods, possibly derived originally form the Greek for 'stone'.The daughter of Menelaus and Helen was named Hermione and it was taken up by English speakers in medieval times.

Hernanda
Origin: Spanish
Meaning 'adventurous life'.

Hero
Origin: Greek
The name of the lover of Leander,

also famous as the heroine of Shakespeare's comedy *Much Ado About Nothing*. The name has never enjoyed popularity among English speakers, however, and remains obscure.

Herta
See Eartha

Hesba
Origin: Greek
From the Greek *hespera*, meaning 'western', this has been an uncommon name since its first appearance in the nineteenth century.

Hester
See Esther

Hestia
Origin: Greek
Meaning 'star'.

Hetta
See Hedda

Hilary m/f
Diminutives: Hil, Hilly, Hils
Variants: Hillary, Ilar (Welsh)
Origin: Latin
From the Latin *hilaris*, meaning 'cheerful', which lent itself to the Roman Hilarius, from which we get Hilary. In medieval times, it was taken up mainly as a name for

boys subsequently fell into decline. It was revived in the nineteenth century as a name for both sexes.

Hilda
Variants: Hylda, Hilde (German)
Origin: Old German
From *hild*, meaning 'battle', developed initially as a diminutive of such names as Hildegard. Taken up as a first name in medieval times, it was less frequent by the Tudor era. In the early twentieth century, it enjoyed a revival but has since become rare.

Hilma *See* Wilhelmina

Hina
Origin: Hebrew
Meaning 'a female deer'.

Hirkani
Origin: Indian
Meaning 'like a diamond'.

Hollis
Origin: English
Meaning 'of the holly grove'.

Holly
Origin: English
Developed either from the vocabulary word 'holy' or else taken from the name of the tree. By the latter half of the nineteenth century, the name

was in use on both sides of the Atlantic and, towards the end of the twentieth century, it enjoyed a peak in popularity. A famous bearer of the name is actress Holly Hunter.

Honesty
Origin: Latin
From the ordinary vocabulary word 'honesty', this name is pretty self-explanatory.

Honey
Origin: English
From the vocabulary word 'honey', perhaps also developed as a diminutive of Honoria (see Honor). Use of the name was popular after the release of Margaret Mitchell's *Gone With the Wind*.

Honi
Origin: Hebrew
Meaning 'gracious'.

Honor
Diminutives: Nora
Variants: Honora Annora, Honora, Honorine
Origin: Latin
Either from the vocabulary word 'honour' or from the Roman name Honoria. Records of the name among English speakers date back as far as 1066.

Famous bearers of the name include actress Honor Blackman.

Hope
Origin: English
One of the 'virtue' names popular with English Puritans in the seventeenth century; also from the Old English word *hope*, meaning 'enclosed valley'. The name is now more popular in the USA than anywhere else.

Hortense
Variants: Hortensia
Origin: Roman, probably from the Latin
Likely from the Latin *hortus*, meaning 'garden' via the Roman Hortensia, this has been in use among English speakers since the nineteenth century but has never been very common.

Hosanna m/f
Variants: Hosannah
Origin: Hebrew
From the Hebrew meaning 'save now' or 'save pray', its biblical associations meant it was taken up as a name as far back as the thirteenth century and was used for both sexes. From the seventeenth century, it has been reserved largely for girls.

Howin
Origin: Chinese
Meaning 'loyal swallow'.

Hulda
Origin: German
Meaning 'loved one'.

Humayra
Origin: Muslim
Given by the Prophet Mohammed to his wife Aisha, the name's actual meaning is unclear.

Huriyah
Origin: Arabic
Meaning 'virgin of paradise'.

Hyacinth
Diminutives: Hy, Sinty (Ireland)
Variants: Hyacintha, Jacinta, Jacinth
Origin: Roman legend
A youth accidentally killed by Apollo in Roman legend, this name was once used for boys, but since its use among English speakers in the nineteenth century as part of the fashion for using the names of plants and flowers, it has been regarded as exclusively for girls.

Hyone
Origin: Greek
Meaning 'a dream from the sea'.

Hypacia
Origin: Greek
Meaning 'highest'.

Ianira
Origin: Greek
Meaning 'enchantress'.

Ianthe
Variants: Iantha, Ianthina, Janthina, Janthine
Origin: Greek
Meaning 'a violet-coloured flower'.

Icasia
Origin: Greek
Meaning simply 'happy'.

Ida
Origin: Uncertain
Either from the Old Norse legend of the goddess Iduna or from the Old German *id* ('work' or 'labour') or *itis* ('woman'). Could have links with Mount Ida in Crete and in Ireland. It could also be said to derive from *ita* ('thirsty'). The name came to England with the Normans but, after the fourteenth century, it became rare.

Idalia
Origin: Spanish
Meaning 'of a sunny disposition'.

Idell
Variants: Idella
Origin: English
Meaning 'prosperous'.

Idonea
Origin: Nordic
Meaning 'renewal', suggesting new birth.

Idoya
Origin: Spanish/Basque
In tribute to the Basque Virgin of Idoia. Idoia is a place name, meaning 'pool' or 'pond'.

Iduna
Variants: Idonia, Idonie
Origin: Norse
Meaning 'lover'; alternatively, it can be said to mean 'the keeper of the golden apples of youth'.

Ierne
Origin: Latin
Meaning 'person from Ireland'.

Igraine
Origin: Irish
From the Gaelic meaning 'full of grace'.

Ilana
Origin: Hebrew
From the Hebrew, meaning 'tree', therefore perhaps suggesting long life.

Ilka
Origin: Slavic
Meaning 'flattering'.

Ilona
See **Helen**

Ilsa
See **Elizabeth**

Imala
Origin: Native American
Meaning 'determined'.

Iman
Origin: Arabic
From the Arabic, meaning 'faith' or 'belief'. Perhaps the most famous bearer of the name is supermodel Iman, who is married to rock star David Bowie.

Imara
Origin: Hungarian
Meaning 'great ruler'.

Imelda
Origin: Old German
From the Old German name Irmhilde, from *irmin* or *ermin* ('entire' or 'whole') and *hild*, meaning 'battle', can be translated as 'all-conquering'; initially popular among Roman Catholics as a tribute to St Imelda Lambertini, it has made occasional appearances among English speakers, principally in Ireland, during the twentieth century. Famous bearers of the name include politician Imelda

Marcos and actress Imelda Staunton.

Imke
Origin: Old German
A German name that evolved as a diminutive of Imma, itself a form of **Irma**.

Imogen
Diminutives: Immy
Origin: Latin or Gaelic
This appears to be a printing error, when the original name Innogen, taken either from the Latin *innocens* ('innocent') or the Irish Gaelic *inghean* ('maiden', 'girl' or 'daughter'). It is likely the error was made during the first printing of Shakespeare's play *Cymbeline*, when the 'nn' was replaced with 'm', becoming Imogen. A well-known bearer of the name is actress Imogen Stubbs.

Ina
Origin: Celtic
Originally a variant of **Ena**, but also used as a diminutive of such names as **Georgina** and **Edwina**. Used by English speakers in the nineteenth century, but has since become rare. *See also* **Agnes**

Inari
Origin: Finnish
Meaning 'from the lake'.

Inaya
Origin: Arabic
Meaning 'taking care'.

Indrajeet
Origin: Sanskrit
This Indian name means 'conqueror of the god Indra'.
See also **Inderjit**

India
Origin: English
Most likely to be taken as a name due to interest in Indian culture, which reached a peak in the 1970s, but could also be partly down to a character in Margaret Mitchell's bestselling novel *Gone With the Wind*.

Indiana m/f
Origin: English
A fairly recent name that came into use either as a variant of **India** or named directly for the US state of Indiana. In the early twentieth century, it was used exclusively for girls, but since the *Indiana Jones* films were released in the 1980s, it has also been acceptable for boys.

Indigo
Origin: Latin
Named after the colour.

Indira
Origin: Sanskrit
Indian name from the Sanskrit meaning 'splendour' or 'beauty'. Famous bearers of the name have included Indian Prime Minister Indira Gandhi.

Inez
See **Agnes**

Inge
Variants: Inja
Origin: Scandinavian
Meaning 'a person protected by Ing, the goddess of peace'; other sources say Ing is the name of a Norse fertility god.
See also **Ingrid**

Inger
See **Ingrid**

Ingrid
Diminutives: Inga, **Inge**, **Inger**
Origin: Scandinavian
Derived from Ing (goddess of peace, or fertility god, depending on the source) and *frithr* ('beautiful') or *rida* ('to ride'). A few English speakers used the name in the thirteenth century, but was taken up more widely in the mid-nineteenth century.

Iniga
Variants: Ignatia

Origin: Latin
Meaning 'fiery ardour'.

Innes m/f
Origin: Scottish
This name developed first as an anglicization of Aonghas or Aonghus (*see* Angus).

Inola
Origin: Native American
This name comes from the Cherokee word for 'fox', suggesting wiliness and cunning.

Ioanna
Origin: Greek
Meaning 'grace'.

Iola
Variants: Iole
Origin: Greek
Meaning 'the colour of the clouds at dawn'.

Iolanthe
Origin: Greek
Meaning 'violet flower', this name was one of those of a fashion popular at the end of the nineteenth century based on flowers and plants.
See also Yolanda and Violet

Iona
Origin: Scottish or Greek

An English name developed from the Scottish Iona, named for the island, which was originally called Ioua ('yew-tree island'), possibly changed to Iona through a misspelling; alternatively, from the Greek *ion*, meaning 'violet'.

Irene
Diminutives: Rene, Renie
Variants: Irena, Irina (Russian)
Origin: Greek
From the Greek *eirene*, meaning 'peace', it was taken up as a name by English speakers around the end of the nineteenth century and enjoyed a peak in the 1920s, but is now uncommon.

Iris
Origin: Possibly Greek
Common across western E urope after the name of the flower, though possibly inspired by the Greek goddess of the rainbow. Part of the late Victorian fashion for naming children after flowers and plants, this name became less common after the 1930s.

Irma
Variants: Erma
Origin: Old German
From the Old German *ermen*,

meaning 'whole', the name was used occasionally among English speakers towards the end of the nineteenth century. Initially a diminutive of German names beginning with the prefix Irm-, it was popular in the USA for a time, but the twentieth century saw its gradual decline.

Irvette
Variants: Irvetta
Origin: English
Meaning 'sea friend'.

Isa m/f
Origin: Old German
Meaning 'lady of iron will', suggesting determination. From Old German *isan*, meaning 'iron'. Also a diminutive form of Isabel.

Isabel
Diminutives: Isa, Izzy, Ib, Bella
Variants: Isobel, Ysobel, Ishbel
Origin: Hebrew
Used by English speakers as early as the medieval period, this is a Spanish equivalent of Elizabeth, and was among the most popular names during the thirteenth and fourteenth centuries. Revived in the nineteenth century but went into decline in the twentieth.

I

Isabella
Diminutives: Izzy, **Bella**
Origin: Hebrew
This Italian equivalent of **Elizabeth**, made occasional appearances among English speakers as early as the twelfth century and continued to be popular, particularly in Scotland, until the twentieth century.

Isadora
Diminutives: Issy, Izzy, **Dora**
Variants: Isidora
Origin: English
First developed as a feminine version of Isidore and made its first appearances in the nineteenth century. The most famous bearer of the name so far has been dancer Isadora Duncan.

Iseult
See **Isolda**

Isha
See **Aisha**

Ishana
Origin: Hindi
Meaning 'desire'.
Ishbel
See **Isabel**

Isibeal
Origin: Irish
See **Elizabeth**

Isis
Origin: Egyptian
Named for the goddess of the same name.

Isla
Origin: Scottish
This name apparently dates only as far back as the 1930s, named for the Scottish island of Islay, though also considered a diminutive form of **Isabella**. A well-known bearer of the name is folk singer and TV presenter Isla St Clair.

Ismat m/f
Origin: Arabic
From the Arabic *isma*, meaning 'infallibility' or 'safeguarding', suggesting protection and strength.

Ismay
Origin: Uncertain
Records of the use of this name go back as far as the thirteenth century and it is sometimes linked with **Esme**.

Ismene
Origin: Greek
The name's meaning is unknown but is usually linked to the Oedipus myth as the name of the daughter of Oedipus and Jocasta. Since the nineteenth century, this name has made only occasional appearances.

Isolde
Variants: Isolda, **Ysolde**, **Essylt** (Welsh)
Origin: Celtic or Old German
From Iseult or Yseult, from the Celtic for 'beautiful' or 'fair'. Alternatively, from the Old German Isvald, from the words for 'ice' and 'rule'. A famous bearer of the name appears in the tale of *Tristan and Isolde*.

Italia
Origin: Italian
The Italian word for 'Italy'.

Ivana
Diminutives: Iva
Variants: Ivanna
Origin: Slavic
Meaning 'God is gracious'.

Iverna
Origin: Latin
An old name for Ireland.

Ivonne
See **Yvonne**

Ivory
Origin: Uncertain
Either from the Welsh for 'high-born lady' or straight from the vocabulary word 'ivory'.

Ivy
Origin: English
Towards the end of the nineteenth century, it became fashionable to name children after plants and flowers, and this name developed as a result. Since its peak in the 1920s, it has fallen from favour.

Ixia
Origin: Greek
From the Greek for 'mistletoe'.

Izora
Origin: Arabic
Meaning simply 'dawn'.
See also **Dawn**

Izzy
See **Isabel**, **Isadora**

Jacinda
Variants: Jacinta, Yacinda
Origins: Greek
Meaning simply 'beautiful'.
See also **Hyacinth**

Jackie
See **Jacqueline**, **Hyacinth**

Jacqueline
Diminutives: **Jackie**, **Jacqui**
Variants: Jaclyn, Jacaline, Jaqueline, Jackelyn
Origin: Latin
A diminutive of Jacques, the French equivalent of **James**,

records exist of its use as early as the thirteenth century, but it was only during the middle of the twentieth century that it became popular.

Jacquetta
Variants: Jacquenetta (historical, to describe a country wench)
Origin: Latin
Used by English speakers since medieval times, it was popular in the twentieth century.

Jade
Origin: Spanish
From the stone, the name of which came from the Spanish *pietra de ijada*, meaning 'stone of the bowels', due to its supposed magical effect on intestinal disorders. Taken as a name among English speakers in the late nineteenth century, it became popular again after rock star Mick Jagger chose the name for his daughter.

Jaden m/f
Variants: Jaydn, Jaiden
Origin: English, from Spanish
A more elaborate variant of **Jade**.

Jagoda
Origin: Slavonic
This name means 'strawberry'.

Jaime m/f
Variants: Jaimee, Jaimey, Jaymee
Origin: Biblical or French
Sources differ as to the meaning and origin of this name. Related to **James**, it is biblical; however, as French, it simply means 'I love'.

Jaimica
Origin: Spanish
The feminine of **James** (disciple of Jesus) and **Jacob** (supplanter).

Jakinda
See **Hyacinth**

Jala
Variants: Jalah
Origin: Arabic
The meaning of this name is disputed.

Jalaya
Origin: Sanskrit
Meaning 'lotus blossom'.

Jalila
Origin: Arabic
Meaning simply 'great'.

Jan m/f
Variants: Janna
Origin: English, from various other names.
Developed as a diminutive of several different names, including **Janet**, **Janice** and **Janine**, or names such as **Jane** or **Jean**.

Janaki
Origin: Sanskrit
An Indian name from the Sanskrit *janaka*, which means 'a descendent of Janaka').

Jancis
Origin: English
A name that combines such names as Jane and Frances or Cicely (*see* Cecilia). First appearing in the 1920s, possibly invented by Mary Webb for her novel *Precious Bane*. One famous bearer of the name is wine expert Jancis Robinson.

Jane
Diminutives: Janie, Janey, Jaynie
Variants: Jayna, Jayne, Janice, Shena, Yoanna
Origin: Hebrew
This name is derived – via the Old French Jehane (ultimately from Johannes) and the Greek Iōannēs – from the Hebrew Yochanan, meaning 'Yahweh [God] is merciful'. It is thus the feminine form of John. In use by English speakers by the sixteenth century, it gradually became more popular than such names as Jean and Joan. In nineteenth-century fiction, it was often used as the name for housemaids and returned to mainstream use in the twentieth century.
See also Janet, Janice, Sian, Siobhan

Janet
Origin: English, from Latin or French
Originally a diminutive of Jane, this name was popular from medieval times but then fell into decline, except in Scotland, until the nineteenth century. Since the 1950s and 1960s, it has been in another decline.

Janice
Diminutives: Jan
Variants: Janis
Origin: English, from Latin or French
Originally a diminutive form of Jane, this may have first been recorded in the novel by Paul Leicester Ford, *Janice Meredith*. After that, it became popular but has since suffered a decline.

Janine
Diminutives: Jan
Variants: Jannine, Janene, Janina (rare)
Origin: French, from the Hebrew
Originally used as an anglicized version of Jeanine, itself from the masculine name Jean. Alternatively, meaning 'God is gracious'. The 1930s and 1960s were peaks of popularity for the name.

Jannali
Origin: Australian
The aboriginal word for the moon, this is also a place near Sydney.

Janthina
Origin: Greek
A violet-coloured flower.

Jarah
Variants: Jara
Origin: Hebrew
Meaning 'honey'.

Jarita
Origin: Sanskrit
A Hindi name meaning 'a famous bird'.

Jarmila
Origin: Slavic Meaning 'spring'.

Jasmine
Variants: Jasmin, Yasmine, Jessamine, Jessamyn
Origin: Persian
From the flower of the same name, ultimately from the Persian *yasmin*, adopted by English speakers in Victorian times in keeping with the fashion of the time of using flowers and plants as names. The name is now less frequent.

Jaspreet
Variants: Jasprit
Origin: Punjabi
Meaning 'virtuous'.

Jaswinder
Origin: Sanskrit
From the Sanskrit *jasu* 'thunderbolt') and Indra, the name of a god, thus interpreted as 'Indra of the thunderbolt'.

Jawahir
Origin: Arabic
Meaning 'jewels'.

Jay m/f
Diminutives:
Variants: Jaye, Jai
Origin: English
The name evolved as a diminutive of such names as Jane, though it has been assumed that it is a tribute to the bird. As a first name for boys, it was in use in the nineteenth century, though it has also been said that in medieval times it was used as a nickname for anyone who talked a lot. The twentieth century saw the name first being used for girls.

Jaya
Origin: Indian
Developed as a feminine equivalent of Jai or Jay.

Jaye See Jay

Jaylo
Variants: J. Lo, Jalo, J-Lo
Origin: American
After the shortened name of the singer Jennifer Lopez.

Jean
Origin: Latin or French
From the same root as Jane, by which the name has been eclipsed since its peak in the 1930s.

Jeanie
See Jeanette

Jeannette
Diminutives: Jeanie, Jinty, Netta, Nettie
Variants: Jennet, Genette
Origin: French
First developed as a diminutive of the French Jeanne, its use was recorded in Scotland long before it was taken up as a name among English speakers in the twentieth century.

Jemima
Diminutives: Jem, Jemmy, Mima
Origin: Hebrew
A biblical name from the Hebrew meaning Yemimah, though it is unclear whether this means 'wild dove' or 'bright as day'. It has remained popular since English Puritans took up the name in the seventeenth century.

Jemma
See Gemma

Jena
Variants: Jenna, Genna
Origin: Arabic
Meaning 'small bird'.

Jennifer
Diminutives: Jenny, Jenni, Jen
Variants: Jenifer
Origin: English
Originally developed as a variant of the Cornish Guinevere and was established as a name in the eighteenth century, but did not become common until the twentieth. A famous bearer of the name is comedienne Jennifer Saunders.
See also Gaynor

Jera
Origin: Old English
From *jera*, which was the Old English word for 'year'.

Jerarda
Origin: Old German
The feminine form of Gerard.

Jerusha
Variants: Jerushah
Origin: Hebrew
Meaning 'the married one'.

Jeryl
Origin: English
Meaning 'spear ruler'.

Jesca
Variants: Jescah
Origin: Hebrew
Meaning 'God sees'.

Jessamine
See **Jasmine**

Jessica
Diminutives: Jess, Jessie
Origin: English
This name appears to have been an invention by Shakespeare for the name of Shylock's daughter in *The Merchant of Venice* and thus has associations with Jews. It seems to have been based on **Jesca** or Iscah. Famous bearers of the name include actress Jessica Lange.

Jethetha
Origin: Hebrew
Meaning simply 'princess'.

Jetta
Variants: Jette, Jettie
Origin: Danish
Meaning 'coal black'.

Jewel
Origin: Latin
Meaning 'most precious one'; named for the stones used for decoration.

Jill or Jillian
See **Gillian**

Jimena
Origin: Spanish
Meaning 'heard', it is unclear why this was used as a first name, but perhaps it has religious undertones, suggesting a prayer has been heard.

Jinan m/f
Origin: Arabic
Meaning 'paradise' or simply 'garden', this is a common name in Middle Eastern countries.

Jinx
Variants: Jynx
Origin: Latin
Given to a girl who is so beautiful she can enchant people.

Joakima
Variants: Joachima
Origin: Hebrew
Meaning 'the Lord's judge'.

Joan
Origin: Latin
First name derived from Johannes, records of this name go back to the Middle Ages. It was imported from France as Jhone or Johan and the modern spelling dates back to the fourteenth century. Between the sixteenth and nineteenth centuries, the name fell into decline and was overtaken by such names as **Jane**. It enjoyed a revival in the 1920s and 1930s, possibly due to the canonization of Joan of Arc in 1920. Perhaps the most famous modern bearer of the name is actress Joan Collins.

Joanna
Diminutives: Jo
Origin: Latin
An English variant of **Joan** derived from the Latin from the Greek Ionna and as a feminine version of **John**. Until the eighteenth century, it was usually spelt Johanna, and after the eighteenth century, it began to replace **Joan** as the dominant form of the name. Famous bearers of the name include actress Joanna Lumley and novelist Joanna Trollope.

Joanne
Diminutives: Jo
Variants: Jo-Anne, Jo Anne
Origin: Old French

Another feminine equivalent of **John**, this name derived from the Old French, as opposed to **Joanna**, which derived from the Latin. In the 1970s, it enjoyed a peak in popularity, but has since fallen into decline. A famous bearer of the name is actress Joanne Whalley-Kilmer.

Jocelyn m/f
Diminutives: Jos, Joss
Variants: Jocelin, Joselin, Joselyn
Origin: Disputed
From the Old Norman Joscelin, this was taken up as a name by English speakers. The Norman name itself may have come from the name of a Germanic tribe, the *Gauts* or *Gautelen* ('little Goths'). Other sources say it comes from the Breton Jedoc or the Old German Josse.

Joci
Origin: Latin
Meaning 'happy'.

Jocosa
See **Joyce**

Jocunda
Origin: Latin
Meaning 'full of happiness'.

Jody m/f
Variants: Jodi, Jodie
Origin: English

Once used as a name for both boys and girls, the name derived as a diminutive of such names as **Josephine**, **Judith**, **George** and **Jude**. In the 1950s, it was taken as a girls' name, being especially popular in the USA and Canada. Actress Jodie Foster is a famous bearer of the name.

Joelle
See **Joel**

Joely
See **Jolie**

Jofrid
Origin: Teutonic
Meaning 'a lover of horses'.

Joie
Origin: French
Meaning 'joy', 'happiness'.

Jolene
Variants: Joleen
Origin: Disputed, but likely Middle English
Meaning 'He will increase'.
Or a contraction of **Joanna** and **Darlene**, or Jo and **Marlene**. Many people know the name from the Dolly Parton song 'Jolene'.

Jolie
Diminutives:
Variants: **Joely**, Joly, Jolee

Origin: English
This name evolved as a variant of such names as **Julia**. It appears to be a twentieth-century invention.

Joni
Diminutives: Jo
Origin: Latin
Developed as a variant of **Joan**, this name was taken up in its own right in the 1950s, particularly popular in the USA and Canada. The most famous bearer of the name is probably singer-songwriter Joni Mitchell.

Jonquil
Origin: English
Part of the Victorian fashion for using plant and flower names as names for children, this one was less popular and reached its peak in the 1940s and 1950s, since when its use has declined.

Jora
Variants: Jorah
Origin: Hebrew
Meaning 'autumn rain'.

Jordan m/f
Diminutives: Judd
Variants: Jordyn
Origin: Hebrew
From the name of the river in the Holy Land, which came from the

Hebrew *hayarden*, which means 'flowing down'. Brought to England by the Crusaders, though it was originally given only to boys who had been baptized in the river Jordan. Since its revival in the nineteenth century, it has been used as a name for girls as well, and in 2001 it stood in the top thirty names. Model Katie Price took the moniker Jordan, which gave it another boost.

Jordana
See Jordan

Josephine
Diminutives: Josie, Josette, Posy
Variants: Josepha, Josephina
Origin: Hebrew
With its roots in the Hebrew Yoseph, this name seems to have been first used among English speakers around the middle of the nineteenth century. Famous for being the name of Napoleon's wife.
See also Joseph

Jovanna
Origin: Serbian
The feminine form of Jovan, meaning 'God is gracious'.

Joy
Diminutives:
Variants: Joye, Joie, Joya

Origin: French
Derived from the vocabulary word 'joy' and as a diminutive of Joyce, this was in use as early as the twelfth century and was popular among Puritans in the seventeenth century. Though irregular, it has remained in use, with a small increase in popularity around the mid-twentieth century. A well-known bearer of the name was naturalist Joy Adamson.

Joyce
Origin: Disputed
As with Jocelyn, this may have been an anglicization of the Norman French Josce or the Breton Jodoc, meaning 'lord', though these days, it is more commonly lined with the vocabulary words 'joy' or 'rejoice'. The name originally came to England with the Norman invasion, it vanished in the fourteenth century, reappeared in the seventeenth and was common in the nineteenth. Since the 1920s, its use has declined.

Juanita
See Juan

Jubilee
Origin: Probably Hebrew
Meaning 'horn of a ram'. Alternatively, it is perhaps used simply as the ordinary vocabulary word, especially if a baby is born around the occasion of a jubilee.

Judith
Diminutives: Judy
Variants: Yehudi
Origin: Hebrew
Biblical, from the Hebrew Yehudith, meaning either a woman from Judea or a Jewish woman. The name was borne by the niece of William the Conqueror, but did not appear frequently until the seventeenth century. Shakespeare's second daughter was named Judith. It is sometimes encountered as an anglicization of the Irish Siobhan.

Jula
Origin: Zimbabwean
Meaning simply 'depth'.

Jules m/f
See Julian, Julia, Julie

Julia
Diminutives: Jules
Variants: Julie
Origin: Roman
Evolved as a feminine form of Julius and was adopted by English speakers in the sixteenth century. In the second half of the twentieth century, it enjoyed a revival, especially in the 1960s,

but **Julie** has remained the more popular form of the name.

Juliana
Diminutives: Liana
Variants: Julianna, Julianne, Julie Ann
Origin: Roman
A feminine version of the masculine Julianus, records of this name go back as far as the twelfth century. The eighteenth century saw a resurgence but after the nineteenth it became rare.

Julie
Origin: French, from Roman
Taken up as a name around the end of the nineteenth century, it gradually became more common than **Julia** and remains popular to this day. Well-known bearers of

the name include actresses Julie Andrews and Julie Walters.

Juliet
Diminutives: Jules
Origin: Italian
From the Italian Giulietta, the name was promoted among English speakers by the popularity of Shakespeare's *Romeo and Juliet*. The name has been in regular use since, with the most recent peak being the 1960s.

Jun
Origin: Chinese
Meaning 'truthful'.

June
Origin: English
Named after the month, likely taken up as a name in the early

twentieth century, but became less frequent after the 1930s. Actress June Whitfield is one famous bearer of the name.

Juniper
Origin: Latin
It is not know what the Latin *juniperus* means. In the Bible, it is given as a translation of the Hebrew *rothem*, which is the name of a desert shrub. It gave its name to the bush, from which we get the first name, though it has never been common.

Justine
Diminutives: Justie, Justy
Origin: Latin
A feminine form of **Justin**, it developed from Justina, the name of a fourth-century martyr. In the nineteenth century, it was taken up by English speakers and enjoyed a peak in the 1970s. A well-known bearer of the name is singer and guitarist Justine Frischmann.

Jyoti
Origin: Sanskrit
An Indian name derived from the Sanskrit *jyotis*, meaning 'light', this was adopted as a first name quite recently and is sometimes also used as a name for boys.

Kabira
Origin: Arabic
Meaning 'powerful'.

Kachina
Origin: Native American
Meaning 'a sacred dance'.

Kady
Origin: Irish or Greek
Possibly derived from the Irish Gaelic *ceadach* ('first'), but could also have evolved as a diminutive of Katie (*see* Catherine).

Kaela
Variants: Kaelah, Kaylah, Keyla, Keylah
Origin: Hebrew
Meaning 'sweetheart'.

Kai m/f
Variants: Kaj
Origin: Sources vary
Possibly from the Hawaiian meaning 'sea', the name could also come from the Scandinavian name of uncertain meaning, possibly from Old Norse *katha* ('chicken') or Roman Caius.

Kailash m/f
Origin: Sanskrit
Indian, from the Sanskrit *kailasa*, but the meaning of this is uncertain. Shiva's paradise is known as Kailash.

Kaisa
Origin: Scandinavian
A Scandinavian name meaning 'pure'.

Kala
Variants: Kaela, Kaiala, Kaila
Origin: Sanskrit
Meaning 'black one' or 'dark one'. (*See* Kali, below.)

Kali
Origin: Hindi
Meaning 'the dark one', this is the name of a Hindu goddess.

Kalila
Variants: Kalilah
Origin: Arabic
Meaning simply 'loved'.

Kalinda
Origin: Hindi
Meaning 'of the sun'.

Kalista *See* Calista

Kalma
Origin: Teutonic
Meaning 'calm'.

Kalya
Origin: Sanskrit
Meaning 'healthy'.

Kama
Origin: Sanskrit
The Hindu god of love, similar to Cupid

Kamala
Origin: Sanskrit
This actually means 'deep red' but the name comes from the lotus flower. The name of Shiva's wife.
See also **Gauri**

Kamari
Origin: Swahili
Meaning 'like the moon'.

Kameko
Origin: Japanese
Meaning 'the child of a tortoise'; the tortoise is a Japanese symbol of longevity.

Kamila
Variants: Kamilah
Origin: Arabic
Meaning 'whole' and 'complete'.

Kana
Origin: Welsh
Meaning 'beautiful'.

Kanda
Origin: Native American
Meaning 'magical power', perhaps as a means of bestowing this power on the child.

Kane
Origin: Japanese
Meaning, curiously, 'ambidextrous'.

Kanisha
Variants: Quanisha
Origin: American
This name is derived from Tanisha, altered to the fashion for names beginning with 'k'.

Kanti
Origin: Sanskrit
An Indian name taken from the Sanskrit *kanti*, which means 'beauty', making the reasons for using this as a first name self-explanatory.

Kanya
Origin: Thai
Meaning 'young lady'.

Kareela
Origin: Australian
Meaning 'southern wind'.

Karen
Origin: Scandinavian
See **Catherine**

Karenza
Variants: Carenza
Origin: Gaelic
Meaning 'loving'. A well-known bearer of the name is Carenza Lewis, an archaeologist on TV's *Time Team*.

Karida
Variants: Karidah
Origin: Arabic
Meaning 'virginal'.

Karima
Variants: Karimah
Origin: Arabic Meaning 'noble'.

Karissa
Origin: Greek
Meaning 'dear', 'darling'.

Kasey
See **Casey**

Kate
See **Catherine**

Katherine
See **Catherine**

Kathleen
See **Catherine**

Katrina
See **Catriona**

Kaulana
Origin: Hawaiian
Meaning 'famous'.

Kay
See **Catherine**

Kayla
See **Kayleigh**

Kayleigh
Variants: Kayley, Kaleighy, Kayla, Kayly, **Keeley**
Origin: Irish
This is derived from the Irish O Caollaidhe (meaning a 'descendant of Caoladhe') and may have been made popular among English speakers due to combinations of such names as **Kelly**, **Kylie** and **Lee**. It was especially popular in the 1970s and 1980s.

Keanna
Origin: Hawaiian
Meaning 'cool breeze over the mountains'; the feminine version of **Keanu**. Alternative sources have suggested it comes from the German for 'bold' or the Irish for 'beautiful'.

Keeley
Origin: Irish
Probably derived from the Irish Keelin and **Kayleigh**. A well-known bearer of the name in recent times has been the actress Keeley Hawes.

Kei
Variants: Keikann, Keiana, Keionna

Origin: Japanese
Meaning 'reverent'.

Keighley
Origin: English
Pronounced 'keethly', this derives from the Yorkshire place name and was possibly originally an altered form of **Keeley**.

Keiko
Origin: Japanese
Meaning 'happy child'.

Keira
Variants: **Kiara**, Ciara
Origin: Irish

A form of Ciara, meaning 'small and dark'.

Keisha
Variants: Kesha
Origin: African-American
Meaning 'favourite'.

Keita
Origin: Scottish
Meaning 'from the woods'.

Kelda
Variants: **Kelly**
Origin: Norse
Meaning 'a bubbling spring'.

Kelly m/f
Variants: Kelley, Kellie
Origin: Irish
This name has been used for both sexes since the 1950s, adapted form the Irish form Ceallagh, which means 'strife', 'warlike' or 'war'. Actress Grace Kelly may have been an influence on its popularity, one reason, perhaps that it is now reserved almost exclusively for girls. *See also* **Kelda**

Kelsey m/f
Variants: **Kelsie**, Kelcey
Origin: Old English
From the Old English Ceolsige, from *ceol* ('ship') and *sige* ('victory'), suggesting a maritime or naval history for this name.

Kelsie
See **Chelsea**, **Kelsey**

Kendall m/f
Diminutives: Ken
Variants: Kendal, Kendell, Kendyll
Origin: English or Norse
From the town in Cumbria meaning 'valley of the river Kent', this was taken as a first name about halfway through the nineteenth century. Other sources claim it comes from the Old Norse *keld*, meaning 'spring' or from the Old Welsh

name Cynnddelw, of which the meaning is unknown. Other sources claim the name means 'ruler of the valley'.

Kennedy m/f
Origin: Irish
Taken from the Irish Cinneidigh, from *ceann* ('head') and *eidigh* ('ugly'), thus rendering it a little hard to understand why this has been used as a first name. Also as an anglicized version of the Scottish Gaelic Uarraig. It is mainly a boys' name, only occasionally bestowed on girls.

Kenya
Origin: African
From the country of the same name.

Kenzie
Origin: Scottish
Meaning 'fair-skinned'.

Keren
Origin: Hebrew
Meaning 'horn of antimony'.

Kerry m/f
Variants: Kerrie, Kerri, Keri, Ceri (Welsh)
Origin: Irish
Probably derived form the county of the same name, itself being the home of the 'descendants of Ciar'

or 'dark one'. It was taken as a first name for boys in the early twentieth century. It established itself as a boys' name in Australia before coming to be used as a girls' name among other English speakers, and it peaked in popularity between the 1960s and the 1980s.

Kesi
Origin: Swahili
Meaning someone who was born during hard times.

Kessi
Origin: Ashanti
Meaning simply 'chubby baby'.

Khadija
Variants: Khadiga, Khadijah, Khadeejah
Origin: Arabic
Meaning 'premature child', records of the name go back to pre-Islamic times and was the name of Mohammed's first wife, making it consistently popular up to the present day.

Kiah
Variants: Kia
Origin: African
Meaning 'season's beginning'.

Kiara
See **Keira**

Kiku
Origin: Japanese
Meaning 'chrysanthemum'.

Kim m/f
Diminutives: Kimmy, Kimmie
Variants: Kym
Origin: English
Originally a diminutive form of **Kimberley**, this name emerged as a name in its own right near the end of the nineteenth century, though it was mainly given as a name to boys.

Kimberley m/f
Diminutives: **Kim**
Variants: Kimberleigh, Kimberly (chiefly in USA and Canada)
Origin: English
Named for the South African town, itself named after John Wodehouse, 1st Earl of Kimberley. This ancestral home was named for the Old English, meaning 'Cyneburga's wood'. The name was a tribute to the army's relief of Kimberley from siege after the Boer War.

Kimi
Variants: Kimiko, Kimia
Origin: Japanese
Meaning 'righteous'.

Kina
Origin: Greek
Meaning 'Christian'.

Kiona
Origin: Native American
Meaning 'brown hills'.

Kira
Origin: Persian
Meaning 'the sun'.

Kirima
Origin: Eskimo
Meaning 'a hill'.

Kirsten
Diminutives: Kirby
Variants: Kirstin, Kirsty, Kirstyn
Origin: Norse
Meaning 'the anointed one'.
See also **Christine**

Kita
Origin: Japanese
Meaning simply 'north'.

Kitty
See **Catherine**, **Kathleen**

Kohana
Origin: Japanese
Meaning 'little flower'.

Koleyn
Origin: Australian
Meaning 'born in winter'.

Kolina
Origin: Swedish
See **Catherine**

Komala
Variants: Komal
Origin: Sanskrit
Meaning 'tender', 'charming'.

Koren
Origin: Greek
Meaning simply 'beautiful maiden'.

Krishna m/f
Variants: Kistna, Kishen, Kannan
Origin: Sanskrit
From the Sanskrit *krsna*, which means 'black' or 'dark', this is the name of the most revered of the Hindu gods. As such, it is a popular name for both girls and boys in India.

Krista
See **Christine**

Krystal
See **Crystal**

Kuki
Origin: Japanese
Meaning 'snow', suggesting purity.

Kumari
Origin: Sanskrit
A feminine form of the masculine **Kumar**, from the Sanskrit *kumara*, meaning 'boy' or 'son'. The feminine form is taken to mean 'warrior' or 'maiden'.

Kwai
Origin: Chinese
Meaning 'rose-scented'.

Kyle m/f
Origin: Gaelic
Taken from the surname based on the Ayrshire place name, derived from the Gaelic *caol* ('narrow'). In the 1940s, English speakers took it as a boys' name, but in the 1960s it was used as a girls' name and is often used as a diminutive of **Kylie**.

Kylie
Variants: Kyly, Kilie, Kyleigh
Origin: Scottish or Irish
Commonly believed to be taken from the Aboriginal word for 'boomerang', it is more likely that this name developed from names such as **Kyle** and **Kelly**. It became popular in the 1980s due to it being the name of then-soap star Kylie Minogue.

Kyna
Origin: Gaelic
Meaning 'great wisdom'.

Kyra
Variants: Kyria
Origin: Greek
Meaning 'female ruler'.

Lacey
Variants: Lacy (m)
Origin: Norman
This has made occasional appearances as a name since medieval times, named for Lassy in Calvados.

Lady
Origin: English
Some sources say this means 'bread kneader', but it is more likely to come from the vocabulary word 'lady', to suggest elegance and grace.

Lahela
Origin: Hawaiian
See Rachel

Laidh
Origin: Hebrew Meaning 'lioness'.

Laila
Variants: Leila, Leilah, Lela, Lila
Origin: Arabic
Meaning 'night', this probably refers to black or dark hair.

Lainey
Variants: Laine, Laney
Origin: French
Meaning 'bright light'.

Lani
Variants: Lanie
Origin: Hawaiian
Meaning 'sky'.

Laoise
Origin: Irish
From the Irish county of Laios.
See also Lucy

Lara
Origin: Greek or Latin
From the Russian Larissa, itself from either the Greek city ('citadel') or the Latin for 'cheerful' or 'famous'. This is also found as a diminutive of Laura. The name Lara became popular in the late 1960s and 1970s after the release of *Doctor Zhivago*.

Larissa
See Lara

Lata
Origin: Sanskrit
From the Sanskrit *lata*, which is the name of a creeping plant and because of this, it has come to be associated with curves and thus feminine beauty.

Latifa
Variants: Latifah
Origin: Arabic
Meaning 'gentle and pleasant'. Perhaps the most famous bearer of this name in recent years has been the actress, rapper and singer Queen Latifah.

Latoya
Origin: Spanish
Meaning 'victorious one'.
The name has become famous through Latoya Jackson, sister of Michael Jackson.

Laura
Diminutives: Lolly, Lorita, Lauretta
Variants: Lauri, Lowri, Lori, Lora
Origin: Latin
Meaning 'laurel' or 'bay', this name emerged among English speakers in the sixteenth century, enjoying peaks in popularity in the nineteenth century and in the 1960s.
See also Lauren

Laurel
Diminutives: Laurie
Variants: Laurelle
Origin: Latin
From the laurel tree, this name has become increasingly frequent since the mid-twentieth century.

Lauren
Variants: Loren (m, rare)
Origin: Latin
First developed as a diminutive of Laura, this name appeared with increasing frequency from the 1960s onwards, made famous by actress Lauren Bacall. It reached a peak in the 1990s.

What's My Name?

Lauretta
Diminutives: Laurie, Lorrie
Variants: Lorette, **Loretta**
(USA and Canada)
Origin: Latin
First developed as a diminutive
of **Laura**, it first appeared during
the Middle Ages, but did not
become common until the
nineteenth century.

Lavinia
Diminutives: Vinnie, Vinny
Variants: Lavina, Lavena
Origin: Roman
From the name of an ancient
Roman town, the meaning of which
has been lost. The legendary wife
of Aeneas, thus the mother of all
Rome, the name was popular
during the Renaissance but went
out of favour until the eighteenth
century.

Leah
Variants: Lea, **Lee**
Origin: Hebrew
The meaning of this name is

disputed, and is said to mean
'antelope', 'gazelle' or 'cow'.
Another derivation suggests it
means 'languid' or 'weary'. It
appears in the Bible as the name
of Jacob's first wife and was
subsequently popular with English
Puritans in the seventeenth
century. Nowadays, it is most
commonly used in Jewish
communities.

Leandra
Origin: American or Greek
Sources vary as to the origin of this
name: it could be a combination of
Leah and **Sandra**, or it could be

a feminine version of the Greek name **Leander**.

Leanne
Variants: Lianne, Leigh-Ann, Lee-Ann, Leanna
Origin: Uncertain
Either from the French Julianne or made of a combination of **Lee** and **Anne**. This name appeared among English speakers in the 1940s and has become popular in Australia. Since the 1960s, use of the name has increased.

Lecia
Origin: Latin
A pet form of Felicia, meaing 'lucky'. *See* **Felicity**

Lee m/f
Variants: **Leah**
Origin: English
From the Old English *leah*, meaning 'wood' or 'clearing'. A name for boys since the nineteenth century and for girls since the early twentieth.

Leela
Variants: **Lila**
Origin: Sanskrit
An Indian name from the Sanskrit *lila*, meaning 'play'. In its original spelling of **Lila**, it is usually interpreted as meaning 'love-play'.

Lei
Origin: Hawaiian
The Hawaiian word for a garland of flowers.

Leila
See **Laila**

Leilani
Variants: Lillani, Lullani
Origin: Hawaiian
Meaning 'heavenly blossom'

Lena
Variants: Lina, Leni
Origin: Various
Originally a diminutive of such names as Helena (*see* **Helen**), it was taken up for use as a name in its own right in the middle of the nineteenth century. A famous bearer of the name was singer and dancer Lena Zavaroni.

Lenora
Diminutives: **Nora**
Variants: Leanora, Leonora
Origin: Greek
Originally a variant of Eleanora via **Eleanor**, it first appeared in the nineteenth century.

Leontine
Variants: Leontyne
Origin: Latin
Originally taken as an English version of Léontine, itself from the Latin (*leo*, meaning 'lion') via the Italian Leontina. Alternatively, it could have come fom a combination of Leonora (*see* **Lenora**) and Clementine. It was in use as an English name by the nineteenth century.

Leslie m/f
Diminutives: Les
Variants: Lesley
Origin: Scottish, possibly from the Gaelic
Derived from Lesslyn, a place in Aberdeenshire, which may have got its name from the Gaelic *leas cuilinn* ('garden of hollies'). Its use as a first name was recorded in the eighteenth century, for which the Robert Burns poem 'Bonnie Lesley' may have been partly responsible. A famous bearer of the name is actress Leslie Ash.

Letitia
Diminutives: Lettie, Tish, Tisha
Variants: Leticia, Laetitia, Lecia
Origin: Latin
From the Latin *laetitia* ('joy' or 'gladness'), this name has been in use since medieval times, but the twentieth century saw the beginning of its gradual decline. A famous bearer of the name is actress Letitia Dean.

Lexia
Variants: Lexi, Lexie, Lexy
Origin: Greek
A pet form of **Alexandra**, meaning 'the defender of mankind'.

Lia
Origin: Various
A diminutive of such names as Rosalia (Italian), since the 1950s, this has also been found as a diminutive of names such as **Amelia** and **Delia**. Alternatively, Italian, from the Greek meaning 'bringer of the gospel'.

Liama
Origin: English
Meaning 'faithful guard'.

Liana
Variants: Lianna
Origin: Various, depending on the root name
A derivative of such names as **Juliana**, this spelling is rare among English speakers.

Libby
See **Elizabeth**

Liberty
Origin: Latin
From the Latin word for 'free'.

Liese
Variants: Liesel, Liesl

Origin: German
Meaning 'promised to God'.

Lila
Variants: Lilia
Origin: Arabic or Sanskrit
Meaning 'night'; Sanskrit, meaning 'full of life', 'playful'.
See also **Leela**

Lilith
Origin: Hebrew
This deeply biblical name has been interpreted in various ways: 'serpent', 'belonging to the night', 'screech owl', 'storm goddess' or 'night monster'. However, they are all seen as negative, because this was the name of Adam's first wife. This was not taken as a name until the twentieth century because of its negative connotations. Can also be used as a variant of **Lily**.

Lillian
Diminutives: Lil, **Lily**
Variants: Lilian, Lillias
Origin: Various
Thought to be a diminutive of **Elizabeth** or to be a combination of **Lily** and **Anne**. As Liliana, it had been known in Italy since the sixteenth century. After its peak in the late nineteenth century, it has been in decline since the 1920s.

Lily
Diminutives: Lil
Variants: Lillie, Lilly, Lilla, Lila
Origin: English
Named for the flower as part of the Victorian fashion for naming children after plants and flowers. The music hall song 'Lily of Laguna' helped promote the name at the end of the nineteenth century. Also found as a diminutive of **Elizabeth**.
See also **Lillian**

Linda
Diminutives: Lin, **Lynn**, Lindy
Variants: Lynda, Lenda
Origin: Uncertain
This name may have started out as a diminutive of **Belinda** and other names with the same ending. It could also be from the Spanish *linda*, meaning 'pretty', the Italian *linda*, meaning 'neat' or from the Old German *lindi* ('snake'). The name was popular in the 1950s and 1960s when it was one of the top five names in the English speaking world.

Linden
Variants: Lindon
Origin: Old English
Sometimes used as a variant of **Linda**, this is also the common name for the lime tree

(*linde* in Old English), so could count as a 'flower' name. *See also* Lyndon.

Lindsey m/f
Diminutives: Lin, Lyn
Variants: Lindsay, Linsay, Lynsey, Linzi
Origin: English
From the Lincolnshire place name Lindsey, meaning 'island of Lincoln' or 'wetland of Lincoln'. It was taken as a first name in the nineteenth century, initially for boys, but now mainly used as a girls' name and is rare among boys.

Linette
Variants: Lynette, Linnette
Origin: Welsh, French
Meaning 'idol' in Welsh or the name of a bird in French.

Liora
Variants: Liorah, Lior
Origin: Hebrew
Meaning 'I have light'.

Lisa
Diminutives: Liz, Lisette, Lysette
Variants: Liza, Leesa
Origin: Hebrew
Developed initially as a diminutive of Elizabeth, it emerged as a name in its own right in the 1960s. Famous bearers of the name include singer Lisa Stansfield.

Lisbeth
See Elizabeth

Lissa
See Melissa

Lissandra
Variants: Lisandra
Origin: Greek
Meaning 'defender of man'. *See also* Lysander

Liv
Origin: Nordic
From the Old Norse *hlif*, meaning 'protector' or 'defence'. The link with 'life' from *liv* is now also made. Featured in Norse legend, the name was revived in the nineteenth century. A well-known bearer of the name is actress Liv Tyler.

Livia
Diminutives: Livy, Livvy
Origin: Roman
Possibly from the Latin *lividus*, meaning 'blueish' or 'leaden-coloured'; also used as a shortened form of Olivia, itself made popular through Shakespeare's use of the name in *Twelfth Night*.

Liz
See Elizabeth

Llawela
Variants: Llawella
Origin: Welsh
Meaning 'like a ruler'.

Logan m/f
Origin: Scottish
Taken from the place in Ayrshire, the name may originally have come from the Gaelic word for 'hollow'. The name remains largely confined to Scotland and is occasionally used for girls, though mostly it is a boys' name.

Lois
Diminutives: Lo
Origin: Greek
From the Greek *loion*, meaning 'good' or 'better', this can also be found as a diminutive of Louise or Louisa. It was taken up by English speakers in the seventeenth century, as Lois was the name of Timothy's mother in the Bible. More frequent in North America than the UK, the 1920s were the name's heyday. A well-known beaer of the name is Lois Lane, the character from *Superman*.

Lola
Diminutives: Lolita
Variants: Lolicia

Origin: Spanish
First developed as a diminutive of **Dolores**, also found as a diminutive of Carlotta (*see* **Charlotte**). Long established in Spanish-speaking countries, it has been used occasionally by English speakers since the nineteenth century.

Lone
Origin: Danish
Developed as a diminutive of such names as Magdelone.

Lora
See **Laura**

Lorelei
Variants: Lorelia, Lorelie, Lorilyn, Lurleen
Origin: Teutonic
Meaning 'river siren', named after the maiden of the Rhine, who lured people to their deaths.

Loretta
See **Lauretta**

Lorna
Origin: English
This name was invented by novelist R.D. Blackmore for *Lorna Doone*, based on the Scottish place name Lorn, perhaps in order to bring to mind the Old English *lorn* ('forsaken', 'lost') and the Marquis of Lorne. The success of the book meant the name was hugely popular from that point on.

Lorraine
Diminutives: Lori, Lorri
Variants: Lauraine, Lorain, Lorayne
Origin: Various
Derived from a Scottish surname that may itself have derived from the French province of Lorraine, from the Latin Lotharingia ('land of the people of Lothar'). Often assumed to be a variant of **Laura**, was taken up in the nineteenth century, enjoyed a peak in the 1950s and 1960s but has since declined. A famous bearer of the name is actress Lorraine Chase.

Lottie
See **Charlotte**

Louisa
Diminutives: Lou, Louie
Variants: Louiza, Luisa
Origin: Old German
A feminine form of **Louis**, this was a popular name in the nineteenth century after its adoption in the eighteenth. Since the early twentieth century, it has been eclipsed by **Louise**. A notable bearer of the name was writer Louisa May Alcott.
See also **Lois**

Louise
Diminutives: Lou, Louie
Origin: Old German
Since the early twentieth century, the name has mostly eclipsed **Louisa**. Likely to have made its first appearance among English speakers in the seventeenth century, gave way to **Louisa** in the eighteenth century and re-emerged at the end of the nineteenth. Increased in popularity in the UK from the 1950s and reached a peak in the 1980s. A well-known bearer of the name was actress Louise Brooks.

Lourdes
Variants: Lurdes (Spanish)
Origin: French
A Spanish name taken from the famous French shrine, mainly used by Catholics and rarely found among English speakers.

Lowri
Variants: Lowry
Origin: Welsh
A regional variant of **Laura**, a well-known bearer of the name is TV presenter Lowri Turner.

Luanne
Diminutives: Lu
Variants: Luana, Luanna
Origin: Unclear
This name seems to be without meaning and is used in Italy and the UK. It appears to have been invented for the film *The Bird of Paradise* as the name of a Polynesian maiden.

Lubna
Origin: Arabic
From *lubna*, meaning 'storax tree'. Known from the legend of Lubna and Qays, a couple forced to divorce because they were childless.

Lucia
Diminutives: Luce
Variants: Lucina (Roman)
Origin: Latin
From the Latin *lux*, meaning 'light', which meant this name was possibly reserved for children who were born at dawn. Taken up by English speakers towards the end of the nineteenth century, often as an alternative to **Lucy**.

Lucille
See **Lucy**

Lucinda
See **Lucy**

Lucretia
Variants: Lucrece (French), Lucrezia (Italian)
Origin: Unknown
A Roman name developed as a feminine form of Lucius, but of unknown origin beyond this. Between the sixteenth and eighteenth centuries, the name appeared occasionally among English speakers, but because of its associations with Lucretia Borgia, believed to have been involved incestuously with her father and brother, it has never been common.

Lucy
Diminutives: Luce
Variants: **Laoise**, Lucie, Lucette
Origin: Latin
An English variant of **Lucia**, the name became popular in the eighteenth century in North America and in the UK, reaching peaks in both at the end of the nineteenth and twentieth centuries.

Luiseach
Origin: Irish
A feminine form of **Lugh**, which comes from the Irish Gaelic word for 'oath'.

Luna
Variants: Lunete
Origin: Latin
This is the name of the Roman moon goddess.

Lynn m/f
Variants: Lin, Lyn, Lynne
Origin: Various root names
Developed as a diminutive of such names as Lynda (*see* **Linda**) and **Lindsey**, it is used as a masculine name in Wales but rarely outside that country. It enjoyed a peak as a name for girls (how it is mostly used) in the 1950s and 1960s. A well-known bearer of the name is actress Lynn Redgrave.

Lyris
Variants: Lyra
Origin: Greek
Meaning 'she who plays the harp'.

Maaia
Origin: Maori Meaning 'courage'.

Mabel
Diminutives: Mab, Mabs
Variants: Mable, Mabelle (also from the French *ma belle*)
Origin: Old French
Derived from the Old French *amabel* or *amable* ('lovely' or 'loveable'); between the twelfth and fifteenth centuries, the name was common, was revived in the nineteenth century, but after a peak between 1870 and 1920, it suffered another decline.

Machiko
Origin: Japanese
Meaning 'beautiful woman'.

Mackenzie m/f
Origin: Scottish
Meaning literally 'son of Kenneth', this name is more frequently used for girls in Canada, where it is most closely associated, and is said to refer to the Mackenzie river.

Macy
Variants: Macey, Maci, Macie
Origin: French
Meaning 'Matthew's estate'.

Madeleine
Diminutives: Mad, Madge, Maddie, Maddy
Variants: Madolina, Madlyn
Origin: Hebrew
From the Hebrew name Magdalene, meaning 'of Magdala' (which is a town on the Sea of Galilee). Other versions of the name were imported from France in the thirteenth century when veneration of Mary Magdalene was at a peak. The nineteenth century saw the name become popular again and Madeleine has been the most common spelling since the start of the twentieth century.

Madhur
Origin: Sanskrit
An Indian name derived from the Sanskrit *madhura* ('sweet'), as a first name this is a relatively recent introduction. A well-known bearer of the name is cookery writer Madhur Jaffrey.

Madia
Variants: Madiah
Origin: Arabic
Meaning 'praiseworthy'.

Madison
Diminutives: Maddie, Maddy
Variants: Maddison
Origin: Hebrew or English
Either from Magdalen (*see* **Madeleine**) or meaning 'son of Maud'. Prevalent in the USA, where it has been popular since the early nineteenth century, via the country's fourth president, James Madison.

Maeve
Variants: Maev, Maeve, Meaveen, Medbh, Mab
Origin: Irish Maedhbh, possibly from the Gaelic *meadhbhan*, which means 'intoxication', suggesting the name means 'she who intoxicates'. Perhaps the most famous bearer of the name is novelist Maeve Binchy. Queen Mab was the queen of the fairies as described by Mercutio in Shakespeare's *Romeo and Juliet*.

Maggie
See **Margaret**

Mahala
Diminutives:
Variants: Mahalah, Mahali, Mahalia, Mehala
Origin: Hebrew
From the Hebrew, which is thought to mean 'tenderness' (though other sources say it is based on a musical term or on a word which means 'barren'. Appearing in the seventeenth century, it is now most common in the USA.

Mahina
Origin: Hawaiian
Meaning 'halo of the moon'.

Maia
Variants: Maja, Maya
Origin: Greek or Latin
Meaning 'nurse' or 'mother', Maia was the oldest and most beautiful of Atlas's daughters, and gave her name to the month of May. It could also be derived from the Sanskrit word meaning 'illusion'. Notable bearers of the name include writer and poet Maya Angelou.

Mairead
Origin: Irish
See Margaret

Maisie
Variants: Mysie
Origin: Greek
A diminutive form of the Scottish name Mairead, a Gaelic version of Margaret, this was fashionable among English speakers in the late nineteenth century and reached a peak in the 1920s, but declined after the 1930s.

Malina
See Malcolm

Mallika
Variants: Malika
Origin: Sanskrit
Meaning 'jasmine flower'. As Malika, it is Hungarian and means 'hard-working'.

Mallory m/f
Variants: Malory (f)
Origin: Norman
From a Norman French nickname meaning 'unlucky' or 'unhappiness', form *malheure*. Mostly used as a boys' name, it is occasionally used for girls. Many people will know it as the name of the female lead in the film *Natural Born Killers*.

Mandara
Origin: Hindi
Meaning simply 'calm'.

Mandy
See Amanda

Mani
Origin: Chinese
Meaning 'mantra'.

Manpreet
Origin: Punjabi
Meaning 'full of love'.

Mara
Variants: Marah
Origin: Hebrew
Meaning 'bitter', though often used as a variant of Mary, this has made infrequent appearances among English speakers since the seventeenth century. In the Bible,
Ruth's mother-in-law Naomi calls herself Mara in protest at being treated badly by God.

Marcella
Variants: Marcelina, Marcelle, Marsha, Marcy
Origin: Latin
Derived as a feminine form of Marcus.

Marcia
Variants: Marcy
Origin: Latin
Derived from the Latin as a feminine form of Marcus, which means 'warlike'.

Margaret
Diminutives: Madge, Maggie, Margy, Meg, Peggy
Variants: Margareta, Mairead, Margo, Marjorie
Origin: Greek
From the Greek *margaron* ('pearl'), the English and Scottish version of the Roman name Margarita could go back even further, to Hebrew or Persian roots. First taken up as a name in Scotland in the eleventh century, it made its way to other English speakers in medieval times. One of the most enduring of girls' names, though it has been in decline since the early twentieth century.

Margot
Variants: Margo, Margaux (rare)
Origin: Greek
Adapted from the French Marguerite, this appeared in medieval times but remained rare until the nineteenth century, when it increased in popularity. Famous bearers of the name include ballerina Dame Margot Fonteyne.

Maria
Diminutives: Mitzi, Ria
Variants: Marie, Mary, Mariah
Origin: Hebrew
The origin of Mary, this name can be traced back to its origins in the Hebrew Miryam. Taken up as a name in the sixteenth century and remained fashionable until the nineteenth century, but the English Mary has always been more popular. It is interesting to note that the pronunciation has altered over the years, from 'Mar-eye-a' to 'Mar-ee-a'.

Mariah
See Maria

Marian
Variants: Marianne, Marion (m)
Origin: Hebrew
Sometimes considered a combination of Marie and Ann, this is an English version of the French Marion. Use of the English version was popular in medieval times, in part due to the legend of Robin Hood and Maid Marian.

Marianne
Variants: Mariane, Maryanne, Mary-Anne, Mariana (sixteenth century), Marianna, Marian
Origin: Hebrew
Often used as a combination of Mary and Anne, it was taken up in the eighteenth century. A famous bearer of the name is Marianne, a character in Jane Austen's novel *Sense and Sensibility*.

Marie
Diminutives: Mimi
Variants: Maree, Mari
Origin: Hebrew, via Latin
The French version of Mary, this was initially taken up as a first name in the USA in the nineteenth century, and reached a peak in the 1960s and 1970s. Notable bearers of the name have included physicist Marie Curie.

Marika
Origin: Hebrew
A Slavonic variant of Maria, now recognized as a name in its own right.

Marilyn
Variants: Maralyn, Marolyn, Marylin, Merrilyn
Origin: Various
Based on a combination of **Mary** and **Ellen**, or simply **Mary** with –lyn as a suffix. A relatively recent name dating back only as far as the early twentieth century, but it was popular in the 1950s due to the high-profile actress Marilyn Monroe (Norma Jean Baker).

Marina
Diminutives: Rena
Origin: Latin or Roman (*see* **Marius**)
A feminine version of family name Marinus, this name has obvious associations with the sea. Records of its use go back to the fourteenth century, perhaps inspired by Greek martyr St Marina.
See also **Marni**

Marini
Origin: Swahili
Meaning 'healthy and pretty'.

Marjorie
Diminutives: Marje, Marge, Margy
Variants: Marjory, Marsali (Scottish Gaelic)
Origin: Greek
An English version of Marguerite (*see* **Margaret**), this has been regarded as a name in its own right since at least the thirteenth century, the earliest record going back to 1194 (as Margery or Margerie). The current spelling was adopted in Scotland in the late thirteenth century. The old spelling disappeared in the eighteenth century, only to be revived when the name became more popular again in the early twentieth.

Marlene
Diminutives: Marla, **Marley**
Variants: Marlena, Marleen
Origin: Biblical
A German diminutive form of Mary Magdalene, this was in use by English speakers by the 1930s on the back of the popularity of actress Marlene Dietrich.

Marley m/f
Origin: Old English
From the place name meaning 'pleasant wood', this is a surname as well as a first name. Its popularity in recent decades is undoubtedly a tribute to reggae star Bob Marley.

Marni
Variants: Marnie
Origin: Uncertain
Possibly derived as a variant of **Marina**, its promotion was helped by the Hitchcock film *Marnie*. Marnie Nixon provided the singing voice for Audrey Hepburn in *My Fair Lady*.
See also **Marina**

Marsha
See **Marcia**, **Marcella**

Marta
See **Martha**

Martha
Diminutives: Marti, Mattie
Variants: Marthe (French, German), **Marta** (Italian, Scandinavian)
Origin: Aramaic
From the word for 'lady' or 'mistress', this was the name of Lazarus's sister. Because of its biblical associations, it was popular with Puritans in the seventeenth century and in the USA it enjoyed a huge resurgence in the nineteenth century, in tribute to Martha Washington. Since the mid-twentieth century, its use has declined.

Martina
Diminutives: Marti
Variants: Martine
Origin: Roman
A feminine equivalent of **Martin**, first used by the Romans and

taken up by English speakers around the mid-nineteenth century. A famous bearer of the name is tennis star Martina Navratilova.

Mary

Diminutives: Mae, Molly, Minnie
Variants: Mara, Marie, Maire (Irish), Mairi (Scottish)
Origin: Hebrew
Ultimately believed to come from the Hebrew for 'to swell' or 'full/good', thus it has associations with motherhood and pregnancy, a claim that is backed up by its proximity to 'mother' in various languages. May have ancient Egyptian roots (meaning 'beloved of Amun', an Egyptian god). Its obvious biblical connection makes it popular among Christians. It was well-established by the twelfth century, then lost ground before becoming popular again in the eighteenth century. Since the 1920s, it has been eclipsed by Marie.

Matilda

Diminutives: Matty, Maud, Patty, Tilly
Variants: Mathilda
Origin: Old German
This name came to be used by English speakers via the Normans, as William the Conqueror's wife was named Matilda. From the Old German *macht* ('might') and *hiltja* ('battle'), its meaning is self-explanatory. After the Middle Ages, it lost ground but was revived in the eighteenth century until it fell from favour again in the early twentieth. A famous use of the name is the children's book *Matilda* by Roald Dahl.

Maud

Diminutives: Maudie
Variants: Maude
Origin: Old German
Originally a diminutive of Matilda, it has come to be seen as a name in its own right. In the nineteenth century, Alfred, Lord Tennyson helped revive the name through his poem 'Maud', though it is now seen as rather old-fashioned.

Maureen

Diminutives: Mo, Reenie
Variants: Maurene, Moreen
Origin: Hebrew
From the Irish Mairin, which is itself derived from Mary. It was taken up as a name towards the end of the nineteenth century and was especially popular in the 1930s, but it is now in decline except in Scotland and Ireland.

One famous bearer of the name is actress Maureen Lipman.

Mavis

Diminutives: Mave
Origin: Old French
Derived from the Old French word *mauvis*, meaning 'thrush', it made its appearance among English speakers around the end of the nineteenth century due to the popularity of the Marie Corelli novel *The Sorrows of Satan,* in which there was a character named Mavis Clare. Since its peak in the 1930s, it has suffered a decline.

Maxine

Diminutives: Maxie, Mickie
Variants: Maxene
Origin: Latin
Ultimately derived from the Latin *maximus* via the boys' name Max, the name began to emerge in the 1930s and remained popular until the 1960s, when it started to suffer a decline.

May

Variants: Mae
Origin: Various sources
A diminutive of Margaret or Mary and also treated as a name in its own right, named for the month or alternatively for the hawthorn or may blossom.

Maya *See* **Maia**

Meagan
Origin: Welsh
See **Margaret**

Meena
Origin: Sanskrit
This is an Indian name derived fm the Sanskrit *mina* ('fish'), this is the name of the daughter of Usha, goddess of the dawn, in Indian mythology.

Meg *See* **Margaret**

Mehri
Origin: Persian
Meaning 'kind'.

Melanie
Diminutives: Mel
Variants: Melany, Mellony
Origin: Greek
From the Greek *melas*, meaning 'black' or 'dark', this was a name reserved for children with dark hair or dark eyes. Records of its use go back to medieval times, though it did not become popular until the seventeenth century.

Even then, it was mainly confined to the south-western counties of England until the 1960s. Since then, it has become widespread among Engllish speakers generally. A famous bearer of the name is actress Melanie Griffith.

Melantha
Origin: Greek
Meaing 'dark flower'.

Melina
Origin: Greek
Meaning 'honey'; perhaps suggesting sweetness or the colour of a child's hair. Alternatively, it can be a diminutive of such names as **Emmeline** and **Melinda**.

Melinda
Diminutives: Mel
Variants: Malinda
Origin: Possibly Latin
It is thought perhaps this name derives from the Latin *mel*, meaning 'honey', but it is also a diminutive of such names as **Belinda**. A famous bearer of the name is model Melinda Messenger.

Melissa
Diminutives: Mel, **Missy**, Lissa
Origin: Greek
From *Melissa* ('bee') via *mel* ('honey'), this name has been in

use among English speakers since the sixteenth century. In the second half of the twentieth century, it became popular, especially in the USA and Australia.

Melody
Variants: Melodie
Origin: Greek
From the Greek *melodia* ('singing of songs') via the English 'melody', this name first appeared at the tail end of the eighteenth century and was especially popular in the 1920s. It enjoyed another resurgence in the 1950s.

Mercedes
Diminutives: Mercy, Sadie
Origin: Latin
Taken from the Spanish *merced*, meaning 'mercy', itself taken from the Latin *mercedes* ('ransom', 'wages'), the link being the sacrifice of Christ being seen as a ransom for the sins of humankind. Also linked to the Spanish reference to the Virgin Mary as *Maria de las Mercedes*, thus its popularity among Catholics, though people today assume it is linked more closely to the car manufacturer.

Mercia
Origin: Latin and English
From the Latin meaning

'merciful', also named for the ancient English kingdom of Mercia, itself from the Old English *merce*, meaning 'people of the borderland'.

Mercy
Diminutives: Merry,
Variants: Mercia (rare)
Origin: Latin
Sometimes treated as a diminutive of Mercedes, also named for the virtue thereby making it popular among Puritans in the seventeenth century, though it has since fallen from favour.

Meredith m/f
Diminutives: Merry
Variants: Meridith, Meridyth, Meredyth
Origin: Welsh
Based on the Welsh *mawredd* ('greatness') and *iudd* ('chief' or 'lord'), the name being Maredudd or Meredydd. Sometimes used as a masculine name, but it is far more common among women.

Meri
Origin: Finnish
Meaning 'from the sea'.

Merle m/f
Origin: Various sources
Often seen as a version of

the French *merle*, meaning 'blackbird', it could also be a diminutive of such names as Muriel and Meryl (itself a diminutive of Muriel).

Merry
Origin: Various
This name emerged as a diminutive of several other names, including Mary and Mercy. In the nineteenth century it began to gain ground, especially after the publication of *Martin Chuzzlewit* by Charles Dickens. More usually, it is found in the USA as a form of Mary, and the pronunciation is identical.

Meryl
See Muriel

Mesha
Origin: Hindi
Meaning someone born under the constellation of Aries.

Mia
Origin: Spanish or Italian
Most likely based on the Spanish or Italian *mia* ('mine'), this name is also used as a diminutive of Maria. A famous bearer of the name is actress Mia Farrow; it enjoyed a huge boost in 2001 after actress Kate Winslet chose the name for her daughter and it

entered the top thirty names for that year.

Michaela
See Michael

Michelle
Diminutives: Chelle, Shell
Variants: Micheline (rare)
Origin: Hebrew
From the French Michèle, a feminine form of Michael, the French name was adopted in the 1940s but was soon eclipsed by its anglicized spelling. Between 1950 and 1980, the name was popular, partly (after 1965) due to the popularity of the Beatles song 'Michelle'. A famous bearer of the name is actress Michelle Pfeiffer.

Mika
Variants: Micah
Origin: Hebrew
Meaning 'one who resembles God'.

Miki
Origin: Japanese
Meaning 'stem' (the reasoning for this name, given the meaning, is unclear).

Mildred
Diminutives: Millie, Milly
Origin: Old English
From the Old English Mildthryth, from *milde* ('mild') and *thryth*

('strength'). Revived in the seventeenth century and again in the nineteenth, in the USA it enjoyed a peak in the twentieth century, but the opposite happened in the UK.

Milena
Variants: Milana, Milada, Mladena
Origin: Czech
From *mil*, meaning 'grace' or 'favour', treated as a diminutive of Maria in Italy since 1900.

Miley
Origin: American
Meaning simply 'smiley', this name has been made famous in recent years by pop star Miley Cyrus.

Miliani
Origin: Hawaiian
Meaning 'gentle caress'.

Millicent
Diminutives: Millie, Milly
Variants: Melicent, Melisant
Origin: Old German
From the Old German Amaswint (*amal*, 'industry' and *swind*, 'strong'), meaning 'hard worker', via the French Mélisande. It travelled from France to England in the twelfth century (as Melisende or Melisenda), but fell from favour in the seventeenth century. In the

nineteenth century, it enjoyed a revival, but it is rare again today.

Mimi
Origin: Italian
Meaning 'bitter'.
See also Marie, Mary

Minette
Origin: French
Meaning 'faithful defender'; also a term of endearment for a kitten. Perhaps the most famous bearer of the name is crime writer Minette Walters.
See also Henrietta

Ming
Origin: Chinese
Meaning 'bright'.

Minnie
See Wilhelmina

Mione
Origin: Greek
Meaning 'small'.

Miranda
Diminutives: Mira, Mandy, Randy
Origin: Latin
From *mirari*, meaning 'to wonder at', so translated as 'adorable'. Shakespeare used the name in *The Tempest* and was thus taken up widely among English speakers. Since the nineteenth century, its

popularity has been increasing. Famous bearers of the name include actress Miranda Richardson.

Miren
Variants: Mirien
Origin: Hebrew
Meaning 'bitter'. The name derived from the same root as Mary.

Miri
Origin: Romany
Meaning 'mine' or 'of me', this name is also a diminutive of Miriam.

Miriam
Diminutives: Mitzi
Variants: Myriam, Mariam
Origin: Hebrew
From the original name Maryam (of uncertain meaning) and closely related to Mary, this name is usually translated as meaning 'to swell', 'good' or 'full'. Its original root may be Egyptian. Miriam was a biblical prophetess and the sister of Abraham and Moses. Always a favourite within Jewish communities, it was taken up by English speakers in the seventeenth century. Famous bearers of the name include actress Miriam Margolyes and TV presenter Miriam Stoppard.

Misaki
Origin: Japanese
Meaning 'beautiful blossom'.

Missy
See Melissa

Misty
Origin: English
Derived from the ordinary vocabulary word, it first appeared as a name in the 1970s, influenced by the 1971 film *Play Misty For Me*.

Mitzi
See Maria, Mary, Miriam

Modesty
Origin: Latin
Related to the Roman Modestus, this is another 'virtue' name; this one, however, did not emerge until the twentieth century.

Mohala
Origin: Hawaiian
Meaning 'flowers in bloom'.

Moira
Variants: Moyra
Origin: Hebrew
From the Irish Maire, itself from Mary. Since the nineteenth century the name has established itself among English speakers, particularly in Scotland. Notable

bearers of the name include newsreader Moira Stewart.

Molly
See Mary
Mona
Variants: Moyna
Origin: Irish
From Muadhnait, from the Gaelic *muadh*, meaning 'good' or 'noble', also found as a diminutive of Monica. Towards the end of the nineteenth century, it spread from Ireland into other English-speaking areas, at a time when Irish names were in fashion.

Monica
Diminutives: Mona, Monny
Variants: Monique (French)
Origin: Greek or Latin
It has been suggested this name can be traced to the Greek *monos* ('alone') or the Latin *monere* ('to advise' or 'warn'). Taken up by English speakers around the end of the nineteenth century, it decreased in popularity in the 1930s, though it has remained fairly steady since then.

Morag
Origin: Scottish
From the Gaelic *mor*, meaning 'large' or 'great', though it

has also been suggested it comes from the Gaelic word for 'sun'. Possibly a Scottish variant of **Mary** or **Sarah**. Predominantly Scottish, its use has increased throughout the twentieth century.

Morgan m/f
Variants: Morgana
Origin: Uncertain
From the Welsh Morcant, possibly from *mor* ('sea') and *cant* ('edge' or 'circle'), though this is not certain. Possibly meaning 'seabright', the name has a long history in Wales.

Morrighan
Origin: Irish

Named for the Irish goddess of warfare and death.

Moselle
Variants: Mosella, Mozel, Mozella
Origin: Hebrew
Meaning 'taken from the water'.
See also **Moses**

Muriel
Variants: Merrill, **Meryl**
Origin: Gaelic
From the Scottish and Irish Gaelic *muir*, meaning 'sea' and *gael* ('bright'). In use in England by around 1066, it increased in frequency in the nineteenth century and was especially popular in Scotland for centuries.

In the 1920s and 1930s it reached a peak, but has since gone into slow decline. A famous bearer of the name is writer Muriel Spark.

Myfanwy
Diminutives: Myfy, **Fanny**
Origin: Welsh
From *my* ('my dear') and *manwy*, meaning 'precious' or 'fine'; may alternatively have developed from *menyw* ('woman'). Little known before the twentieth century, it is largely confined to Wales and is best known to English speakers as the the name of a character in Dylan Thomas' *Under Milk Wood*, Myfanwy Price.

Myla
Origin: English. Meaning 'merciful'.

Mylene
Origin: GreekMeaning 'dark'.

Myrtle
Variants: Myrtill, Myrtilla, Mertle, Mirle
Origin: English
From the Victorian fashion for naming children after plants and flowers, its popularity has declined since the mid-twentieth century.

Myune
Origin: Australian
Meaning 'from the clear water'.

Naamah
Variants: Nama, Namah, Namana
Origin: Hebrew
Meaning 'beautiful' or 'pleasant'.

Nadia
Variants: Nadya, Nada, Nadine
Origin: Arabic or Russian
Either from the Arabic word for 'moist with dew' or from the diminutive of the Russian name Nadezhda, meaning 'hope'. Virtually unknown before the twentieth century, the Ballets Russes tours promoted Russian names in Europe, after which Nadia became popular in English- and French-speaking countries.

Nadine
Variants: Nadda, Nadeen
Origin: Russian
Meaning 'hope'.
See also **Nadia**

Nadira
Origin: Arabic
Meaning 'precious' or 'rare'.

Nafisa
Origin: Arabic
Meaning 'precious'.
See also **Nadira**

Nahida
Variants: Nahidah
Origin: Persian
Named for the Persian goddess of beauty and love.

Najila
Origin: Arabic
Meaning 'one with beautiful eyes'.

Nalani
Origin: Hawaiian
Meaning 'the calmness of the heavens'.

Nan
See **Ann**, **Anne**, **Nancy**, **Nanette**

Nancy
Diminutives: **Nan**, Nance
Variants: Nancie, Nanci, Nanny
Origin: English, from Hebrew
This probably developed as a diminutive form of **Ann** and was recognised as a name in its own right in the eighteenth century. In the mid-twentieth century, it became especially popular in the USA and Canada, though its recent links with the homosexual community has led to a severe decline. Charles Dickens used the name in his novel *Oliver Twist* and the first female MP in Britain was Nancy Astor.

Nanette
Origin: Hebrew
This name probably developed as a diminutive form of **Ann** and, in the eighteenth century, it began to be used as a name in its own right.

Nani
Origin: Hawaiian
Meaning 'beautiful'.

Naomi
Variants: Naomia (rare)
Origin: Hebrew
Biblical name from the Hebrew meaning 'my delight', or 'sweetness', 'pleasure'. Naomi was Ruth's mother-in-law in the Old Testament and a common Jewish name, which was taken up by Puritans in the seventeenth century. Since the 1970s, it has been popular among non-Jews, especially in Australia. A famous bearer of the name is supermodel Naomi Campbell.

Nara
Origin: Celtic
Meaning simply 'happy'.

Nata
Origin: Sanskrit
Meaning 'dancer'.

Natalie
Diminutives: Talia, Talya, Tally
Variants: Natalia, Nathalie
Origin: Latin

Deriving originally from the Latin *natale domini*, meaning 'birthday of the Lord', records of use of the name in Britain date only to the nineteenth century, though it was the name of a fourth-century saint. A famous bearer of the name is actress Natalie Portman.

Natalya
See Natalie

Natania
Variants: Natanya, Nataniah
Origin: Hebrew
Meaning 'a gift from God'.

Natasha
Diminutives: Tash, Tasha
Variants: Natacha, Natassia
Origin: Russian, from Latin
Developed initially as a variant of Natalya (*see* Natalie) and went on to become a name in its own right in English-, German- and French-speaking countries. The 1960s and 1970s in Britain saw a resurgence of the name, partly inspired by the TV adaptations of Tolstoy's *War and Peace*. A famous bearer of the name is actress Nastassia Kinski.

Natesa
Origin: Hindi
Meaning 'godlike', this is another name for the goddess Shakti.

Natsu
Origin: Japanese
Meaning 'summer'.

Nayana
Origin: Sanskrit
Meaning 'lovely eyes'.

Nazira
Variants: Nazirah
Origin: Arabic
Meaning 'an equal'.

Neala
Variants: Neila, Nelia
Origin: Irish
This Irish name is a feminine version of Neil or Neal, meaning 'champion'.

Neassa
Origin: Irish
A character from Irish folklore.

Neema
Origin: Swahili
Meaning 'born in good times'.

Neha
Origin: Sanskrit
An Indian name which is derived from the Sanskrit word for 'rain'.

Nell
Variants: Nelly, Nellie
Origin: Various
Now considered to be a name in its own right, this began as a diminutive of such names as Eleanor and Helen. With its heyday in Victorian England, it has suffered a decline since the 1930s. Famous bearers of the name have included Nell Gwyn, the lover of Charles II.

Nenet
Origin: Egyptian
The name of the goddess of the sea.

Neola
Origin: Greek
Meaning 'young and new'.

Neoma
Origin: Greek
Meaning 'the new moon'.

Nereida
Origin: Greek
From the Spanish, meaning 'sea nymph'.

Nerissa
Origin: Greek
Probably from the Greek *nereis* ('sea nymph'), the name is believed to have been an invention by Shakespeare for *The Merchant of Venice*.
See also Nereida, Nerys

Nerys
Origin: Probably Welsh
Likely to have derived from the Welsh *ner*, meaning 'lord', and interpreted as 'lady'. Also a diminutive of **Nerissa**. Nerys is little known outside Wales, but a famous bearer of the name is actress Nerys Hughes.

Neva
Variants: Nevada
Origin: Spanish
Meaning 'as white as the moon'.

Nevada
See **Neva**

Nevina
Origin: Spanish
Meaning 'worshipper of St Nevin'.

Niamh
Diminutives: Nia (Wales)
Origin: Irish
From the Gaelic meaning 'brightness' or 'radiance', this is popular in Ireland but rare elsewhere. The name of a pagan goddess and has links with the legend of Tir nan Og. Famous bearers of the name include actress Niamh Cusack.

Nicola
Diminutives: Nick, Nicki, Nicky, Nikki

Variants: Nichola, Nicole
Origin: Greek
Originally a feminine version of **Nicholas**, the name is quite common among English speakers. It has been in use since the twelfth century and enjoyed a peak in the 1970s. A famous bearer of the name is actress Nicole Kidman.

Nieta
Origin: Spanish
Meaning 'granddaughter'.

Nigella
See **Nigel**

Nike
Origin: Greek
Meaning 'victorious'.

Nikhita
Origin: Sanskrit
Meaning 'the Earth'.

Nima
Origin: Hebrew
Meaning 'thread', presumably a thread which ties the child to its ancestors.

Nina
Variants: Nena, Ninette
Origin: Uncertain
Possibly derived from such names as **Ann** or as a diminutive of names ending in the suffix -nina. Alternatively, it could have derived from the Spanish *nina*, meaning 'little girl'. Famous bearers of the name include jazz singer Nina Simone.

Nirah
Origin: Hebrew
Meaning 'light'.

Nisha
Origin: Sanskrit
Meaning 'night'.

Nissa
Origin: Scandinavian
Meaning 'a friendly elf', who can be seen only by lovers.

Nita
Origin: Hebrew
Developed as a Spanish variant of **Ann**.

Nitha
Origin: Scandinavian
Meaning 'elf'.

Nixie
Variants: Nissie, Nissy
Origin: Teutonic
Mwaning 'water sprite'.

Noel m/f
Variants: Noele, Noeleen, Noelene, Noelle

Origin: French

From *Noël*, meaning 'Christmas', given to children born around this time, up to the seventeenth century, it was given to both girls and boys, though since then it has been reserved almost exclusively for boys.

Noirin
See **Nora**

Nona
Diminutives: Nonie
Origin: Latin
From the Latin *nonus*, meaning 'ninth'. In the nineteenth century, when people had more children, the name was usually reserved for the ninth child. As such, it is rarely used today.

Nora
Variants: Norah
Origin: English or Roman
An Irish name developed from **Honor**. Also treated as a shortened form of such names as **Eleanor**.

Nordica
Origin: Scandinavian
Meaning 'from the north'.

Noreen
See **Nora**

Norma
Origin: Latin
From the Latin *norma*, meaning 'standard', 'pattern', 'rule'. Especially in Scotland, it is sometimes considered as a feminine version of **Norman**. It became popular in the early nineteenth century and reached a peak in the 1920s, but it has become relatively rare since then.

Normandie
Origin: French
From the province of the same name.

Nuala
Origin: Irish
From the Gaelic meaning 'white shoulder'.
See also **Fenella**

Nur m/f
Variants: Nura (f)
Origin: Arabic
Meaning 'light'.

Nuria
Origin: Spanish
From the Catalan name for the Virgin Mary, Our Lady of Nuria. It refers to the statue of the Madonna which was blackened by candle smoke, in Nuria, Gerona.

Nydai
Origin: Latin
Meaning 'from the nest'.

Nydia
Origin: English
This name was invented by writer Edward Bulwer-Lytton for *The Last Days of Pompeii*.

Nyree
Origin: Maori
Meaning 'from the sea'.

Nyssa
Origin: Greek
Meaning 'goal'.

Obelia
Origin: Greek
Meaning 'needle'.

Ocean m/f
Variants: **Oceana**
Origin: English
From the ordinary vocabulary word 'ocean', this name may have been inspired by Oceanus, the name of a Greek sea-god.

Oceana
See **Ocean**

Octavia
Diminutives: **Tavie**
Origin: Latin
From the Latin *octavus*, meaning

O

'eighth', this name was often reserved for the eighth-born child, meaning it's obviously a much rarer name nowadays.

Odessa
Origin: Greek
Originally from the Greek meaning 'colony' or 'quest', it is now associated with Black Sea Town, the Ukrainian town that was once a Greek colony.

Odette
Variants: Odetta
Origin: Old German
From the Old German *od*, meaning 'riches', came the French boys' name Oda, from which we get Odette, which seems to have been imported into English-speaking countries near the end of the nineteenth century.

Odile
Variants: Odilia
Origin: German
Either from the German name

Otto (*see also* **Odette**), or from *othal*, Old German, meaning 'fatherland'. Often seen as a feminine version of Odell.
See also **Ottilie**

Odina
Origin: Norse
A feminine form of Odin, named after the Nordic god.

Ofrah
See **Oprah**

Okalani
Origin: Hawaiian
Meaning 'from heaven'.

Oksana
Origin: Russian
Meaning 'praise to God'.

Oleander
Origin: Latin
Named after the shrub, this may have been another of the names taken up by the Victorians as part of the fashion for plant and flower names for children.

Olesia
Origin: Greek
Meaning 'defender of mankind'.

Oletha
Origin: Scandinavian
Meaning 'nimble-footed'.

Olina
Origin: Hawaiian
Meaning one who is full of happiness.

Olive
Variants: Olivette
Origin: Latin
Derived from the Latin *oliva* ('olive tree'), records of versions of this name date as far back as the thirteenth century. Its associations with peace meant it was revived in the nineteenth century and reached a peak in the 1920s before being eclipsed by **Olivia**. A famous bearer of the name is the protagonist of the Minette Walters novel *The Sculptress*.

Olivia
Diminutives: Libby, Livvy
Origin: Latin
This name was promoted by Shakespeare's play *Twelfth Night*, but remained infrequent until the 1970s. A famous bearer of the name is actress and singer Olivia Newton-John.

Olwen
Variants: Olwin
Origin: Welsh
From the Welsh *ol* ('footprint') and *wen* ('blessed' or 'white'). In Welsh legend, Olwen's footprints sprouted clover. Popular for a

brief period in England after the translation of *The Mabinogion*, the name remains mostly confined to Wales.
See also Olwyn

Olympia
Variants: Olympe (French)
Origin: Greek
From the Greek Olympus, home of the gods. The name has never been common and is known through the painting *Olympia* by Manet, which caused a scandal when it was exhibited in 1865. A famous bearer of the name is actress Olympia Dukakis.

Oma
Variants: Omie
Origin: Arabic
From the Arabic, meaning 'leader'.
See also Omar

Omega
Origin: Greek
The last letter of the Greek alphabet, sometimes used as a name for last-born children.

Omyra
Origin: Latin
Meaning 'scented oil'.

Oneida
Origin: Native American
Meaning 'long-awaited'.

Onyx
Origin: Latin
After the stone of the same name.

Oona
See Una

Oonagh
See Una

Opal
Variants: Opaline
Origin: Sanskrit
An Indian name, from the Sanskrit for 'precious stone', this name was taken up by English speakers in the nineteenth century, when it was fashionable for children to be named after jewels. Particularly appropriate for girls born in October, the name is rarely encountered outside the USA.

Ophelia
Diminutives: Philia
Variants: Ofelia, Ofilia
Origin: Greek
Probably from Ophelos, meaning 'profit' or 'help', though a less plausible root could be *ophis*, which means 'a serpent'. Probably a sixteenth-century invention, it is best known among English speakers as the name of the tragic heroine in Shakespeare's *Hamlet*. Until the nineteenth century, the name was rare, but has since made a comeback.

Oprah
Variants: Ofrah, Orpa, Ophrah, Orfa
Origin: Hebrew
The meaning of this name is unknown, with conflicting views on the subject. In the Old Testament, it is Orpah (a man's name). TV presenter Oprah Winfrey is so-named due to a misspelling on her birth certificate.

Ora
Origin: Obscure
Possibly from the Latin *orare* ('to pray'), or may be a diminutive of names such as Cora and Dora.

Orabela
See Ora

Oralie
Variants: Oralee
Origin: Obscure
Sometimes treated as a variant of Aurelia.

Orchid
Origin: Greek
From the flower of the same name, possibly as part of the Victorian fashion for naming children after plants and flowers.

Orela
Origin: Latin
Meaning 'divine pronouncement',
'the oracle'.

Orena
Variants: Orenah, Orenne
Origin: Hebrew
From the Hebrew, meaning
'pine tree'.
See also **Irene**

Oriana
Variants: Orianna
Origin: Latin
Meaning 'golden dawn'.
See also **Dawn**

Orinthia
Variants: Orinda
Origin: Greek
From *orinein* (to excite'). Orinda
was the pseudonym of writer
Katherine Philips, whose
nickname was 'The Matchless
Orinda'. George Bernard Shaw
used the name for a character in
The Apple Cart (*see* **Orithna**).

Orithna
Origin: Greek
Sources say it was invented by
Shaw for *The Apple Cart*, but the
name was **Orinthia**. Orithna was
the mythical daughter of the King
of Athens.

Orla
Variants: Orlaidh, Oria, Orlagh
Origin: Irish
From the Gaelic for 'golden
princess', the name is confined
to Ireland. A well-known bearer
of the name is news reporter
Orla Guerin.

Orlanda
See Roland

Orlenda
Origin: Russian
Meaning 'eagle', perhaps
suggesting strength and grace.

Orna
Variants: **Ornice**
Origin: Irish
Meaning 'olive-coloured'.

Ornice
Origin: Irish and Hebrew
Meaning 'olive-coloured'
(*see* **Orna**) or 'from the
cedar tree' (Hebrew).

Orsa
Variants: Orsaline
Origin: Latin
Meaning 'little bear'.

Osanna
Origin: Latin
Meaning 'filled with mercy'.

Osla
Origin: Old Norse
Meaning 'consecrated to God'.

Osnat
Origin: Hebrew
Meaning 'favourite of the deity'.

Ottilie
Variants: Otilie, Otillia
Origin: German
This name was derived from
Odile and is the name of the
seventh-century patron saint of
Alsace, thereby being common to
both France and Germany. It is
rare in English-speaking countries.

Ouida
Origin: Old German
From a childish mispronunciation
of **Louisa**, this variant of the
name was developed in French-
speaking countries.

Owena
Origin: Welsh
Meaning 'born to a noble
warrior' or 'well born'.

Owissa
Origin: Native American
Meaning 'bluebird', the bringer
of spring.

Ozette
Origin: Native American
From the village of the same
name.

Paciane

Origin: Latin
A French name from the Latin, meaning 'peace'.

Padma m/f

Variants: Padmavati, Padmini
Origin: Sanskrit
An Indian name derived from the Sanskrit *padma*, which means 'lotus'. Nowadays, it is reserved almost exclusively for girls and is found in ancient Sanskrit literature.

Page

See **Paige**

Paidrigin

Origin: Latin
A feminine version of **Padraigh**, from the Irish Gaelic.
See also **Patrick**

Paige

Variants: **Page**, Paget
Origin: English
From 'page', meaning 'servant', this was originally a surname and has recently been taken up as a first name. Despite medieval pages always being young men, the name is now reserved exclusively for girls.

Paisley

Origin: Scottish
From the town of the same name.

Paka

Origin: Swahili
Meaning simply 'kitten'.

Palila

Origin: Tahitian
A name given to someone 'with a spirit as free as a bird'.

Pallas

Origin: Greek
Meaning 'wisdom and knowledge'.

Paloma

Origin: Spanish
Meaning 'a dove'.

Pamela

Diminutives: Pam, Pammy
Variants: Pamala, Pamila, Pammala
Origin: English
This name was invented by poet Sir Philip Sidney in *Arcadia* in 1590, who took it from the Greek *pan* ('all') and *meli* ('honey'), suggesting sweetness. A famous bearer of the name is comedienne and psychologist Pamela Stephenson.

Pandora

Diminutives: Pan
Origin: Greek
From the Greek *pan* ('all') and *doron* ('gift'), Pandora was the first mortal woman in Greek mythology and is famous for the legend of Pandora's box. Because of the negative associations, it was not taken up by English speakers until the twentieth century. It is well known in the UK thanks to the character in Sue Townsend's *Adrian Mole* books.

Paniz

Origin: Persian
Meaning 'candy', 'sweets'.

Pansy

Origin: French
From the French *pensée,* which means 'thought', this name was taken up as part of the fashion in the nineteenth century for naming children after flowers and plants. Never as popular as **Poppy**, it has since become a term for an effeminate man, which seems to have sealed its fate.

Panthea

Origin: Greek
Meaning 'of all the gods'.

Panya

Origin: Swahili
Meaning 'little mouse'.

Paris m/f

Origin: Greek and French
It was Paris who abducted Helen of Troy, so it is possible that the name is derived from this, though

P

Babies' Names ☼ Girls

it seems far more likely that it is simply a tribute to the French capital city. A famous bearer of the name is socialite and model Paris Hilton.

Parker m/f
Origin: English
This surname has been in use as a first name, chiefly in the USA, since the nineteenth century.

Parvaneh
Origin: Persian
Meaning 'butterfly'.

Parvati
Origin: Sanskrit
Meaning simply 'mountain climber' or 'of the mountain'.

Pascale
Variants: Paschal
Origin: Latin
A French name which is derived from the Latin *Paschalis*, meaning 'Easter' (*see* **Eostre**), this name was first taken up by Christians and given to boys born at this time of year. Later popular in medieval Cornwall and today retains its links with Catholicism.
See also **Pascal**

Pasha
Origin: Greek
Meaning simply 'of the sea'.

Pat
See **Patricia**

Patience
Diminutives: Pat, Patty
Origin: Latin
From the Latin *pati* ('to suffer'), this name was popular with early Christians and was taken up by English and American Puritans in the sixteenth and seventeenth centuries. Once given to both sexes but now reserved exclusively for girls, this remains fairly popular.

Patrice
See **Patricia**

Patricia
Diminutives: Paddy, Pat, Patrice, Patsy, Pattie, Tricia
Origin: Latin
From the Latin *patricius* ('nobleman') and a feminine version of **Patrick**, this name was written in Roman records to distinguish female from male members of noble families. It was not taken up as a name among English speakers until the eighteenth century, though it was not until the birth of Queen Victoria's granddaughter that it became more widespread. In the 1950s, it reached a peak but has since declined. Actress

Patricia Hodge is one famous bearer of the name.

Patsy
See **Patricia**

Paula
Origin: Latin
A feminine version of **Paul**, from the Latin *paulus*, meaning 'small'. Several Christian martyrs bore the name and it was in use among English speakers by medieval times, but it was only in the 1950s that it became popular. It seems to have been in decline since the 1970s.

Pauline
Variants: Paulene, Pauleen, Paulanne
Origin: Latin
A feminine version of **Paul**, this French version took over from the Roman Paulina after the nineteenth century. Popular first in the USA.

Pavla
See **Paula**

Paxton m/f
Origin: Latin
Meaning 'peaceful town'.

Pearl
Diminutives: Pearly, Perlie
Variants: Pearle, Perla

Origin: English
Taken up as a first name in the nineteenth century, the jewel itself represents unhappiness, but that has not diminished its popularity. Famous bearers of the name have included writer Pearl Buck.

Pageen
Origin: Irish
See **Margaret**

Peggy
Variants: Peggie, Peg
Origin: Greek
This name has been treated as a name in its own right, though it began (and is well known to be) a diminutive of **Margaret**. Records of its use as a name date to the sixteenth century, but it was not popular until the 1920s, when it reached a peak, though it has since been in decline. Famous bearers of the name have included actress Dame Peggy Ashcroft.

Pelia
Origin: Hebrew
Meaning 'marvel of God'.

Penelope
Diminutives: Pen, **Penny**
Origin: Probably Greek
The origin of this name is uncertain, though it seems to come from the Greek *pene* ('bobbin', 'thread') or *penelops*, a breed of duck. Penelope was the wife of Odysseus and was taken up by English speakers in the sixteenth century. Its popularity has been consistent and it reached a peak in the 1950s and 1960s. Sometimes seen as an anglicization of the Irish Fionnuala (*see* **Fenella**). Famous bearers of the name include actress Penelope Cruz.

Penny
See **Penelope**

Peony
Origin: English (possibly from Greek)
Taken up as a name as part of the Victorian fashion for naming children after plants and flowers, this one has never been popular. The flower may have been named for Palon, the gods' physician.

Perdita
Diminutives: Purdie
Origin: Latin
From the Latin *perditus*, meaning 'lost', it is thought that Shakespeare invented the name for the play *The Winter's Tale*. Though never common, it has appeared sporadically since then. In Dodie Smith's novel *The Hundred and One Dalmations*, one of the dogs is named Perdita.

Perla
See **Pearl**

Perry m/f
Origin: Old English
From the Old English word *pirige* ('man who lives by a pear tree') and as a diminutive of other names. Also from the French, meaning 'pear tree'.

Petra
Diminutives: Pet
Variants: **Petrina**, Petrona
Origin: Latin
This is a feminine form of **Peter**. In 1812, the ruins of Jordanian city Petra were discovered and this boosted the popularity of the name, though it appears not to have been taken up by English speakers until the 1940s.

Petrina
See **Petra**

Petula
Diminutives: Pet
Variants: Petunia
Origin: Uncertain
Possibly from the Latin *petere* ('to attack' or 'to seek'), from where we get 'petulant', or alternatively it could just have

been named after the petunia flower. This seems to have been a twentieth-century invention, and perhaps the most famous bearer of the name is singer Petula Clark.

Phaedra
Origin: Greek
Meaning 'shining brightly'. In Greek mythology, Phaedra fell in love with her stepson, who rejected her.

Philana
Variants: Phila
Origin: Greek
Meaning 'the lover of mankind'.

Philippa
Diminutives: Pippa
Variants: Phillipa, Philipa
Origin: Greek
A feminine version of Philip, it was introduced initially in medieval times to distinguish men and women who were named Philip. Famous bearers of the name in history have included the wife of poet Geoffrey Chaucer, but it was not until the nineteenth century that the name became more widespread. A well-known bearer of the name in more recent times is TV presenter Philippa Forrester.

Philomena
Diminutives: Phil, Philly
Variants: Philomene, Philomina,
Filomena
Origin: Greek
From *philein* ('to love') and *menos* ('strength'), Philomena was the name born by a saint. It was thought another had been found, but the inscription on the second saint's tomb was not definitive. Because of this, the name fell into decline, though it still makes occasional appearances.

Phoebe
Variants: Phebe, Pheobe
Origin: Greek
From the Greek *phoibe*, which means 'shining' or 'bright'; Phoebe was the legendary daughter of Uranus and Gaia. Reaching a peak in the nineteenth century, since when it has been less popular, though it enjoyed a resurgence in the 1990s. Sometimes seen as a diminutive of Euphemia.

Phoenix m/f
Origin: Arabian
Alluding to the Arabian bird of legend, Phoenix appears to have emerged as a first name quite recently. Melanie B from the Spice Girls named her daughter Phoenix Chi in 1999.

Phyllida
Diminutives: Phil, Phillie, Philly
Variants: Phillida
Origin: Greek
Originally a variant of Phyllis, this emerged as a name in its own right in the fifteenth century and was popular among English speakers in the seventeenth century. Famous bearers of the name include actress Phyllida Law.

Phyllis
Diminutives: Phil, Phillie, Philly
Variants: Phillis, Philis, Phyliss
Origin: Greek
From the Greek *phullis*, meaning 'green branch' or 'foliage'. Variants such as Felis and Phillice emerged when the name was confused with Felicia. The eighteenth century saw a decline in popularity but it was revived again in the nineteenth and enjoyed a peak in the twentieth. A notable bearer of the name is actress Phyllis Logan.

Pia
Origin: Latin
From the Latin *pia*, meaning 'godly', 'pious' or 'dutiful', a feminine equivalent of Pius, which is now defunct. With occasional appearances in the twentieth century, especially since the 1970s, it remains less common in the UK than in other countries.

Piety
Origin: English
Adopted by the Puritans in the seventeenth century, this fell into disuse long ago.

Pippa
Diminutives: Pip
Origin: Greek
Initially treated as a diminutive of **Philippa**, it is now seen as a name in its own right and became popular with English speakers after the publication of Robert Browning's *Pippa Passes* in 1841.

Pixie
Variants: Pixy
Origin: Uncertain
Another name for a mischievous fairy, it has been suggested (but not proven) that the name comes from the Celtic *pict sidhe*.

Pleasance
Variants: Pleasant (rare)
Origin: Old French
From *plaisance*, meaning 'pleasure', this name was brought to England with the Norman invasion.

Polly
Diminutives: Pol, Poll
Variants: Pollie
Origin: Latin
A variant form of **Mary**,

influenced by **Molly**, it has been suggested that it is not dependent on or derivative of Mary but comes from a long-forgotten source.

Poni
Origin: African
Meaning 'second daughter'.

Pooja
Variants: Puja, Pujita, Poojita
Origin: Hindi
Meaning 'worship' or 'worshipped'.

Poonam
Variants: Punam
Origin: Hindi
This Hindi name means 'the full moon'.

Poppy
Origin: English
From the Old English *popaeg* and was introduced near the end of the nineteenth century. Popular in Edwardian times, it reached a peak in the 1920s, despite its associations with poppy fields after the First World War.

Portia
Origin: Latin
An anglicization of the Latin name Porcia, a feminine form of a Roman family name which probably derived from the Latin *porcus* ('pig' or 'hog').

Another sourse suggests it originally meant 'safe harbour'. Shakespeare's heroine was named Portia in *The Merchant of Venice*, meaning it has been used occasionally ever since.

Posy
Variants: Posie
Origin: English
This flower name began to be used as a first name in the 1920s and sometimes treated as a diminutive of **Josephine**.

Prabha
Origin: Hindi, meaning 'light'.

Pratibha
Origin: Sanskrit
An Indian name from the Sanskrit *pratibha* meaning 'light' or 'wit', this seems to have been a medieval introduction.

Precious
Origin: Latin
From the Latin meaning 'great worth', this name is quite self-explanatory.

Preeti
Origin: Hindi
Meaning 'love'.

Priela
Origin: Hebrew
Meaning 'the fruit of God'.

Priscilla

Diminutives: Pris, Prissy, Cilla
Variants: Prisca
Origin: Latin
From the Latin *priscus*, meaning 'old' or 'ancient', suggesting a long life. The name was taken up by Puritans in the seventeenth century and was fashionable again in the nineteenth, but since the 1960s, it has been less popular. Perhaps the most famous bearer of the name in recent years is Priscilla Presley.

Priya

Variants: Priyal
Origin: Sanskrit
An Indian name from the Sanskrit *priya*, which means 'beloved'.

Priyal *See* Priya

Prudence

Diminutives: Pru, Prue, Purdy
Origin: Latin
Based on the Roman name Prudentia, Prudence made a few appearances in medieval England before being adopted by the Puritans in the seventeenth century. It is one of the few of these 'virtue' names which have stood the test of time (unlike Abstinence and Repentance, for example), though it is used less frequently nowadays than previously.

Prunella

Diminutives: Pru, Prue
Origin: Latin
This name derives from the Latin *pruna*, meaning 'little plum', and was adopted by English speakers in the nineteenth century, though the word itself had been known before that as a fabric, a flower and a bird. A famous bearer of the name is actress Prunella Scales.

Punita

Origin: Hindi
Meaning 'pure'.

Purity

Origin: English
Based on the ordinary vocabulary word 'purity', the meaning of this name is self-explanatory.

Qadira

Origin: Arabic
Meaning 'powerful'.

Queenie

Variants: Queeny, Queena (mainly USA, rare)
Origin: Latin or Old English
Initially used as a diminutive of Regina, it may actually derive from the Old English *cwene* ('woman'). Popular in medieval times, it was revived in the nineteenth century in reference to Queen Victoria. As a result, it has since been used as a nickname for people called Victoria.

Querida

Variants: Cherida
Origin: Spanish
Meaning 'beloved one'.

Quinn m/f

Origin: Irish
Derived from a surname from the Irish Gaelic meaning 'counsel'.
See also Quentin

Quisha

Origin: African
Meaning 'physical and spiritual beauty'.

Quita

Origin: French
Meaning 'tranquil'.

Rabiah
Origin: Arabic
Meaning simply 'garden'.

Rachel
Diminutives: Rach, **Rae**, **Shelley**
Variants: Rachael, Racheal, Rachelle, **Raquel** (Spanish)
Origin: Hebrew
From the Hebrew meaning 'ewe', symbolizing gentleness. In the Old Testament, it appears as Rahel and, as a result, Christians, Jews and Muslims all took up the name. In the seventeenth century, it became popular with the Puritans, and it reached peaks again in the nineteenth and twentieth centuries and has been especially popular since 1970. Sometimes treated as an anglicization of Raoghnald, from the Norse Ragnhildr.
See also **Rochelle**

Rachida
Origin: Arabic
Meaning 'wise'.

Radha m/f
Origin: Hindi
Meaning 'prosperous', 'successful'.

Radhiya
Origin: Swahili
Meaning 'pleasant', 'friendly'.

Rae
Origin: Middle English
Meaning 'a doe', 'female deer'.
See also **Rachel**

Rahil
Variants: Raheel, Raheela
Origin: Arabic
An Arabic form of **Rachel**.

Rahima
Variants: Raheema, Raheemah
Origin: Arabic
Meaning 'compassionate', 'merciful'.

Raina
See **Regina**

Rainbow
Origin: English
From the ordinary vocabulary word 'rainbow'.

Raiona
Origin: Maori
Meaning 'lion'.

Raisa
Variants: Raisah
Origin: Hebrew
Meaning 'rose', St Raisa was martyred in the fourth century.

Raissa
Variants: Raisse
Origin: French
Meaning 'the believer'.

Rajani
Origin: Sanskrit
Meaning 'night', perhaps given to a baby with dark hair or eyes.

Rama
Variants: Ram
Origin: Sanskrit
An Indian name from the Sanskrit *rama*, meaning 'pleasing', this was the name of Vishnu in classical texts. It is also found as part of several compound names beginning 'Ram-'.

Ramona
Diminutives: **Mona**, **Rama**, Ramonda
Origin: Teutonic
Meaning 'wise protector'.
See also **Raymond**

Rana
Variants: Ranee, **Rani**, Rania, Ramique, Rayna
Origin: Sanskrit
Meaning 'a queen', 'of royal birth'.

Randy m/f
See **Miranda**

Rani
See **Rana**

Ranita
Variants: Ranite
Origin: Hebrew
Meaning 'joyful song'.

Raphaela
See **Raphael**

Raquel
See **Rachel**

Rasha
Origin: Arabic
Meaning 'a young gazelle'.

Rathnait
Origin: Irish
From the Gaelic meaning 'little graceful one'.

Raven m/f
Origin: English
This name has been popular among African-Americans since 1989, when an actress named Raven appeared in *The Cosby Show*.

Raya
Origin: Hebrew and Javanese
Meaning 'friend' (Hebrew), 'greater' (Javanese).

Rayne m/f
Origin: Scandinavian
Meaning 'mighty'.

Razina
Origin: Arabic
A Muslim name, meaning 'contented'.

Reanne
See **Rhiannon**

Reba
See **Rebecca**

Rebecca
Diminutives: Becky, Becca, **Reba** (uncommon)
Variants: Rebeccah, **Rebekah**
Origin: Hebrew (from Aramaic?)
Meaning either 'heifer' or 'binding', 'knotted cord' (suggesting marriage), the name is probably much older with an Aramaic source and appears in the Old Testament as **Rebekah**. In England and America in the sixteenth and seventeenth centuries, it became popular with Puritans due to its biblical associations. After Daphne du Maurier's *Rebecca* was published, the name received a new lease of life, and the 1970s saw a huge revival. Famous bearers of the name include actress Rebecca De Mornay.

Rebekah
See **Rebecca**

Rechaba
Origin: Hebrew
Meaning 'horse woman'.

Reese
Origin: Welsh
Meaning 'zealous' and 'fiery'. A famous bearer of the name is actress Reese Witherspoon.

Regan
Origin: Latin
Probably derived originally from **Regina**, though possibly linked to the Irish surname Regan or Reagan. In *King Lear*, Shakespeare used the name for the second daughter of the king.

Regina
Variants: **Reina**
Origin: Latin
From the Latin *regina*, meaning 'queen', the religious associations of this name (one of the Virgin Mary's titles was *Regina Coeli*, 'Queen of Heaven') made it a popular name during medieval times. After the Reformation, it fell from favour but was revived in the eighteenth century, reaching a peak in the nineteenth in tribute to Queen Victoria.

Reina
See **Regina**

Renata
See **Renee**

Renee
Variants: **Renata**, Reenie, Rena, Rene (m)
Origin: Latin
From the Latin *renatus*, meaning 'reborn', it was popular among early Christians and was taken up for use by the Puritans in the seventeenth

century. In Canada and the USA, its use was frequent due to the influence of missionary St René Groupil, who was killed by members of the Iroquois tribe. Taken up again in the twentieth century, especially popular in Australia.

Renie
See **Irene**

Reshma
Variants: Reshmam, Reshmi
Origin: Sanskrit
Meaning 'silken', perhaps referring to a child's smooth skin.

Reta
See **Margaret**

Reyhan
Origin: Turkish
Meaning 'a sweet-smelling flower'.

Rhea
Variants: Rea
Origin: Greek
Meaning 'Earth Mother', the mother of Zeus. A famous bearer of the name is actress Rhea Perlman.

Rhedyn
Origin: Welsh
Meaning 'fern'.

Rhiannon
Variants: Riannon, **Rhianna**

Origin: Welsh
Probably derived from the Celtic *rigantona*, a royal title, meaning 'great queen', the Welsh name means 'nymph' or 'goddess'. It has become more widespread in recent years, and is no longer confined to Wales.

Rhianwen
Variants: Rhianwyn
Origin: Welsh
Meaning 'pure maiden'.

Rhoda
Origin: Greek
From the Greek, meaning either 'a woman from Rhodes' or 'rose', both derived from *rhodon* (meaning 'rose', the name of the island coming from the same word). In the Bible, Rhoda was the name of a maidservant.

Rhonda
Origin: Welsh
From *rhon* ('pike', 'lance') and *da* ('good'), this has made occasional appearances as a first name since the early twentieth century. Likely to have been influenced by **Rhoda**, as well as the Rhondda valley. In the 1960s, heavy industry declined in this area and made the name less attractive in the UK.

Rhonwen *See* **Rowena**

Ria
Origin: Various
From the Spanish, meaning 'the river'. Also treated as a diminutive of such names as **Mary**, **Maria** and **Victoria**.

Rihana
Variants: Rhiana, **Rhiannon**, Riana, Rianna
Origin: Arabic
Meaning 'sweet basil', the herb.

Rika
Origin: Swedish, meaning 'ruler'.

Riley m/f
Origin: English
From the Old English *ryge* ('rye') and *leah* ('meadow' or 'clearing'), this was taken up both as a first name and a surname. It may also have derived from Reilly in Ireland, or be descended from the Irish first name Raghallach, the meaning of which is uncertain.

Rilla
Variants: Rille, Rillette
Origin: Teutonic
Meaning a stream or a brook.

Rima
Variants: Rimah
Origin: Arabic
Meaning 'antelope'.

Rio m/f
Variants: River
Origin: Spanish
A relatively recent name, this comes from the Spanish word for 'river' and its popularity was no doubt boosted by the 1982 hit 'Rio' by Duran Duran.

Riona *See* Catriona

Risa
Origin: Latin
From the Latin *risa*, meaning 'laughter'.

Risha
Origin: Hindi
A name given to a child born under the sign of Taurus.

Rissa
See Nerissa

Rita
Origin: Greek
Originally a Spanish and Italian variant of Margarita (*see* Margaret), now considered a name in its own right, adopted by English speakers in the twentieth century. A famous bearer of the name was actress Rita Hayworth.

Riva
Origin: French
Meaning 'riverbank' or 'shore'.

River m/f
Variants: Rio, Riviera
Origin: English
From the ordinary vocabulary word 'river'. A famous bearer of this name was actor River Phoenix.

Roberta
Diminutives: Bobbie, Berta
Variants: Robertina (rare)
Origin: Old German
A feminine form of Robert, this was introduced in the 1870s and was especially popular in Scotland and the USA, partly due to the musical *Roberta* by Jerome Kern. Famous bearers of the name include Roberta Flack.

Robin m/f
Variants: Robyn, Robynne, Robina (all f only)
Origin: Old German
This name developed as a diminutive of Robert, but it has been in use as a name in its own right for a significant length of time. Coming to England from France in the medieval period, it emerged as a boys' name and it was only in the 1950s that it began to be bestowed on girls, possibly influenced by the garden bird, making it less popular for boys.

Rochana
Origin: Persian
Meaning 'sunrise'.
See also Dawn

Rochelle
See Rachel

Rohan m/f
Variants: Rowan
Origin: Disputed
Some sources link this name to the French place name and surname, though others say it comes from the Irish Gaelic for 'red'. The name is popular in India, and comes from the Sanskrit *rohana* ('ascending'). The variant Rowan is perhaps derived from the tree of the same name.

Roisin
Origin: Irish
From *rios*, the Irish Gaelic for 'rose', this name means 'little rose'.

Rolanda *See* Roland

Romaine
Origin: Latin
Meaning 'Roman woman', this is the feminine equivalent of Roman.

Romola
Variants: Romella, Romelle, Romula
Origin: Latin
Meaning 'lady of Rome'.

Romy
See **Rosemary**

Ronnie
See **Veronica**, **Rowena**

Rosa
See **Rose**

Rosalie
Origin: Latin
This name replaced Rosalia, a Roman tomb-decorating festival, in around the middle of the nineteenth century.
See also **Rose**

Rosalind
Diminutives: Ros, Roz
Variants: Rosaline, **Rossalyn**, Roslyn, Rosaleen
Origin: Old German
From the Old German name Roslindis, from *hros* ('horse') and either *lind* ('soft', 'tender') or *linta* ('lime'), thereby meaning a horse shield made of lime. Introduced into Spain by the Goths, whence it acquired a rather more attractive meaning, 'pretty rose' (from *rosa* and *linda*). Brought over from Normandy in the eleventh century, it would not appear frequently until the sixteenth century. After a decline, it was back in fashion in the twentieth century.

Rosamund
Diminutives: **Rosa**, **Rose**, Roz
Variants: Rosamond
Origin: Old German or Latin
From the Old German *hros* ('horse') and *mund*, meaning 'protection', though there is also a suggestion that it comes from the Latin *rosa mundi*, meaning 'rose of the world'. Entering Britain with the Normans, it has been used as a name ever since.

Rose
Variants: Rosie, Rosy, **Rosa**, Rosetta, **Roisin**
Origin: Old German
From the Old German *hros* ('horse') or *hrod* ('fame'), it is now more associated with the Latin *rosa*, the flower. As Roese and Rohese, it entered Britain with the Normans and has remained popular ever since. Enjoying peaks in the nineteenth and twentieth centuries, notably in the 1990s.
See also **Rosemary**

Roseanna
Variants: Roseanne, Rozanne, Rosanne
Origin: German and Hebrew
Originally a combination of **Rose** and **Anna**, this name was adopted in the eighteenth century and has remained popular.

Famous bearers of the name include actress Rosanna Arquette.

Rosemary
Diminutives: **Rose**, Rosie, **Romy** (rare)
Variants: Rosemarie
Origin: Latin
From the Latin flower name *ros marinus*, meaning 'sea dew', also considered as a combination of **Rose** and **Mary**. In the late nineteenth century, it became popular as part of the fashion for using plant and flower names for children. It remained popular until the 1960s, but has been in decline since then.

Rossalyn
See **Rosalind**

Rowan m/f
Variants: Rowanne, **Rohan**
Origin: Irish
From the Gaelic Ruadhan, meaning 'little red-haired one', though it is sometimes derived from the alternative name for the mountain ash. Popular in Ireland due to two early saints bearing the name, it made its way to England in the twentieth century.

Rowena
Diminutives: Ron, **Ronnie**, Rona, Rhona

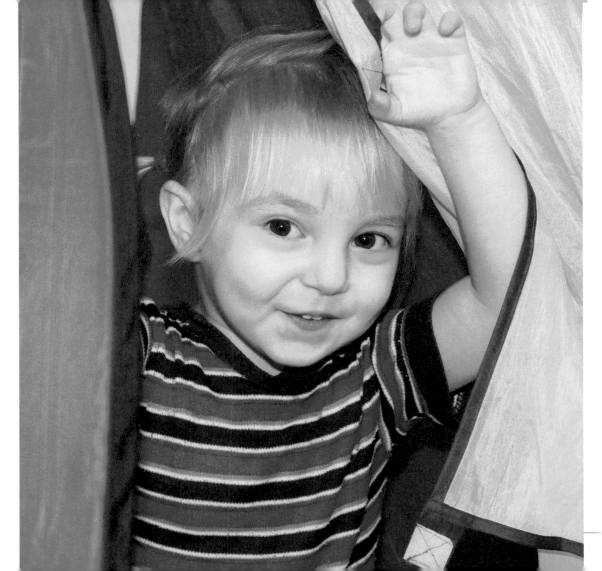

Variants: Rowina
Origin: English or Celtic
This name derives either from the Old English *hrod* ('fame') and *wynn* ('joy') or from the Welsh name **Rhonwen**, from *rhon* ('lance') and *gwen* ('fair' or 'white'). Having been in disuse for a considerable length of time, it was revived in the nineteenth century thanks to Sir Walter Scott using the name for a character in *Ivanhoe*.

Roxanne
Diminutives: Roxie, Roxy
Variants: Roxane, Roxana
Origin: Persian via Latin
Deriving from the Persian name Roschana meaning 'dawn' or 'light' (or Roshanara, meaning 'light of the assembly'). Alexander the Great's wife was called Roxana, and the name became popular following Daniel Defoe's novel *Roxana*. The most well-known form, Roxanne, was popularized by Edmond Rostand's novel *Cyrano de Bergerac*.

Ruby
Variants: Rubie, Rubina
Origin: Latin
From the Latin *rubeus*, meaning 'red', this was taken up for use as a first name in the nineteenth century but went into decline after the 1920s. Famous bearers of the name include comedienne Ruby Wax.

Rue
Variants: Roo
Origin: English or Hebrew
Sometimes considered as a diminutive of **Ruth**, this is also a plant name and only emerged as a first name among English speakers in the twentieth century.

Rufina
Origin: Latin
From the Roman name Rufinus, meaning 'reddish' or 'rosy', this name is popular in Russia but has made only sporadic appearances among English speakers.

Rukiya
Origin: Swahili
Meaning 'to arise'.

Rukmini
Origin: Sanskrit
An Indian name derived from the Sanskrit *rukmini*, which means 'adorned with gold'. In the *Mahabharata* as the name of one of the lovers of **Krishna**.

Rula
Origin: Latin
Meaning 'a sovereign', one who rules by right. A famous bearer of the name is actress Rula Lenska.

Rupak
Variants: Rupali, Rupashi, Rupashri
Origin: Sanskrit
Meaning 'beautiful'.

Rupinder
Origin: Sanskrit
An Indian name derived from the Sanskrit *rupa* ('beauty') and *indra* ('mighty'), thereby translated as 'great beauty'. This name is found most commonly among Sikhs.

Ruri
Origin: Japanese
Meaning 'emerald', perhaps given to a child with green eyes.

Rusty m/f
Variants: Rustie
Origin: American
Referring to someone with red hair. A famous bearer of this name is actress and chef Rustie Lee.

Ruth
Diminutives: Roo, Ruthie
Origin: Hebrew
This name has uncertain meaning, but is usually interpreted as meaning 'vision of beauty' or 'friend'.
See also **Rue**

Sabah
Variants: Saba
Origin: Arabic
From the Arabic meaning 'morning'.

Sabella
See **Isabella**

Sabina
Diminutives: Sabbie, Sabby, Bina
Variants: Sabine
Origin: Roman
Meaning 'Sabine woman', the Sabines being an Italic race absorbed into the Romans, mostly by force. This has never been widespread among English speakers.

Sabrina
Origin: Welsh
This Welsh name has been in occasional use among English speakers since the nineteenth century. According to legend, Sabrina, Locrine's illegitimate daughter, was drowned in the River Severn by order of Gwendolen, Locrine's widow. The name enjoyed a revival in the 1980s.

Sade
Origin: Yoruba
From the Yoruba name Falasade, which means 'honour bestows a crown', the name was made famous by singer Sade.

Sadella
See **Sarah**

Sadie
Origin: Hebrew
Developed initially as a diminutive of **Sarah** in the nineteenth century and the 1970s saw its popularity peak. Famous bearers of the name include actress Sadie Frost.
See also **Mercedes**

Sadira
Variants: Sadirah
Origin: Persian
Meaning 'lotus tree'.

Saffron
Diminutives: Safi
Origin: English
This has been in use as a first name since the 1960s and is taken from the name of the spice.

Safi
Origin: Hindi
Meaning 'friend'.
See also **Saffron**

Sage m/f
Variants: Saga, Saiga
Origin: Latin or English
From the Latin meaning 'wise and healthy', though it is more likely to be named for the herb.

Sahar
Variants: Sahara
Origin: Arabic
Meaing 'sunrise'.

Sahlah
Origin: Arabic
Meaning 'smooth'.

Sai
Origin: Japanese
Meaning 'intelligence', perhaps with the intention of bestowing this on the child.
See also **Sally**, **Sarah**

Sakari
Origin: Hindi
Meaning 'sweet one'.

Sally
Diminutives: Sal
Variants: Sallie, Salley
Origin: Hebrew
Developed as a diminutive of **Sarah**, this was established in its own right by the eighteenth century and enjoyed a peak in the 1920s and then the 1930s as Gracie Fields sang 'Sally' in 1931. Since the 1960s it has been eclipsed by the original **Sarah**. Notable bearers of the name include athlete Sally Gunnell.

Salome
Origin: Aramaic
The meaning of this name is unknown but it may have links to the Hebrew *shalom*, meaning 'peace'. Common in biblical times, it was popular in the sixteenth and seventeenth centuries with the Puritans. Revived at the end of the nineteenth century by Oscar Wilde's *Salome* and Richard Strauss's opera of the same name.

Samantha
Diminutives: Sam, Sammy
Origin: Hebrew
This is an English, feminine variant of Samuel, that probably first appeared in the southern US states in the eighteenth century but, until the 1960s, it was not widespread. It enjoyed a boost with the Cole Porter song 'I love you, Samantha' in 1956. Famous bearers of the name include model and singer Samantha Fox.

Samimah
Variants: Sameema, Sameemah
Origin: Arabic
Meaning 'sincere' or 'true'.

Samuela
See Samuel

Sanaa
Variants: Sana
Origin: Arabic
Meaning 'brilliance' or 'resplendence'.

Sancia
Origin: Latin
Meaning 'holy'.

Sandeep
Origin: Punjabi
Meaning 'enlightened'.

Sandhya
Origin: Sanskrit
This Indian name is derived from the Sanskrit *sandhya*, meaning 'junction' or 'twilight'. This time of day has special significance for certain religious castes and the daughter of Brahma is named Sandhya.

Sandra
Diminutives: Sandie, Sandy
Variants: Saundra, Sondra, Zandra
Origin: Greek
This name was initially derived as a diminutive of the Italian name Alessandra (*see* Alexandra) and made early appearances among English speakers in the nineteenth century. In the 1930s, it became more widespread and enjoyed a

peak in the 1950s before losing ground once more.
See also Cassandra

Sangeeta
Origin: Hindi
Meaning 'musical'.

Saoirse
Origin: Irish
This name translates directly from the Irish Gaelic as 'saved'.

Sapphire
Variants: Sapphira
Origin: Hebrew
From the Hebrew *sappir*, meaning 'sapphire' or 'lapis lazuli', this name was taken up in the nineteenth century among English speakers as part of the fashion for naming children after jewels, but it remains uncommon. As Sapphira, it appears in the New Testament.

Sarah
Diminutives: Sally, Sassie, Zara
Variants: Sarey, Sarra, Sara, Sarina, Sarita
Origin: Hebrew
Sarah was the wife of Abraham in the Bible, her name meaning 'quarrelsome' or 'contentious' (*sarai*) in Hebrew. Puritans took up the name in the sixteenth

century and reached a peak in the 1870s. In the early twentieth century, its popularity declined before reaching a revival in the 1960s. Again in the 1970s and 1980s, it was among the top girls' names. Famous bearers of the name have included jazz singer Sarah Vaughan.
See also **Sadella**, **Sadie**, **Sorcha**

Saree
Origin: Arabic
Meaning 'most noble'.

Sasha m/f
Diminutives: Sy
Variants: Sacha
Origin: Greek
Initially a diminutive of **Alexander** and **Alexandra**, the variant came from Russia in the early twentieth century via the Ballets Russes.

Saskia
Origin: Dutch or German
The origin of this name is obscure, though it was taken up by English speakers in the 1950s. It may have evoled from the Old German *sachs*, meaning 'Saxon' and notable bearers of the name include actress Saskia Wickham.

Savitri
Origin: Sanskrit
An Indian name derived from the Sanskrit *savitri*, meaning 'of Savitr the sun god'; it has associations with marriage and fidelity.

Scarlett
Variants: Scarlet
Origin: English
A surname which was taken up for use as a first name in the mid-twentieth century, initially reserved for dealers in scarlet cloth or people wearing red clothing (e.g. Will Scarlett). After Margaret Mitchell used the name in *Gone With The Wind* in 1936, people began to use the name. Can also reflect the ordinary vocabulary word 'scarlet', although its use may be controversial for some because of the implication of impropriety via 'scarlet woman'.
See also **Ashley**

Sean m/f
Origin: Hebrew
The Irish version of **John**, this has remained an essentially Irish name, although it has expanded since the 1920s and especially since the 1960s. It is mainly a masculine name, although one notable female bearer of the name is actress Sean Young.

Seda
Origin: Armenian
Meaning 'an echo in the forest'.

Selina
Variants: Selena, Salena, Salina
Origin: Greek or Latin
From the Greek *selene*, meaning 'moon', or the Latin *caelum* ('heaven'), this name was adopted by English speakers in the seventeenth century, increasing in popularity in the nineteenth. Enjoying peaks in the 1830s and the 1980s, a famous bearer of the name is TV presenter Selina Scott.

Selma
Variants: Zelma
Origin: Uncertain
This is from an English surname and sometimes seen as a contracted version of Selima.

Seon
See **Jane**

Seonaid
See **Jane**

Seraphina
Diminutives: Fina
Variants: Serafina
Origin: Hebrew
From the Hebrew *seraphim* ('fiery ones' or 'burning ones'), this is

found in the Bible as the name of an order of angels and was also the name of an obscure fifth-century saint.

Serena
Variants: Serina, Serenah, Serenna (all rare)
Origin: Latin
From the Latin *serenus*, meaning 'calm' or 'serene', this was the name of an early saint and was used by Edmund Spenser in *The Faerie Queene*. Sometimes considered to be an aristocratic name.

Shaela
Origin: Hindi
Meaning 'from the mountain'.

Shafira
Origin: Arabic
Meaning 'honourable' or 'eminent'.

Shahnaz
Origin: Persian
An Indian name derived from the Persian *shah* ('emperor' or 'king') and *naz* ('grace' or 'glory'), translated as 'king's glory'.

Shahrazad
Variants: Shahrizad
Origin: Persian
This Arabic name is derived from the Persian *shahr*, meaning 'city', and *zad*, meaning

'person'. Well known globally as Sheherazade from the *Thousand and One Nights*.

Shaina
Origin: Hebrew
Meaning 'beautiful'.

Shaira
Variants: Shakira
Origin: Arabic
Meaning 'thankful'. The variant **Shakira** has been made famous by the singer of the same name.

Shakira
See **Shaira**

Shakti
Origin: Sanskrit
From the Sanskrit *sakti*, meaning 'power', comes this Indian name which is the name of Shiva's wife and represents various types of power: power by rulers to that wielded by poets and artists.

Shanasa
Origin: Hindi
Meaning 'wished for', 'desired'.

Shani
Origin: Swahili
Meaning 'a marvel', 'a wonder'.

Shania
Variants: Shainya

Origin: Native American, Yiddish
The singer Shania Twain is a famous bearer of this name, which means 'I'm on my way' in the Native American Ojibwa language, and 'beautiful' in Yiddish.

Shanice
Origin: American, ultimately from Latin
A combination of **Janice** and the prefix 'Sha-', this is an African-American invention.

Shannon m/f
Origin: Hebrew
Made up of a combination of Shane (*see* **Sean**) and **Sharon**, though it is often considered to have come from the name of the river in Ireland. Despite the latter theory, the name is little used in Ireland.

Shanta
Origin: Sanskrit
From the Sanskrit *santa* ('pacified', 'calm'), this name appears in the *Mahabharata* and it is said to represent a person who is in full control of their emotions.

Shanti
Origin: Sanskrit
This Indian name is derived from the Sanskrit *santi*, which means 'tranquillity', appearing in various

religious texts and describing the peace achieved through meditation and yoga.

Shari
See **Sharon**

Sharik
Origin: African
Meaning 'a child of God'.

Sharmila
Origin: Sanskrit
An Indian name derived from the Sanskrit *sarman*, which means 'refuge' or 'protection', but sometimes interpreted as 'modest' or 'shy'. Its use as a first name was fairly recent.

Sharon
Diminutives: **Shari**
Variants: Sharron, Sharona, Sharyn
Origin: Hebrew
From the Hebrew name Saron, from *sar* ('singer', 'to sing'). The name of a valley in Palestine featured in the Bible, it was taken up by English speakers in the 1930s, reaching a peak in the 1960s and 1970s. It has since fallen out of favour, however. Famous bearers of the name include actress Sharon Stone.

Shauna
See **Shaun**, **John**

Shayna
Variants: Sheine
Origin: Yiddish
This is a Jewish name from the Yiddish for 'beautiful'.

Shea
Origin: Gaelic
Meaning 'from the fairy fort'.
See also **Shelah**

Sheela
See **Sheena**, **Sheila**

Sheena
Variants: Sheenah, Shena, Sheenagh, Shona
Origin: Various, depending on the source
Meaning 'shining' in Hebrew, this name is also said to have come from the Irish Gaelic Sine, itself from **Jane** or **Jean**.

Sheila
Variants: Sheelagh, Shelagh
Origin: Latin
An Irish version of **Celia**, Sile, in its turn developed into the English Sheila. It appeared among English speakers in the nineteenth century, reaching a peak in the 1930s, and it was then no longer considered to be exclusively Irish. The Australian use of the name as a slang term for a woman has led to the name's decline.

Notable bearers of the name include actress Sheila Hancock.

Shelah
Variants: Shava, **Shea**, Shela, Sheva, Sheya
Origin: Hebrew
Meaning 'asked for'.

Shelby m/f
Origin: Old English
From the Old English, which probably meant 'settlement with willow trees' (other sources say 'from the estate'), it saw its first use as a first name in the USA, after the character of that name in the film *Steel Magnolias*.

Shelley
Variants: Shelly
Origin: English
From the place name in Essex, Suffolk and Yorkshire, the name means 'wood on a slope' and the nineteenth century saw it taken up as a first name. Once a gender-neutral name, it is now reserved exclusively for girls, which is probably due to the influence of **Shirley**.
See also **Rachel**, **Michelle**

Sheridan m/f
Diminutives: Sherry
Origin: Irish
The original meaning of this

Irish surname is uncertain, possibly from the Gaelic sirim, meaning 'to seek', but it has since been taken up as a first name by English speakers. In the mid-nineteenth century, its use was promoted by the playwright Richard Brinsley Sheridan. Mainly a name for boys, though one notable female bearer of the name is actress Sheridan Smith.

Sherry
See **Cherie**, **Shirley**, **Sheridan**

Shirin
Origin: Persian
This Indian name, derived from the Persian *shirin* ('charming' or 'sweet'), was borne by the daughter of the Byzantine emperor Maurice.

Shirley
Diminutives: **Sherry**, Sherri, Shirl
Variants: **Shelley**
Origin: English
English place name from the Old English *scir* ('county' or 'bright') and *leah* ('wood', 'clearing'). Previously reserved for boys, this switched after the publication of Charlotte Brontë's *Shirley* in 1849, when the protagonist's parents decided to keep the name even though the baby was a

girl. Peaking in the 1930s, partly due to actress Shirley Temple, it suffered a marked decline after the 1950s.

Shona
See **Sheena**

Siân
Variants: Sian, Siana
Origin: Latin and Hebrew
This is a Welsh version of **Jane**, itself a version of **Sean**, and was taken up in Wales in the 1940s. It has since become more widespread. A well-known bearer of the name is actress Siân Phillips.

Sidney m/f
Diminutives: Sid, Syd
Variants: **Sydney** (usually f. only), Sydne (f.)
Origin: Old English or Norman
Possibly from the Norman place name Saint Denis, but more likely from the Old English *sedan* ('wide') and *eg* ('river island'), this name became popular in the nineteenth century. As a name for girls, it may have been influenced by **Sidonie**.

Sidonie
Variants: Sidony
Origin: Latin or Greek
A French name, derived from the

Roman Sidonia (Sidon was the capital of Phoenicia), or from the Greek *sindon* ('linen', probably in reference to the shroud of Christ). In the nineteenth century, this French version was adopted by English speakers.

Siena
Origin: Italian
A name derived from the name of the city, which seems to have appeared as a first name in the nineteenth century.

Sierra
Origin: Spanish
This Spanish name means 'mountain range' and seems to have been introduced to English speakers relatively recently.

Sigele
Origin: Malawian Meaning 'left'.

Sigourney
Origin: English
This was a surname taken up as a first name in the 1920s and was used as a character in *The Great Gatsby* by F. Scott Fitzgerald in 1925. The actress Sigourney Weaver made the name popular in the 1990s.

Sile
See **Julia**

Silvia
Diminutives: Syl
Variants: Sylvia, Sylvie (French)
Origin: Latin
From the Latin *silva*, meaning 'wood', this name has been popular in Italy since the Renaissance period due to its connections with the founding of Rome (Rhea Silvia was the mother of Romulus and Remus). Shakespeare used the name in *Two Gentlemen of Verona*, but only in the nineteenth century did use of the name pick up significantly. It has since fallen into decline, however. A famous bearer of the name was suffragette leader Sylvia Pankhurst.

Simone
Variants: Simona
Origin: Hebrew
This is a French version of Simon and was adopted by English speakers in the 1940s and famous bearers of the name have included the writer Simone de Beauvoir.

Sinead
Origin: Irish
See Janet

Siobhan
Variants: Shevaun, Chevonne

Origin: Latin
This is an Irish version of Joan and is more common in Ireland than anywhere else, though it has been used occasionally by English speakers outside Ireland.
See also John, Judith

Siomha
Origin: Gaelic
This name has roots in the Gaelic *maith*, meaning 'good'.

Sirena
Variants: Siren
Origin: Greek
Meaning 'entangler of men', *siren* is also the French word for 'mermaid'. The Sirens in Greek mythology were three island-dwelling sisters whose beautiful singing lured men to their deaths.

Sita
Origin: Sanskrit
From the Sanskrit meaning 'furrow', this Indian name represents the goddess of agriculture.

Skye
Variants: Sky
Origin: Scottish
From the Hebridean island of the same name.
See also Skylar

Skylar
Diminutives: Sky
Origin: Dutch
Meaning 'giving shelter', 'sheltering'.
See also Skye

Solange
Origin: Latin
From the Roman Solemnia, from *solemnis*, meaning 'religious' or 'solemn'.

Soledad
Origin: Spanish
Meaning 'solitude'.

Sonia
Variants: Sonya, Sonja, Sonje
Origin: Greek
This is a Russian diminutive of Sofiya (*see* Sophia). Taken up by English speakers in the early twentieth century, it is now regarded as a name in its own right and enjoyed a peak in the 1960s and 1970s.

Sonya
See Sophia

Sophia
Diminutives: Sonia
Variants: Sofia, Sofie, Sophie
Origin: Greek
Meaning 'wisdom', this name is widespread among numerous

cultural traditions. Taken up by English speakers in the seventeenth century, it was promoted by being the name of James I's granddaughter and reached a peak in the eighteenth century. Since the 1960s, Sophie has become more widely used. Famous bearers of the name include actress Sophia Loren and model and writer Sophie Dahl.

Sorcha
Origin: Gaelic
This name from Scotland and Ireland means 'brightness' and is often treated as a Gaelic variant of **Sarah**. It is sometimes considered as a variant of Clara in Scotland.

Stacey
Origin: Greek
Developed initially from **Eustace**, via the masculine **Stacy**, this is also found as a diminutive of **Anastasia**. It was taken up as a first name in the nineteeth century.

Star
Origin: English
From the ordinary vocabulary word 'star'.

Stella
Origin: Latin
From the Latin *stella*, meaning 'star', the name was originally used as a title for the Virgin Mary (*Stella Maris*, 'Star of the Sea') and was taken up by English speakers in the Middle Ages. It was not until the eighteenth century that it became more widespread. Since the 1920s, it has been in decline.

Stephanie
Diminutives: Steph, Stef, Steffie, Stevi, **Stevie**
Variants: Stefanie, Steffany
Origin: Latin
From the Latin Stephania from **Stephen**, taken up by English speakers in the nineteenth century and, although its use declined in the 1950s, it enjoyed a peak in the 1990s. Well-known bearers of the name include actress Stephanie Beacham.

Stevie
See **Stephanie**

Storm m/f
Origin: English
Derived from the ordinary vocabulary word 'storm', suggesting a lively and passionate personality, this name does not seem to have appeared until the twentieth century.

Suha
Origin: Arabic
Meaning 'star'.

Suki
Origin: Hebrew
This is a Japanese variant of **Susan**.

Sulia
Variants: Suliana
Origin: Latin
Meaning 'downy' and 'youthful'.

Sulwyn
Variants: Sulwen
Origin: Welsh
Meaning 'as beautiful as the sun'.

Sumalee
Origin: Thai
Meaning 'beautiful flower'.

Sumati
Origin: Indian
From the Indian *su* ('good') and *mati* ('mind'), so meaning 'intelligent'. Once a boys' name, it is now used mostly for girls.

Summer
Origin: Sanskrit
This name comes from the ordinary English vocabulary word, which itself comes from Sanskrit.

Sunita
Variants: Suniti
Origin: Sanskrit
Thus Indian name comes from the Sanskrit *su* ('good') and *nita* ('led', 'conducted'), so meaning 'of good conduct'. Originally a boys' name, it has come to be reserved for girls.

Sunny
Origin: Anglo-Saxon
Meaning 'bright and cheerful', of a sunny disposition.

Supriya
Variants: Supriti
Origin: Sanskrit
Meaning 'loved'.

Surinder m/f
Variants: Surendra
Origin: Sanskrit
This Indian name is derived from the Sanskrit and means 'the mightiest of gods' (from *sura*, 'god' and *indra*, 'mighty').

Susan
Diminutives: Su, Sue, Susie, Suzy, Suky
Variants: Suzan
Origin: Hebrew
Originally a diminutive of **Susannah**, this is now accepted as a name in its own right. Appearing first in the seventeenth century, it was the mid-twentieth before it gained popularity and remained popular until the 1980s. Notable bearers of the name include actress Susan Hampshire.

Susannah
Diminutives: Su, Susie, Suzie
Variants: Susanna, Suzanna, Suzanne, Suzette
Origin: Hebrew
Derived from the Hebrew *shoshan* ('lily') via Shushannah, this name was in use by English speakers as early as the thirteenth century and remained popular until the eighteenth, when it was eclipsed and largely replaced by **Susan**. A well-known bearer of the name is actress Susannah York.

Sybil
Variants: Sybilla, Sibyl
Origin: Greek
From the Greek word for 'prophetess', as this name was borne by prophetesses who were guardians of the oracles. A pagan name made acceptable by St Augustine, who included a sybil in *The City of God*. William the Conqueror's daughter-in-law was named Sybil. It fell into disuse after the Reformation but was revived in the nineteenth century.

Sydney *See* **Sidney**

Sylvana
Origin: Latin
Meaning 'from the woods'.

Syna
Variants: Syne
Origin: Greek Meaning 'together'.

Tabia
Origin: Swahili
Meaning 'talented'.

Tabitha
Diminutives: Tabby
Variants: Tabatha
Origin: Aramaic
Meaning 'doe' or 'gazelle',
this name was revived in the
seventeenth century by the
Puritans, inspired by the biblical
story of Tabitha. In the twentieth
century, it went into a severe
decline, partly because of Tabitha
Twitchit, a character in Beatrix
Potter's children's stories. A
famous bearer of the name is
Tabitha King, wife of Stephen
King. *See also* Dorcas

Tahani
Origin: Arabic
Meaning 'congratulations'.

Taima
Variants: Taina
Origin: Native American
Meaning 'a peal of thunder'.

Taite
Origin: English

Meaning 'cheerful'.

Tala
Variants: Talah

Origin: Native American
Meaning 'stalking wolf'.

Talise
Variants: Talyse
Origin: Native American
Meaning 'lovely water'.

Talitha
Origin: Aramaic
Meaning 'young girl'.

Tallulah
Variants: Tallula
Origin: Native American or Gaelic
From the place name, meaning
'running water' (referring to
Tallulah Falls in Georgia), also
treated as a variant form of
Tallula, from the Irish Gaelic
meaning 'lady', 'princess' or
'abundance'.

Tama
Origin: Japanese Meaning '
jewel'.

Tamara
Diminutives: Tammy, Tammie
Origin: Hebrew
This is a Russian variant of the
Hebrew Tamar, meaning 'date
palm' or simply 'palm tree'.
The Puritans introduced the
name in the seventeenth century
and it was subsequently revived
in the twentieth.

Tamika
Variants: Tameka
Origin: American
Meaning 'people'.

Tammy
Variants: Tammie
Origin: Ultimately from Aramaic
This is a diminutive of such
names as Tamara and Tamsin.
A famous bearer of the name is
country singer Tammy Wynette.
See also Thomas

Tamsin
Diminutives: Tammy
Variants: Tasmin, Tamsine,
Tamasine, Tamzin
Origin: Ultimately from Aramaic
This is a Cornish version of the
medieval name Thomasina, and
has been in fashion since the
1950s. Probable influence by
Jasmine led to the variant Tasmin.

Tanisha
Origin: American
Nisha, meaning 'night', with
'Ta-' prefix.

Tansy
Origin: Greek
This name of a flower is derived
ultimately from the Greek
athanasia, meaning 'immortality'.
Also found as a diminutive form
of Anastasia. It was customary

in the sixteenth century to scatter tansy flowers and leaves on the floor as a way of perfuming the room, but its use as a first name dates only to the nineteenth century, probably as part of the fashion for using flower and plant names as first names for children.

Tanya
Variants: Tania, Tonya (*see also* **Antonia**), Tanja (German)
Origin: Unknown, from Russian
This is an anglicization of **Tatiana** and has been considered a name in its own right since the 1940s and has grown in popularity.

Tara
Origin: Irish and Sanskrit
From the Irish word meaning 'hill', we get this first name, which began to make its way into use among English speakers in the late nineteenth century. Other sources suggest links with the Earth goddess Temair, whose name means 'dark one'. In the nineteenth century, the name became more widely known through Thomas Moore's poem 'The harp that once through Tara's halls'. The Sanskrit gave way to an Indian name for both girls and boys. Famous bearers of the name include actress Tara Fitzgerald.

Taryn
Taryn is a made-up name, by actors Tyrone Power and Linda Christianson.

Tasha
See **Natasha**

Tatiana
Diminutives: Tanya
Origin: Unknown
Since the early twentieth century this name has enjoyed considerable popularity among English speakers and may have Asian, Roman or Greek roots.
See also **Titania**

Tatum
Origin: Old English
From a surname which itself derives from the Old English meaning 'homestead of Tata', this name appears to have been coined especially for actress Tatum O'Neal.

Tavie
See **Octavia**

Taylor m/f
Variants: Tayler
Origin: English
Originally a trade name and given only to boys, this surname has come to be an accepted first name for girls as well.

Tegan
Origin: Welsh
From the Welsh Tegwen, itself from *teg* ('beautiful', 'fair') and *wen* ('white', 'blessed').

Tempany
Origin: English
This is an Australian form of **Temperance**.

Temperance
Origin: English
Named for the virtue of the same name, it was adopted in the seventeenth century by the Puritans. It remained in use until the latter years of the nineteenth century, on both sides of the Atlantic, but has since become rare.

Teresa
Diminutives: Teri, **Terri**, Tess, **Tessa**
Variants: Theresa, Theresia
Origin: Probably Greek
From one of two words meaning 'watching', 'guarding', 'reaper' or form the island of Thera. Famous bearers of the name have included Mother Theresa of Calcutta.
See also **Tracy**

Terri
See **Teresa**

Tessa
See **Teresa**

Thandie
Variants: Thandi, Thana
Origin: Arabic
Meaning 'thanksgiving'.

Thea
Origin: Greek
Meaning 'goddess'.
See also **Anthea**, **Theodora**

Thelma
Diminutives: Thel
Origin: English
This is a made-up name, invented by Marie Corelli for her book *Thelma* in 1887. She may have based the name on the Greek *thelema*, meaning 'wish' or 'will'.

Theodora
Diminutives: **Thea**, **Dora**, Theda
Origin: Greek
Sharing the same root as Dorothea (*see* **Dorothy**), this is a feminine version of **Theodore** and means 'God's gift'. It has never been common since it was adopted by English speakers in the seventeenth century.
See also **Thea**

Theone
Variants: Theona

Origin: Greek
Meaning 'in the name of God'.

Thia
See **Anthea**

Thora
Variants: Thyra, **Tyra**
Origin: Norse
A Scandinavian name derived from the legendary Thor, used infrequently by English speakers before the twentieth century and a name which remains linked to actress Dame Thora Hird.

Tia
Origin: Various
This is a name which developed as a diminutive of such names as **Letitia**.

Tiffany
Diminutives: Tiff, Tiffy
Origin: Greek
From the Greek *theos* ('god') and *phainein* ('to appear'), thus meaning 'manifestation of God'. Traditionally reserved for girls born on the Epiphany, now far more widespread. Common in the Middle Ages, it fell into disuse before being revived by the popularity of the film *Breakfast at Tiffany's* in 1961.

Tilly
See Matilda

Tina
Variants: Teena
Origin: Various, depending on root name
Despite originally being a diminutive of names ending in the suffix '-ina', this has since been accepted as a name in its own right. Adopted by English speakers in the nineteenth century, it enjoyed a peak in the 1960s and 1970s. Famous bearers of the name include rock star Tina Turner.

Tira
Origin: Hindi
Meaning 'arrow'.

Tish *See* Letitia

Titania
Origin: Latin
The queen of the fairies and the name of the character in Shakespeare's *A Midsummer Night's Dream*. It may be a corruption of Tatiana.

Toni *See* Antonia

Tori
See Victoria

Tracy m/f
Diminutives: Trace
Variants: Tracey, Tracie
Origin: French
Meaning 'place of Thracius', this was first adopted as a surname and, from the nineteenth century, it was used as a first name among English speakers. Also possibly a diminutive of Teresa, this name was originally bestowed on boys as well as girls, but this has virtually ceased and now it is known as a name for girls. Famous bearers of the name include actress Tracey Ullman and singer Tracy Chapman.

Tricia
See Patricia

Trinity
Origin: Latin
Meaning 'of the three', the popularity of this name probably enjoyed a surge after the release of the 1999 film *The Matrix*.

Trixie
See Beatrice

Trudy
See Gertrude

Tuesday
Origin: English

This name is generally reserved for children born on that day. Famous bearers of the name include actress Tuesday Weld.

Tulasi
Origin: Sanskrit
From the Sanskrit word meaning 'sacred basil', the plant which is used to symbolize the god Vishnu, as Tulsi. The feminine variant is also the name of a goddess.

Turaya
Origin: Arabic
Meaning 'star'.

Twyla
Origin: Middle English
Meaning 'woven of double thread'.

Tyler m/f
Variants: Tylar
Origin: English
From the surname used to denote someone who tiled roofs, this has made occasional appearances as a first name. Actress Mary Tyler Moore is a notable bearer of the name.

Tyra
Origin: Scandinavian
Meaning 'battler'.
See also Thora

Uda
Variants: Udella, Udelle
Origin: Teutonic
Meaning 'prosperous'.

Ulrica
Diminutives: Ulla
Variants: Elrica, Ulrika
Origin: Norse
Originally from the Norse name Wulfric (meaning 'wolf ruler'), the masculine name (Ulric) was borne by three saints, but it is now the feminine form which is more common. A well-known bearer of the name is TV presenter Ulrika Jonsson.

Ulrika
See **Ulrica**

Uma
Origin: English
This name seems to have been invented by Robert Louis Stevenson for his story 'The Beach of Falesa'. Famous bearers of the name include actress Uma Thurman.

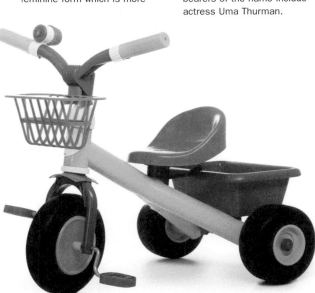

Una
Variants: Juno, Ona, Oonagh, Oona
Origin: Gaelic or Latin
Derived either from the Gaelic *uam* ('sheep') or, as is more likely, from the Latin *unus*, meaning 'one'. Well-known bearers of the name include TV personality Una Stubbs.

Ursula
Origin: Latin
Meaning 'female bear', 'she-bear' (*ursa*), this is also used as a feminine equivalent of Orlando. The fourth century St Ursula influenced people to use the name in the Middle Ages. One famous bearer of the name is science-fiction writer Ursula Le Guin.

Vala
Origin: German
Meaning 'the single one'.

Valeria
See **Valerie**

Valerie
Diminutives: Val
Variants: Valeria
Origin: Latin
From the Latin for 'strong' or 'healthy', this was the name of a powerful Roman family and was introduced to the English-

speaking world in the seventeenth century as Valeria. The end of the nineteenth century saw it give way to Valerie. Notable bearers of the name include TV presenter Valerie Singleton.

Valory
See **Valerie**

Vanessa
Origin: English
This name was invented by satirist Jonathan Swift in the eighteenth century and quickly became popular. It has gained ground in recent years and famous bearers of the name include actress Vanessa Redgrave.

Vanora
See **Genevieve**

Vashti
Origin: Persian
Meaning 'best' or 'beautiful', this biblical name was adopted by the Puritans after the Reformation, though it has never really caught on in European countries.

Venus
Origin: Roman
Named for the Roman goddess of love, this name has appeared infrequently since the sixteenth century, but has never been popular. A famous bearer of the name is tennis star Venus Williams.

Vera
Origin: Russian or Latin
Derived from either the Russian *viera* ('faith') or the Latin *verus*, meaning 'true', this name has sometimes been considered a diminutive of **Veronica** and was taken up in the nineteenth century. Since its peak in the 1920s, it has gone into decline. One famous bearer of the name is wartime singer Dame Vera Lynn.

Verity
Variants: Verily
Origin: Latin
Derived from the Latin *verus*, meaning 'truth', this is one of the 'virtue' names popular with the Puritans in the seventeenth century and remains in use today.

Veronica
Diminutives: **Vera**, Ron, **Ronnie**
Variants: Verona, Veron
Origin: Latin or Greek
Likely to be derived from the Latin *vera icon* ('true image'), though other sources claim it comes from the Greek Pherenika (meaning 'bringer of victory', *see* **Bernice**). St Veronica wiped the face of Christ on the way to his crucifixion and it arrived (as Véronique) in Scotland from France in the seventeenth century. It did not become popular until the nineteenth century, and reached a peak between 1920 and 1960.

Vianne
Origin: Various sources
An American name which uses **Anne** with the prefix 'Vi-'. A famous bearer of this name is the character in *Chocolat* by Joanne Harris.

Victoria
Diminutives: Vicki, Vicky, Vikki, Toria, Tory, **Ria**
Variants: Victorine
Origin: Latin
From the Latin *victoria*, meaning 'victory', this was the name of a Christian martyr but was not well known in England before the nineteenth century, but then became popular after the accession of Queen Victoria to the throne in 1837. The 1970s saw a peak in popularity and it has remained a favourite. A famous bearer of the name is comedienne Victoria Wood.

Vienna
Origin: Latin
Meaning 'geography', this is more likely to derive from the Austrian capital.

Vijaya
Origin: Sanskrit
Meaning 'victory'.

Viola
Origin: Latin
From the Latin *viola*, meaning 'violet', the popularity of this name was given a significant boost with the character Viola in Shakespeare's play *Twelfth Night* in 1601. In the early years of the twentieth century, the name enjoyed a peak, but has since been in decline.

Violet
Diminutives: Vi
Variants: Violette (French), Violetta (Italian)
Origin: Latin
From the name of the flower, this was adopted in the Middle Ages, sometimes being spelt Violante. Since the 1920s, it has suffered a decline.

Virginia
Diminutives: Ginny, Vinnie, Ginger, Jinny
Origin: Latin
From the Roman name Verginius, from the Latin for 'virgin' or 'maiden', Sir Walter Raleigh gave the name to English possessions in America in the sixteenth century, in tribute to Queen Elizabeth I, the Virgin Queen. The first child in Virginia was named Virginia Dare, in 1587. Notable bearers of the name have included writer Virginia Woolf and actress Virginia McKenna.

Vishala
Variants: Vishalakshi ('wide-eyed')
Origin: Indian
Meaning 'spacious', 'immense'. *See also* Vishal

Vita
Variants: Vivianna
Origin: Latin
Meaning 'full of life', 'spirited'.

Viveca
Variants: Vivecca
Origin: Scandinavian
Meaning 'living voice'.

Vivian m/f
Diminutives: Viv
Variants: Vivyan, Vyvyan
Origin: Latin
From the Latin *vivus*, meaning 'lively', 'alive'. Little used until medieval times, the name was initially given just to boys. Records of its use go back to the twelfth century.

Vonda
See Wanda

Wallis
Origin: Scottish or Old French
A variant of Wallace, this is more common in the USA than in the UK and is closely associated with Wallis Simpson, the divorcee who married Edward VIII, causing him to give up his throne.

Wanda
Origin: Obscure
Possibly of Slavonic origin from the tribal name Wend, or from a Polish background (from the name of an eighth-century queen). Another theory is that it comes from the Old German for 'family' or 'young shoot'. It became popular in the nineteenth century, and is considered a diminutive of Wendy. It became well known through the release of the 1988 film *A Fish Called Wanda*.

Wendy
Diminutives: Wend
Variants: Wendi, Wenda
Origin: Probably English
This name was famously invented by J.M. Barrie for *Peter Pan*, published in 1904. However, it has

been speculated that it was used before this as a diminutive of such names as **Gwendolen** and **Gwenda**. It has remained a popular name on both sides of the Atlantic, though it has fallen out of favour since its peak in the 1960s and 1970s. A famous bearer of the name is actress Wendy Craig.

Whitney m/f
Origin: English
Meaning 'at the white island', this name is used for both boys and girls, but is well known by many people as the name of singer and actress Whitney Houston.

Wilhelmina
Diminutives: Willa, Velma, Vilma, Mina, Minnie, **Willa**
Variants: **Wilma**, Williamina
Origin: German
The feminine equivalent of Wilhelm (*see* **William**), the name is not common and is mainly confined to Scotland, Canada and the USA.

Willa
See **Wilhelmina**

Willow
Origin: English
From the Old English *welig*, the Old English name for the tree. It is a relatively recent introduction and remains rare.

Wilma
See **Wilhelmina**

Winifred
Diminutives: Win, Winn, Winnie
Origin: English and Welsh
From the Old English *wynn* ('joy') and *frith* ('peace'); the Welsh root is from St Winifred (**Gwenfrewi**) who was beheaded and then restored to life. More common in the sixteenth century, though since a peak between 1880 and 1930 it has been in decline.

Winona
Variants: Wenona, Wenonah, Winonah, Wynona
Origin: Sioux
Meaning 'eldest daugher', the spelling Winona goes back to the 1881 poem 'Winona' by H.L. Gordon. A famous bearer of the name is actress Winona Ryder.

Winter m/f
Origin: English
From the ordinary vocabulary word 'winter'.

Wynda
Origin: Scottish
Meaning 'of the narrow passage'.

Wynn
Variants: Wyn, Wynne
Origin: Welsh or Old English

Meaning 'white', from the Welsh *wyn*, or from the Old English meaning 'friend'. Also found as a variant of Gwyn.

Xanthe
Origin: Greek
From *xanthos*, meaning 'yellow' or 'golden', several minor characters in Greek mythology bear this name.

Xenia
Variants: Zena, Zenia, Zina
Origin: Greek
From the Greek *xenia*, meaning 'hospitable', this name is very uncommon.

Xoey *See* **Zoe**

Yasmine
See **Jasmine**

Yetta
See **Henrietta**

Ylva
Origin: Old Norse
Meaning 'sea wolf'.

Yoko
Origin: Japanese or Native American
Meaning 'good girl'.
Other sources claim it is a Native American name, meaning 'rain', with Yoki as a diminutive.

Yolanda
Diminutives: Yola, Jola
Variants: Yalonda, Jolantha, Jolan, Yalinda, **Iolanthe**
Origin: Greek or Latin
Either from the Greek for 'violet flower', or Latin from the name of the flower.

Ysabeau
See **Isabel**

Ysolde
See **Isolda**

Yuliana
See **Julia**

Yvette *See* **Yvonne**

Yvonne
Diminutives: Vonnie
Variants: **Yvette**, Evette, **Evonne**
Origin: Old Norse
A feminine equivalent of **Yves**, this has been taken as a first name in English-speaking countries since 1900 and reached a peak in the 1960s and 1970s.

Zara
Variants: Xara
Origin: Arabic
Meaning 'flower' or 'splendour'; also a diminutive of **Sarah**. This name has been used occasionally since the 1960s and when in 1981 Princess Anne gave the name to her daughter, Zara Phillips, the name was given a boost.

Zefiryn
Origin: Greek
The greek god of the west wind; this is a Polish variant.

Zelda
Variants: Zelde
Origin: Obscure
This Jewish name may have come from the Yiddish for 'happiness'; alternatively, it may be a familiar form of the German **Griselda**. The schizophrenic wife of F. Scott Fitzgerald was named Zelda.

Zena
Variants: Zina
Origin: Persian
Meaning 'woman', which may have developed as a familiar form of Zinaida; sometimes regarded as a diminutive of **Xenia** or Rosina.

Zia
Variants: Ziya
Origin: Arabic
This Muslim name comes from the Arabic for 'light' or 'splendour'.

Zoë
Variants: Zoe, Zoey, Zowie
Origin: Greek
This name, which means 'life', was used as an equivalent of **Eve** when the Bible was translated from Hebrew to Greek. In English-speaking countries, it has only been in significant use since the Second World War. In the 1970s, it was among the most popular names for girls. A famous bearer of the name is actress Zoe Wanamaker.

Zofeyah
Origin: Hebrew
Meaning 'God sees'.